Peter FitzSimons was born and bred on a farm at Peats Ridge, the youngest of seven children. After six years of boarding at Knox Grammar School, he went to America for one year on an exchange scholarship and returned to study Arts at Sydney University in 1980 – the same year Nick Farr-Jones arrived there from Newington.

The two played together for the University Firsts Colts team which won the Grand Final that year, and in 1984 both were selected to go on their initial Wallaby tour, rooming together throughout. For the next five years, while Farr-Jones was busy elsewhere, FitzSimons lived in Italy and France playing rugby and writing, before rejoining Nick in the Australian team in 1989; and they played seven Tests together over the next two years.

Peter FitzSimons began writing for the *Sydney Morning Herald* in 1986 and has been with the paper full-time since 1989. The course of his journalistic career since has seen him sending back reports from the bottom of All Black rucks and Sumo wrestlers' armpits, as well as Mother Theresa's sitting room and an interview with then President George Bush. He appears regularly on Channel Nine's *Wide World of Sports* and the *Today* show.

Married in 1992, he lives with his wife Lisa in Sydney and is the author of two other books, *Basking in Beirut* and *Little Theories of Life*.

NICK
THE AUTHORISED BIOGRAPHY
FARR-JONES

PETER FITZSIMONS

ARROW

An Arrow Book
published by
Random House Australia Pty Ltd
20 Alfred Street, Milsons Point, NSW 2061

Sydney   New York   Toronto
London   Auckland   Johannesburg
and agencies throughout the world

First published in 1993 by Random House Australia
Arrow edition 1994

National Library of Australia
Cataloguing-in-Publication Data

FitzSimons, Peter.
  Nick Farr-Jones: the authorised biography.
  Includes index.
  ISBN 0 09 182963 1
  1. Farr-Jones, Nick. 2. Rugby Union football players – Australia –
  Biography. 3. Rugby Union football – Australia. I. Title.
796.333092

Typeset by Midland Typesetters, Victoria
Printed by Griffin Paperbacks, Adelaide
Production by Vantage Graphics, Sydney

Contents

Dedication

To Lisa,
my wife, friend, and fellow-traveller in the journey
that was this book.

Acknowledgements

My warm thanks to those who gave me much-valued help in writing this book. They are all those herein quoted, in particular: Angela Farr-Jones and the Farr-Jones family; and for their help with the manuscript, my thanks especially to Henry Barrkman, Greg Growden, the late Howard Northey, and my wife Lisa. Peter Fenton was kind enough to give his permission to reprint his poem *The Running Game*. Finally, my thanks to my publisher, Matthew Kelly, whose deadlines were commendably malleable.

Foreword

The story of Nick Farr-Jones' life and rugby career is a unique one.

It has been an extraordinary journey. From a practically un-known Second Division player at the end of 1983, he was recognised by the end of 1984 as the most valuable player of the thirty Wallabies who participated in the historic Grand Slam tour.

Nick Farr-Jones was the man who took the initiative and who drove the forwards, giving directions that laid the foundation for so many magnificent victories.

In 1993, he was acknowledged as one of the most respected figures in world rugby, not just for his involvement in Australia's successes of the last few years, nor because he was the first Australian to hold the Rugby World Cup above his shoulders before the world. His universal respect has been earned because of the way he has conducted himself throughout his career and in the role of Australian Captain.

Though a great player, he has undoubtedly excelled in the unofficial role of Ambassador for Australia, indeed for the world of rugby.

To be invited to captain the British Barbarians in the year of the Barbarian Centenary was indicative of the high esteem in which this man is held by his peers.

In a world of sport that is all too frequently pre-packaged, pre-programmed and over professionalised, Farr-Jones' natural humour and grace over the years, evoke the great sporting and traditional memories of previous years, characterised by spontaneity and comradeship. Along the way, he has lived through many historic events in rugby and has many interesting tales to tell.

Although this book is described as 'a biography', I don't think that quite does it justice, for the title connotes an ending of some sort and, in many ways, I suspect, Nick's public life has yet to really begin.

From the unique perspective as long time close friend and Test team-mate, the author Peter FitzSimons has captured the essence of the formative influences on Nick's early life, the behind-the-scenes story of his rugby career and many of the extraordinary things that Farr-Jones has seen and done that have nothing to do with rugby.

The book captures a golden era in Australian rugby, as well as exposing the pressures players experience whilst on tour.

SIR NICHOLAS SHEHADIE AC OBE

CHAPTER ONE

In the Beginning

*'There is no cure to birth and
death save to enjoy the interval.'*
George Santayana

Young Nicholas, all of two years old, had been away from the Christmas lunch table for only a minute when his mother Rosemary went into the suddenly silent adjoining room to check on how he was.

He was blue.

'Actually . . . *navy* blue,' remembers Rosemary Jones.

Flat on his back on the couch in the bay window and choking on part of a 'bon-bon' whistle.

So blue and unmoving was he that for a moment Mrs Jones wasn't sure whether her son was alive or dead.

'I acted instinctively, though, as I've since found out, medically incorrectly,' she recounts. 'You're not meant to put your fingers down someone's throat in a situation like that because you risk lodging the obstruction even deeper down.

'But luckily I had particularly long fingernails at the time, and managed to get my nail hooked on part of the whistle and flipped it straight out of his throat.'

He stirred. He gurgled. He coughed.

To the relieved sighs of the now assembled family, he started gasping for air. Within minutes he was back in the family room, happily running around and totally untroubled by the trauma.

When the person who is now Nicholas Campbell *Farr*-Jones ('Farr' would only be added to his name later, when he went to high school) first resurfaced that Christmas Day of 1964, he found himself to be the second child of Max and Rosemary Jones, a young couple living in Gymea, one of the burgeoning suburbs of southern Sydney.

The story of Max and Ro's romance goes back to the mid 1950s, to the famed Suez Crisis, when Egypt shut down the Suez Canal and Britain and France went to war against her immediately afterwards.

Many travellers were affected, including those in far-off Sydney, Australia, who were booked in to go on the RMS *Himalaya* through the Canal on the way to London. P&O immediately announced that their 28,000 ton ship would go around Africa instead of through the Suez, but it was too late.

Fully three-quarters of the booked passengers decided not to risk running around on the ocean when there was a fully fledged war going on.

The twenty-one-year-old Max Jones decided to go ahead regardless. Having completed sixteen years straight of education, through Eastwood Primary School, the prestigious Fort Street High School, and then Sydney University for his pharmacy degree, Max was in no mood to stay home and twiddle his thumbs when his plan all along had been to go with three friends to London for a couple of years to work, see a bit of Europe in passing, and maybe meet the woman of his dreams, who knows?

Max was of sturdy stock, at least as far back as his grandmother Jessica Farr, who, when she had married his grandfather Frederick Jones, had struck an early blow for feminism in keeping her own name and insisted that their son Reginald, Max's father, be christened Reginald *Farr*-Jones.

So began what would be at least another three generations of name confusion. For simplicity's sake Reg had grown up using only the name Reginald Jones, and had only reactivated 'Farr-Jones' when he started working in his first bank and found another two 'Joneses' working there. Max had stayed as a Jones.

As the time approached for the huge ship to leave the Pyrmont dock it was Max's mother Estelle who started crying first. Pretty soon all three of them—mother, father and son—were crying helplessly as the streamers between the boat and the dock were being thrown, as the brass band began to play and the announcement came that everyone must board.

Gingerly, Max extricated himself from his mother, shook his father's hand, wiped his eyes, looked surreptitiously to his left and right to make sure he hadn't been seen crying, and then took his leave up the gangway.

At that moment, the young Rosemary Burns was in all probability being photographed with her friend Diana Madden by the *Sydney Morning Herald*'s social photographer. The picture the following day shows them holding their hats and beaming with bonhomie.

Blonde and pretty and always well dressed—yet with the svelte body of a born athlete trained hard beneath the frill—Rosemary had just finished her own degree in physiotherapy at Sydney University and she, too, never considered for a moment postponing her trip.

No daughter of the great Noel Burns of Vaucluse, corporate lawyer, great athlete, scion of the Eastern Suburbs and a man who was both respected and a little feared, could ever allow herself to pull out because of something so minor—*pshaw!*—as a war over such a little thing as the Suez Canal.

Her father had originally suggested the trip to try to get her over the death of her beloved border collie Molesworth, and it had worked. Not only would she go on the trip but she would also work while she was away in London.

The odd thing is that Max and Ro should never have previously met, despite spending the last four years at Sydney University together, and both having a particular interest in rugby and tennis. And even though the Suez Crisis had scared away three-quarters of the ship's passengers, heightening immeasurably their chances of meeting, it would still be a good two weeks after the boat had sailed out of Sydney Harbour Heads before the two would clap eyes on each other.

Max remembers the occasion well. Probably because Rosemary was green at the time.

'A couple of days after we left Perth,' Max recalls, 'I was playing quoits on the deck with some friends, and I happened to look up at just that moment when she was coming down from the upper deck. I never saw a woman so seasick—my overwhelming memory is of seeing this moving apparition of blonde and green.'

Rosemary in fact was staggering around on deck for the first time in two weeks, having been all but totally bedridden with seasickness.

So sick, in fact, that when the ship briefly pulled in at Fremantle, before leaving the Australian continent for good, she was too weak even to fulfil her vowed intent of packing her bags and leaving the ship.

She recovered enough a few days out of port to get up and about, and met Max more formally one night at dinner. Usually she and Diana and their other two girlfriends would dine at the officers' table, but this evening, for a lark, they sat down with the young pharmacists.

Max and Ro hit it off right away, albeit initially as nothing more than friends. Although if there was one thing about Max that attracted her, it was that he was so *informal*. One evening at a late-night party in one of the cabins, Max was tired so he just lay down on the floor and slept. On the floor! In the middle of a party! Rosemary had never seen the like.

Their romance developed slowly, Max and his three male friends forming a group with Ro and Diana and their two friends, who were also on the boat. For the rest of the voyage the group danced, played games and partied, still more or less as a group with no particular couples forming. When they reached London on Guy Fawkes Day, 1956, it was understood that as a group they would stay together, although in different houses of course.

Though even at this stage the two were not yet a formal 'couple', it wasn't long after seeing each other in London that they started 'going steady'.

Two years later, after theatre outings, days at Ascot, rowing on the Thames, visits to the opera, wining and dining and trips to Europe for skiing, they decided to write to their parents for permission to get engaged.

That permission forthcoming, Max put the ring on Rosemary's finger on a trip to Paris, and they went to the Moulin Rouge to celebrate with a glass of champagne between them . . . funds being rather embarrassingly short at the time. Soon afterwards they returned to London and set sail for Sydney Town on the Royal Mail Steamer *Oronsay*.

They might have gone over as a group of eight, but coming back there were just the three of them. Max, Rosemary, and Rosemary's Aunt Nancy. Now that she was officially engaged it would have been quite inappropriate for Rosemary to return unchaperoned, and Noel Burns had arranged for his cousin, Nancy Vine, to accompany his daughter on the way home.

In those days a boat bearing gossip columnists and photographers would go out to meet all passenger ships returning from the Mother Country, and have their stories written and cameras at the ready by the time the ship docked at Circular Quay.

Sure enough, the following day 'SOCIALITE SPENDS NIGHT IN TANGIERS GAOL-HOUSE' was the headline of the lead social story, recounting how on a recent trip to the Continent, Rosemary Burns and her fiance Max Jones, together with friends Valerie Stevens and Frank Crosslé, had ventured south to Morocco on a day trip from Gibraltar, missed their ferry back and having decided to sleep on some vacant deck chairs by the beach, were taken to jail by the police for their own protection.

Noel Burns was less than impressed that such a headline should announce the return of his daughter, but there was nothing to be done. At least the next headline about the two was much better, heralding the big society wedding that had taken place the day before at St Michael's in Vaucluse.

Max was lucky. Finally he found just the job he was looking for, managing a pharmacy in the southern Sydney suburb of Cronulla. With the money he would now earn from that, he calculated, he should just be able to afford to buy that house in nearby Gymea that he and Rosemary had loved at first sight. Gymea was just the sort of place to bring up the family the couple hoped to have.

In a kind of forested cul-de-sac, the area had a nice isolated feel about it. By a fortunate quirk of fate, it was the nearby suburb of Miranda that tended to attract the more garish of latterday twentieth-century accoutrements—the large shopping centres, fast food outlets and busy highways.

The Farr-Jones' house was typical of the area. Weatherboard, of simple but spacious design, it had a small decorative garden at the front, while at the back of the house was the traditional Australian backyard.

The backyards tend to grow big out Gymea way, and the one at the Jones' house was a particularly large and healthy specimen. Big enough for Max to grow vegetables in, to help keep down the grocery bill, big enough for the sheets on the Hill's Hoist to blow in the wind without touching anything, and big enough for a bunch of children to play in, should the young couple be so blessed.

And blessed they were; three times.

Young Nick was born on 18 April 1962, after a difficult labour. Suffering from foetal distress, he was brought into the world with the aid of forceps. Named 'Nicholas' because his mother had been so sure that her second baby would be a girl that she had set her heart on 'Nicola', he was as a small baby possessed of a 'totally angelic nature', his mother says. This great placidity wouldn't last long, but it was nice that his parents should at least enjoy a few years of it.

Nick's first memories are of the sound of hammering, awakening him from the almost unconscious existence of very early childhood. It was the sound of workmen nailing wood at the back of the house as they added on another room to cope with the recent arrival of his younger brother Simon. And Simon made three, counting Nick's older brother by a couple of years, Peter.

Nick soon took stock of the rest of his world. That wiry man wearing the white coat, whom he saw only very occasionally but who was always extra affectionate, was Dad.

Max was rarely around the house in those days, working particularly hard running the first All Night Chemist in Sydney at the old Herne Bay Housing Settlement.

Then there was Mum. She'd worked as a physiotherapist briefly after getting married, but with three boys under three years old, thoughts of returning to physiotherapy disappeared. With Max so busy running his pharmacy, she was more often than not alone with the boys and there seemed only one sure-fire way to keep their abundant energy under control as they got older. Have them neutralise each other through games.

Marbles was a good one. They could play that for hours on the kitchen floor as she busied herself around the house, and simply throwing a ball to each other acted as a wonderful sponge for their seemingly overwhelming energy.

Inevitably it acquired its own momentum. From Nick first throwing the ball back and forth to Peter at the age of two, to picking up a tennis racquet at the age of three, to riding on his first tricycle at four, to holding a cricket bat at five, sport in some measure was a constant part of all the boys' lives. Simon couldn't walk of course for the first year of his life, but no problem.

Nick would sit him in a little box on the back of his tricycle and race him round and round the back garden.

That Nicholas would later turn into such a renowned sportsman owes not a little to the fact that these sporting activities were so encouraged in a household where three boys were in close proximity in age. Yet there are plenty of children in similar circumstances who've never won so much as a sausage on the sporting field.

To make a real sporting champion, of course, requires not least a good hand of cards being dealt by the gods of genealogy. Luckily, all the Farr-Jones lads were dealt aces.

Their father Max as a young man had the sinewy build and easy grace that would enable him to go on to become the schoolboy Open Tennis double champion with his brother Ross when they represented Fort Street High School.

While Max would later decide to go into the far more dependable world of pharmacy to make a living, Ross (whose first wife would be Caroline Jones, the well-known ABC broadcaster) was good enough to become a tennis professional, his particular claim to fame being that in his early career he beat the great Fred Stolle, who would later go on to win Wimbledon doubles titles. Max never regretted his move away from tennis into pharmacy, and was awarded a University Blue in tennis together with his degree.

Further out on Max's family tree there was at least one more bloom to show that the genealogical roots of good sport grew strong in his family—John Cuneo, who won a gold medal for Australia in the 1972 Olympics in Yachting, was Max's first cousin.

When it came to pure sporting talent, however, Rosemary could more fairly be ascribed as the wellspring. As a student she was the champion athlete of the exclusive Kambala girls' school in Sydney's east—in her final year becoming the All-Schools 100 yards sprint champion and 50 yards swimming champion.

Rosemary would go on to receive Blues from Sydney University in basketball, swimming and athletics.

Much of Ro's sporting talent, in turn, came from her father, Noel Burns—both genealogically and also through an upbringing that heavily encouraged sporting pursuits. As Rosemary's mother died when Rosemary was born, her father put an inordinate amount of his time and energy into her raising.

One of his great passions outside of the law was sport, and a lot of Ro's childhood was filled with his teaching her not only the skills of various sports, but also how to *win* at them.

And when it came to winning at sport, Noel Burns had a lot of experience to call on.

Seventy years on, *Burns, NR* still holds equal record of winning five individual Greater Public School titles in the one day, and was strongest over the distance of 100 yards and only marginally less powerful over the 220 and 440 yards.

His mentions in the *Sydney Morning Herald* in the early 1920s are numerous, and even the *Bulletin* noted in one of its October editions of 1922 that:

> 'An uncommonly fine young runner in N.R. Burns was the hero of the G.P.S. Sports. Burns, who is a 17 year-old and belongs to Kings School, swept the Board by winning the 100 yards by five yards in 10 3-10 sec., the 220 yards in 23 sec. the quarter-mile in 53 2-5 sec and the 120 yards hurdles in 162-5 sec. His arm-swinging is a bit clumsy but no school athlete of recent years has shown more promise.'

Bar injury he was said to have had a good chance of going to the Paris Olympics of 1924 as a 100-yard sprinter, and a continuation of his enviable athletic career was only curtailed later by a decision to concentrate on law rather than athletics. It was then that he started with the Sydney law firm of Garland, Seaborn & Abbott.

The greatest genealogical background in the world would be no use at all unless the recipient wasn't at least possessed of the heart to explore his potential, and Nick was well provided for in this regard as well.

'It's only hazy now,' he recalls, 'but I remember my grandfather sitting me down as a very young fellow and telling me that, "Nicky, in whatever you do in sport you've got to be able to push your body beyond when your body says stop; you've got to be able to keep going even when your body is *screaming* at you to stop.

' "It'll hurt a lot at first but once you get through it you'll find that even though you think you can't go on, you can." '

Nick took it to heart, he says, 'because it was my grandfather telling me, and whatever he told me I listened to. He was just one of those sort of grandfathers'.

Propitious circumstance also strengthened the boys collectively and Nicky in particular.

Peter was five years old when an attack of bronchitis worsened to become pneumonia. To strengthen him after he was over the worst of it, next summer Rosemary took him to the local swimming pool to build him up in the lungs and body, and the other two boys went along.

A flying fish should fall back into the sea with such enthusiasm . . .

At the end of the hour, it was all Rosemary could do to drag Nick out of the wading pool, even though he couldn't actually swim. The strokes would come soon enough, however, as the family kept returning to the pool to help strengthen Peter's lungs.

While Nicholas did not have an easy style and grace in the water he did have ample enthusiasm and grit, which meant he would always be thrashing in the water long after the other boys were tired.

'I still don't know what it was about Nick at the pool,' Rosemary recalls now, 'but from the moment he walked through the door of that swimming pool he was absorbed by it.'

Just as it was Peter who led the brothers into the world of swimming, it was also Peter who first took them into what would soon become the familiar world of competitive team sports.

By happy coincidence, the same man who had spent the night in the Tangiers gaol-house with Max and Ro, Frank Crosslé, had now moved into the area with his wife Jacqui and one Saturday morning Max received a call from Frank to see if Peter would come down and play in his Cronulla under six soccer side, which he did. The inevitable happened and it wasn't long before they were again short of boys and, as the whole family was already on the sidelines to watch Peter play, Nick went straight into the side and loved it from the first minute.

It was to be one of the few times in Nick's long sporting career that he had to endure a season when he wasn't captain.

The following year Max took over the under six side and because Nick was still young enough he stayed with the under sixes.

So began the association of father and son in the one team, a stormy relationship at the best of times. Max ran a very tight ship at his pharmacy and worked hard at it. Soccer coaching was one of his few leisurely outlets, and he certainly wasn't prepared to take any lip, particularly from his own son.

Yet often, the father would no sooner say, 'Right, boys, we'll finish with a couple of laps around the oval,' than his son would just as likely respond with, 'Get nicked, Dad. We're not doing it.'

Whereupon Max would utter those terrible few words that were to become something of a refrain in Nick's early childhood—'To the car, Nicholas!'

Somewhere along the line, the 'totally angelic' baby had turned into a particularly fractious five year old.

'It was really the only way I could control the little bugger sometimes,' Max says. 'To put him in a confined space like the car and tell him he was not allowed to leave until practice was over was just about the worst punishment imaginable for him because he so liked running around and yapping to the other kids.'

Early on in the season, Max's worst fears were realised when Nick was elected captain of the side on a unanimous vote. Now more confident than ever that he was speaking for the whole side when telling his father to 'get nicked', he became even more polemical than before. And was on the receiving end of 'To the car, Nicholas!' all the more often.

But despite the constant power struggle between father and son the team kept on winning. Finally, at the end of the season, they found that they had made the final against Lilli Pilli, which both were keen to win.

On the Thursday afternoon before the Saturday final, Nick was as usual running around with his brothers after school when they decided to have a race over some huge pipes that were lying side by side on a large building site in the area.

Simon remembers it well: 'As usual, Peter was pulling ahead of Nick and so Nick just tried that bit too hard and then he tripped and went down and really hit his head hard on the metal pipe. He got straight back up and looked at us, like, to see from our faces if he'd really hurt himself, and we were just appalled—there was blood everywhere.

'And as soon as he felt his head and saw the blood, he panicked and ran all the way home.'

As Rosemary recounts, 'We raced him to the doctor for urgent stitching and, because of the extent of the wound, he said there was no way Nick would be playing soccer for two weeks, at least.' Max then rang up a medical friend, Leo Maginnity, who said, "Look, bring him up and I'll give him a skull x-ray, and if there's no fracture or anything like that, I reckon they'll bind him up and he'll be okay."

'So on Saturday morning the poor child was taken up early in the morning for a skull x-ray, there was no actual fracture so they bound him up—he looked like a mummy—and he played.'

One who was playing for Lilli Pilli against Nick that day, is Peter Baker:

'It's something I'll never forget,' he says. 'We ran out on to the pitch and there was this kid with bandages all over his head, and he looked like he should be in hospital or something, and then when the game starts he just ends up going crazy, running everywhere doing everything, telling all the other players in his side where to go and what to do.

'He was a one-man band, making the other ten guys in his team do everything *he* wanted till they got it right. On our side we were just a disorganised bunch of six year olds running everywhere, so we had no chance.'

The side led by Nicky Jones won handsomely.

Next year the fortunes of the losing Lilli Pilli side were to change radically, when the same bandaged-headed kid that had brained them in the final the year before now joined them. It was to be the only time in Farr-Jones's long sporting career that he would change clubs, and he did so on this occasion 'because Lilli Pilli was about ten minutes closer to our Gymea house than the Cronulla RSL side'.

He settled in quickly, with the Lilli Pilli boys remembering him as the funny-looking kid from the previous year who'd played so well, and all immediately began falling into the Farr-Jones thrall. All except one brown-haired kid by the name of Neil Guy. Guy wanted none of this new upstart who'd been in the team only *five minutes*, who already thought he ran the joint, and the two were engaged in constant skirmishes for supremacy.

'The way it worked,' recalls Peter Baker, 'was that during practice the two would always be sniping at each other, saying the other was too slow or too "un-co" [unco-ordinated] and then maybe Nick might give him a bit of a jab in the ribs when they were going for the same ball. Neil would then give Nick a bit of a thump—practice would stop—and the whole team would watch as Nick chased after Neil to give him a thump back, and they'd run up behind the schoolhouse with Nick gaining on him all the time. A minute later, when we were just wondering what had happened to them, Nick would come roaring out the other side, with Neil running after *him* trying to pay Nick back for the thump he'd just received. It used to happen all the time just like that.'

And so it would go.

Neil Guy, now working as a security guard on the Gold Coast, also remembers it well.

'He was just very very sure of himself, always thought he knew the best way to play and to practise, and I'm sure the odd thump never did him any harm.'

CHAPTER TWO

And the
Boys Played On . . .

'We few, we happy few, we band of brothers'.
Henry V

Five-thirty a.m. It was the time of day that the boys both loved and hated. Loved because it was generally the only time on a weekday that they got to see their hard-working father. Hated because he was getting them up to go to wretched swimming training. Things had changed since those first fun days in the pool when they used to just splash about, learning a few strokes and playing around. Somewhere along the line it had all become serious and their dad had started taking them to early morning training sessions, every morning.

The familiar figure moving through the semi-darkness really had no need to follow his familiar routine of gently touching his sons on the shoulders to wake them—they were awakened automatically by the sound of his approaching footsteps, long conditioned as they were to waking up at such an ungodly hour.

Yet it was their father who had the most reason to complain of fatigue. Having usually finished work at 11 p.m. the previous night, then gulped down some midnight dinner and nibbled on a smidgin of TV to relax, he would invariably be able to snatch only some four and half hours' sleep a night if he was lucky.

He, too, often felt rather like a sick'n'sorry parrot in those early mornings. But nothing was going to interfere with taking

13

his sons to swimming training, even if the middle son, for one, 'just detested it'.

'I can remember so often diving in the pool or being thrown into the pool by the coach, swimming up and down, up and down and bawling for ten laps—just bawling and bawling. I don't quite know how I managed to cry with my eyes underwater, but I did,' Nick says.

Many was the time that he resolved to tell his father he didn't want to do it any more, that he didn't like swimming in the morning or racing with his brothers or any of it. Somehow he always felt so happy when he finally got out—so suddenly warm and glowing and glad that it was over—that he never did. Also, the boys perhaps had a sense that with their father working so hard for the family, if one of his pleasures was to take them swimming at first light, then so be it.

'We just revered Dad, simple as that,' says Nick. 'He wanted us to swim so we swam. It didn't matter if we didn't really want to. We shut up.'

Max had a fair idea anyway that his sons weren't rapt in the caper, but was untroubled: 'Sure, they used to hate going to swimming at times, especially when it was cold. But they always came with just a bit of cajoling, and if I was still having trouble then I always promised to buy them some of those soft green frogs or maybe a chocolate bar, and that always made them immediately more interested.'

The hard swimming training for his sons fitted neatly into Max's philosophy that 'life is all *about* winning. I wanted them to know that that's what counts—to be competitive, to get better, to succeed'.

A hard lesson, perhaps, but it was the lesson his father Reg had taught him when he was a lad, and he had always found it salutary.

'I think the competitiveness they learned among them at a young age served them well in later life when they were competing against other adults.'

All the sons agree that his encouragement never overflowed into the full-blown parental pressure to 'succeed at all costs' which so often shows up in psychiatrists' reports of troubled children.

In younger brother Simon's words: 'Mum and Dad thought it was really important to have a go at everything, and to have a *good* go. But they were never pushy. They weren't the type of parents who would stand on the side of the pool or on the sideline at the soccer field and scream to their children and hurl abuse at referees and opposition players. Theirs was far more of a laid-back sort of encouragement.'

Still, there was no point in the brothers having such a high level of fitness and competitive zeal if they didn't have a competitive forum in which to strut their stuff, and in the early days of their childhood Max let the boys loose on the Nippers at the Elouera Beach Surf Club.

Uniquely Australian, the Nippers is a movement whose philosophy is designed to create 'Tomorrow's Lifesavers Today'— the bronzed Aussies of popular mythology.

Practically, this would mean that the boys would compete every Sunday morning of summer in a surf and beach competition, where the aim was to see who could move themselves fastest, furthest and firstest over land and sea. Or any combination of the above.

There was, for example, the famed 'flags' competition. This involved as many as ten boys lying face down side by side on the beach with nine flags behind them at a distance of twenty yards. When the gun went off, the boys had to leap to their feet, turn around and hurtle forwards to claim a flag. Inevitably one boy would miss out. And then they would go again, always with one less flag than there were boys, until there was only one boy left.

This was Nick's particular forte, and he would invariably win, his elbows doing almost as much work in the jostling as his legs were doing in the powering forward. Apart from the pleasure of just winning, the boys also had another, more tangible encouragement to do well.

The system was simple. The more you won the more money you earned. If you got a third, Dad would give you twenty cents; a second was worth fifty cents and a first earned you a whopping one dollar. With eight events it meant that if you had a big day you could pick up as much as five dollars—a far more interesting system than merely giving out pocket money.

The system would also yield results, as every year Nick would be crowned the overall champion in his age group, just as Peter and Simon were in theirs.

His early physical training was to have later benefits. As a Wallaby, the theory of his fellow players was that if you were to drag Farr-Jones out of a London casino at 3 a.m., take the plaster casts off both legs, the drink out of one hand and the cigarette out of the other, then get him out to Twickenham for the Test, he would be ready to play.

The theory may well have been right. Maybe it was, as he says, that the 'early constant training at swimming, in the pool and with the Nippers, sort of hardened my muscles and got my respiratory system working at peak efficiency, which has stood me in good stead since.

'Also it gave me some sense very early on that, just like my granddad had told me, it *was* quite possible to push through pain, come out the other side and things would still be all right. In fact better than all right. The message I got was that it was hardly worth doing training unless you pushed yourself through some sort of barrier.'

Beach-carnival season over meant the return to Miranda Primary School. Academically, Farr-Jones was solid, if not outstanding. But definitely not for him the strict observance of all the petty rules of school-day life. If he felt like reading a *Phantom* comic during English lesson, he did so, albeit under the cover of a regular textbook. If he felt like daydreaming during Maths class and letting his mind wander to the games he would be playing that very afternoon, then he did that too. Even as early as this, Nick was displaying the key personality trait of his father Max that had so attracted his mother—basically doing whatever he felt like doing whenever he felt like doing it, even if as a schoolboy he had to make some arrangements to cover himself. Whether this was passed on genealogically or by filial observation is a moot point, but it was there and would stay with him.

Still, it only took the teacher to announce that their homework would be marked when they brought it in the following day and he would immediately become interested. Because when you looked at in the right way, schoolwork was really like a *competition*, and because they were giving out marks and everything, you might as well do your very best to win it, like his dad had said. Even if you had to improvise on occasion to cover those areas in which you weren't talented.

On one occasion in third class Nick had a project to do which required a lot of drawing, and after a week of trying he realised that he just couldn't do it perfectly. His brother Peter was good at art and he knew they could do a deal whereby they'd complete it by the following morning when it was due.

There was a lot of haggling, but they eventually settled on a price equal to two wins in the Nippers—the princely sum of two dollars. They signed the contracts (their grandfather having once told them that all good deals should be put in writing), with a copy for each, and settled down to work, Nick writing and Peter drawing.

Ten o'clock. Midnight. 2 a.m.

'At three o'clock,' Peter recalls, 'Nick just couldn't go on any more and he said, "I'll give you some more money if you keep going." So I did.'

Nick awoke to start work again at around five o'clock and the two kept working to finish the job just as the sun came up.

Both brothers were satisfied. Peter had three dollars and Nick had his project completely finished. Neither remembers whether their father let them off swimming training that morning but Peter has a clear memory of Nick going off to school 'as happy as Larry'.

Just as Nick was usually as happy as the said Larry every Monday morning of his fourth year at school, when his mother would give him ten cents to pay for his after-school recorder lessons. It was just enough to pay for a drink and a sausage roll, or maybe two packets of straw chips.

The game was up of course at the end-of-year concert. The curtains open, the lights come up on stage and there he is, recorder in hand, as he nervously looks to see where his parents are sitting. There they are, up the back on the right, proudly waiting for the show to begin.

And *now*. The conductor's baton has signalled that they must begin the first cheery bars of 'Merrily We Roll Along' and Nick did the only thing he could do.

'I fudged it. I didn't blow at all on the recorder and just kept moving my fingers up and down, in much the same fashion as the boy beside me was doing, and counted that there'd be enough noise coming from the kids around me that I'd be able to get away with it.'

While he may not have been the leading light of the school's cultural life, he did his best to make up for it with his sporting input.

It was in this fourth year of school that Nick really began to come into his sporting own. While most of the other kids had spent their summers in the traditional Australian way, simply gambolling about in the sun, he and his brothers had again been training and competing hard with the Nippers, and by summer's end Nick was so fit he was dangerous.

From winning just in the internal Miranda Public School competitions, Nick kept winning, and progressing from the school's carnival to the area carnival to the regional carnival until, finally, the biggest moment of Nick's young life arrived.

He found himself on the blocks at North Sydney swimming pool, competing in the state under eights fifty yards freestyle.

Standing. Jiggling up and down. Heart beating furiously. Glancing to the left and right at his fellow competitors. Crouched. Waiting for the gun to go and sort of wishing he didn't have to be under this pressure but still sort of loving it and waiting and . . .

BANG!

He hit the water, stretching his arms and his fingers out before him to their very limit, just like his dad had shown him over breakfast.

Charging up the pool, as his mother remembers it, Nick was just a blur of thrashing water, far less stylish than the two boys in front of him, but probably displacing more water than the two of them put together.

Somehow or other, ten yards from the line, he had gained on these two to the point of drawing even, and then over the final yards he just *willed* himself to the finish ahead of them. The winner, in a time of 38.0 seconds, and new champion of the state under eight titles: Nicky Jones.

It is here, after it was all over, that Nick's memory comes into quite sharp focus.

'I was standing up on this dais on the number one spot, and this lady put a big gold medal around my neck. Then we went home and I was sitting in the car beside Mum, really excited because I couldn't wait to get home to show Dad.'

When he went to school the next day Nick still had the medal on. He also had a headmaster who was so delighted that one of his pupils should have done so well that he escorted him around all the classes to show them the medal—to show them what hard work could achieve.

'I was less enthused about doing that and was more than a little embarrassed about it all, but overall it was just about the best thing that had happened to me up until then.'

And, perhaps, just the thing to give him an early taste for winning bright, shiny and glorious things through sporting endeavour and then getting to hold them up to show everyone. Not to mention the joys of a little media attention . . .

The local Gymea paper, the *Shire Pictorial*, of 15 April 1970 shows Nicky Jones standing side by side with a Margaret Brown atop a headline saying DOLPHINS—TOP SWIMMERS. Another story in the *St George and Sutherland Shire Leader* recorded the following day that 'Nicky's winning time of thirty-eight seconds was close to the record for the event'.

Nick's victory began something of a sporting golden period for himself, his brothers and the school. Just as their mother Rosemary had once won the All-Schools 100 yards swimming *and* running, her sons, together with two others from the school, Paul Bush and Russell Cooper, now began to dominate the state relay titles in both events. In 1968 they won the 4 x 100m relay race at the state athletic titles and also the 4 x 50m swimming. Miranda Primary had never had such a high sporting profile.

In the life of Nicky Jones it was of course heady stuff to be so successful in sport at such a young age. And it seemed inevitable that he should end up putting more of his energy into his sport and less into his studies.

'Nicholas has worked hard this year but still has a tendency to be distracted from the task at hand. His attitude to his teachers is respectful without being obsequious, and he seems to generally get on well with his peers, though he does have a problem with losing his temper.'

The last part of such a report card would have caused the least surprise of all to his parents. Despite all his sporting success and his generally good-natured disposition, there were still frequent outbursts of Nicky's terrible rage. Most of Max and Ro's first-hand experience of their middle son's temper came when they would have to sort out one or other of the constant squabbles happening in their own backyard.

Sure, it was only 'games' the boys were playing, but the common elements of these games were competitiveness and gambling— you didn't just play the game to win, you played it to win *something*.

It had started with marbles on the kitchen floor—your marble against his'n and the winner gets both marbles—and continued in every game they played thereafter, with only the currency changing. Marbles, golf balls, cricket balls, money . . .

Nor did it matter particularly what the game was. The Farr-Jones lads used to bet on snails crawling up a wall. Money being generally scarce at that time, unless they were in the middle of Nipper season, their gambling currency of choice was golf balls. My best golf ball against your best golf ball that my snail will get to the window ledge before yours.

It was a particularly popular game on days when it was a little wet, bringing the snails out in force. The way to do it was to get into the garden before your brothers and find, according to Nick, 'the skinniest, longest snail you could. One that looked like a real "goer"'.

There was a lot of skill in the way you raced your charges. The rules were that you could touch the snails, but only on one or other of their antennae at a time so as to make him change his course. Here too there was a skill: 'If he was veering badly off track you had to touch him to get him back; but if you touched him too hard, then the snail would go back into its shell and you were history—you'd lose the race unless you could quickly get him to come back out.'

As the brothers got older and stronger the games got ever more vigorous. Backyard games the world over tend to be miniature mirrors of the wider sporting scene around them and the Jones backyard was no exception. The mainstream Sydney of that time had a steady sports diet of cricket and tennis in the summer, and one or other of the football codes in the winter. Rugby League was far and away the most popular of the latter and the brothers hero-worshipped some of the players from this code. And no one more so than a man by the name of Vince Farrar, who played for the Cronulla-Sutherland side, which was the Rugby League team closest to Gymea.

The aforesaid Mr Farrar was notable, Peter says, because 'he was such a rotund little front-rower, who would keep taking the ball up and keep getting "creamed" by the opposition. He never tried to sidestep or anything like that, he just kept taking it up, taking it up, and always getting creamed.'

Soon after seeing Farrar play for Cronulla, when on one occasion their father took them to see a local game, the brothers started playing 'Vince Farrar' in their backyard.

A game of 'Vince', involved each of the three boys getting ceremonially dressed in their league jerseys, and going out to the backyard to play man-on-man rugby league. Brother against brother in the backyard, with one brother on the sideline waiting to take on the winner, the aim of the game was to score three tries for a win.

The try line was three paces inside the back fence and four paces from the house at the other end and the 'out' lines were the rockeries that lined the edges of the garden.

And anything went. Full-on front tackles were the desired way to stop your man, but if that didn't work it was quite acceptable to push him into the rockery. At least it was acceptable to Nick.

'Nick,' says Peter, 'was absolutely without mercy in those tackles, and if a rockery beckoned then he didn't hesitate. In we'd go, pushed straight into it by Nick, just so he could stop us.'

The kid who had been such a handful for his father at soccer training was more than a handful now for his brothers. Partly because the only way Nick could compete with Peter's extra two year's growth and arguably greater athletic talent was to develop a killer instinct.

Terrible fights would of course ensue during games of Vince and more often than not the game would finish in some sort of a stoush. Either Nick had gone too far—executing too brutal a tackle—or, God forbid, Nick had lost a game and thrown a tantrum or whatever else he could get his hands on just to get back at his brothers for beating him.

On one notable occasion Nick had lost a game to Peter in a tight one and the thing that happened to be closest at hand was a tomahawk.

Simon, who had been watching from the sidelines recalls: 'Nick just had that look in his eyes that he got when he was about to blow up, and I remember when I saw him get that look, and then eye the tomahawk, I thought *uh-oh* and just started running to get out of the way.'

Peter: 'I saw Nick pick up the tomahawk and remember thinking, "Jeez, he's not really going to throw that is he?" and then, "Oh MY GOD he is!" and I started running like crazy, swerving from side to side trying to get away from him, and I'd just swerved to the left when this axe went whistling past my right ear and into the fibro shed Dad had just built down in the backyard.'

Nick: 'The main thing is it missed him.'

(On another occasion when Simon had refused to continue

playing cricket with Nick after beating him in a game of one-on-one, Nick had hurled a stump after him and severed his Achilles tendon, putting him in hospital for a couple of days.)

If Rosemary heard some sort of a noise and screaming out the back, it wasn't exactly an unusual noise when her sons were playing in the backyard. She would, she says, 'keep a rolled newspaper handy to sometimes slow them down a bit; but when it came to actually stopping them fighting, Max was the one'.

Peter Baker, by now one of the more frequent playmates in the backyard, concurs.

He remembers frequently being so shocked by the ferocity of their 'games' that he found himself 'praying their father would return to stop the carnage!'

As to Max, he was less than impressed to find his fibro shed damaged when he returned, but brotherly solidarity was still strong enough that even when it came to the matter of a tomahawk being hurled at a head, he never did find out the full story of how a couple of panes of his precious fibro shed got broken.

When night would fall, the brothers Jones reluctantly headed for bed and put a stop to their games. Unless of course their mother and father had gone out for the evening, leaving them in the hands of a babysitter. In which case they could always find a way to play a game of Vince in one of the bedrooms, Nick's bedroom at the back of the house being the favourite because it was slightly bigger and afforded more room to manoeuvre.

It also served well because it was furthest from the babysitter sitting in the front room.

The rules were different in the room, of course. Instead of 'one-on-one' it was 'one-on-two', and the way to score a try was for the one with the ball to succeed in getting it on the bed while the other two did everything they could to stop him. There was only one way to do that; put your head down and charge.

So they put their heads down and charged. Inevitably damage resulted. Sometimes to the furniture, more often to the boys.

The other variation in this room game, which would later prove useful in Nick's rugby career, was that it was quite allowable to rip the ball off the attacker and then go straight ahead to score yourself.

'I've often thought,' says Farr-Jones now, 'that whatever skills I've been able to acquire in mauling the ball came originally from that game. Whether you're trying to get it off someone in the middle of a muddy maul, or trying to get it off one of your brothers in the middle of the back bedroom, it's much the same thing. Get the ball, come what may.'

This innate competitiveness extended even to the simple act of watching television. It was all but impossible for the three brothers simply to sit down and watch the rugby league on the television as did the rest of the population. That would be too boring by half. Instead, each brother would have to 'go' for one or other of the teams. Older brother Peter barracked for the Canterbury-Bankstown Bulldogs; Simon went for the Balmain Tigers and Nick for the South Sydney Rabbitohs.

In the Christmas of 1968 their father Max gave each boy a styrofoam surfboard with their club colours and mascot motif upon it. Needless to say they had only taken possession of the boards for mere hours before they were down in the surf having competitions as to who could ride the board for the longest, who could catch the most difficult wave, who could catch the *biggest* wave, and on and on.

As usual Peter won all or nearly all of the competitions, while Nick, as was his wont, raged at bitter fate that had given him the undoubted slowest of the surfboards. Simon was content to eke out his wins wherever he could, though he learned from bitter experience not to be too vainglorious about it all, for fear of a thumping.

On one particular day Simon got it wrong. Fate had ordained that Balmain would play South Sydney in the grand finals of the 1969 series, and Souths were the 'red-hot favourites'. Sitting down to watch the game, Nick couldn't have been happier.

He loved that team. Simple as that. There was just something about them. He loved the personalities of the players, the way they played, the way they walked onto the field. Loved 'em. He was so happy because he knew that today they just couldn't lose and were going to beat Simon's team, which would make the victory even more sweet. He just couldn't wait for his Souths to *really* humiliate Simon's Balmain.

Souths lost. 11–2. Never even looked like winning. Sitting down watching, Nick could barely speak he was so furious. Just let Simon say one thing, *one thing*, and he'd go for him.

It didn't come. Simon may have been young but he still had the good sense to keep his counsel at a time like this.

But it still didn't save him.

Nick didn't like the way he *looked* at him and, without a word, jumped up, chased him into the backyard and pummelled him fiercely till his fury was spent.

When put in the dock over his childhood atrocities against his brothers, Farr-Jones is defensive but untroubled.

'I don't know why I was like that. It only used to happen when I was uptight or losing, but I suppose I got uptight fairly easily . . . It's just that I'm extremely competitive and I didn't like losing. During the game, if I got behind or there was a threat of losing, I just used to up the ante as far as aggression went, to a point where my brothers couldn't match it. But I mean at the same time I was very, very close to my brothers and we loved each other madly and we would do anything for each other, really anything. It was just that I had a very bad temper.'

There was also this: Nick drew a great distinction between what was acceptable behaviour with his brothers and what was acceptable to the rest of the world.

'I still think I was a good sportsman as a kid. I captained the local soccer team and I think I always accepted losses well, at least when in the presence of the opposing team. But there's a difference when you're playing against third parties as opposed to playing against your brothers. A big difference.'

'When I was playing against other people I tried to be fair and I tried not to cheat and I tried not to injure anyone or use illegal tactics, and I think I accepted losses quite well; but against my brothers, I tried to cheat, I was illegal, I hated losing, I didn't take losing well.'

In the end the brothers didn't really mind. Nick was just like that and because he was your brother you accepted it and just worked your way around it. As Peter says, 'It was just one of those things that, whereas some families filled in their time reading or studying or going for walks or whatever, what we most liked to do was prove ourselves to each other. Sometimes it would get out of hand a bit—the competitiveness of it particularly— but you really didn't mind because you were right into it too and through it all we were very, very close.'

So close they even developed their own kind of language. It all began when, on a weekend away, they heard a friend of their father refer to his wife as the 'trouble'n'strife', the phone as the 'Al Capone', a cheque as a 'Gregory Peck', and so on.

Delighted by it, the Jones boys soon set about renaming everything they could think of after their own fashion.

In short order, instead of playing snooker they would play 'Jo Palooka', to have 'a leak', they'd have a 'Werris Creek'. Their father wouldn't drink a beer, he'd have a 'schmeer', and so on.

In all, the Joneses of Gymea were a very self-contained family, generally happy in their own company. Max was always at the pharmacy, of course, working from early until late, but that was by necessity and not choice. So it was to Rosemary that fell much of the actual bringing up of the boys.

Life inside the house was in marked contrast to the wildness that reigned in the backyard. Meal-times were actually quite formal, with the boys sitting up at the table, always with shirts and long pants on, never shorts or T-shirts, and whatever the games that had been going on previously the boys always washed themselves down before dinner.

But never washed up afterwards. Nor did they make their beds or do anything that came under the category of 'domestic chores', other than the odd carwash or lawnmow. That was just the way of things. Max worked at the pharmacy, Rosemary worked in the home, and the boys played games.

Soccer remained Nick's game of choice through his early childhood, as he continued to play with the Lilli Pilli side and then the wider Sutherland representative side.

Peter Baker, by now something of a 'fourth brother', played beside Nick all the way and remembers his role in the team well. 'He was a sort of "nice bully" . . . You knew that when Nick was nearby you'd really better be going hard for the ball or otherwise he'd sort of *look* at you . . .'

As captain of the local side Nick could choose more or less the position he wanted to play, and where else could he choose but the position of centre-forward? From here he could control the action, send the ball out to wherever he wanted. Occasionally he'd drop back to centre-defender, where he could equally control the back game.

His aim was not just to be a good soccer player, but to be the best.

On one occasion Peter happened to notice Nick out in the backyard after breakfast, just bouncing the ball up and down on his foot, and thought nothing of it until he happened to pass again about three hours later and saw Nick still at it, trying to get the ball under total control so it would never touch the ground.

'His single-minded determination to control the ball was amazing.'

It was also in the realm of soccer that Nicholas found his all-time great heroes and the year's great sporting events. Rugby tests could come and go on the sporting calendar and the brothers would only vaguely be aware, if at all, but come soccer's FA Cup final, and it was like Christmas—only eighteen days to go, only seventeen days to go, sixteen days to go, etc.

When the big day came the three brothers would head to Peter Baker's house and excitedly wait up discussing who was going to win.

A frequent topic of conversation, as Peter Baker recalls it, was 'how wonderful it would be to walk up those stairs and get the trophy from the Queen'.

'Childish stuff, I guess, but as kids it was the most magnificent thing we could ever contemplate, the best thing in life that could possibly ever happen to us, even though we knew it was impossible.'

It was possible, however, to win the local version of the FA Cup, which was the state-wide Champion of Champions soccer competition, in which Lilli Pilli was entered in 1969.

They trained hard and after three months of knock-out competition the Lilli Pilli side made the grand final—with only one problem. Their star player and captain, Nick, was with his family on the ski slopes at Thredbo on the day the final was due to be played.

Problem solved. Nicholas was flown up for the occasion. All of ten years old, he caught the plane from the snow, was picked up at the airport by Rosemary's brother Neil, who took him to Guildford, where he captained the side; they won the day, Nick made a speech, Uncle Neil took him back to the airport and he flew back down to Thredbo in victory.

All in a day in the life . . .

'The funny thing is that I can't remember much about the soccer that day at all,' says Nick, 'but I've got a really clear memory of going absolutely nuts inside because Uncle Neil was driving so slowly to get to the game. Really, he drove with about fifty metres of space between him and the next car and I wanted to say to him, "Uncle Neil, for Pete's sake WILL YOU MOVE UP A BIT!" But of course I couldn't and just had to sit there as quietly as I could.'

Farr-Jones's great heroes of early youth were, predictably from the sporting realm: the great Australian cricketer Sir Donald Bradman and the American golfer Jack Nicklaus. Despite Sir Donald's having retired two decades earlier, Nick still clamoured for his parents to get him books about the great man and always pretended to be him when it was his turn to bat in the backyard cricket.

As for Jack Nicklaus: 'I just thought he was the absolute *man*,' Nick says. 'Not only a wonderful sportsperson, but he had that aura of being a charming man, a great man, a person who had tremendous influence in his sport.'

As far as rugby was concerned there was barely a player Nick could name, let alone idolise.

'It just didn't really register with us back then,' he says. 'I was right into soccer, lived for the FA Cup final, and we watched a bit of rugby league or golf if Jack Nicklaus was playing. Rugby was a game we knew was out there but didn't really have any idea about.'

In all the boys' sporting endeavours there was a constant presence other than their parents': their grandfather, Noel Burns. One of the principal pleasures in his later life was following the sporting pursuits of his grandsons and he was the most faithful of spectators whenever they competed for the school.

'He'd tell them they could do anything, anything they wanted to do in sport,' Rosemary says, 'because they were good; they were great. As soon as he'd find they were interested in a sport he'd acquire all the literature on it, read up on it himself, give them the books and buy them all the equipment.'

'When we were into cricket,' Peter recalls, 'we all got a cricket kit with pads, bats, gloves, the works. When we started to get interested in tennis, we all got new tennis racquets for Christmas with books on tennis.'

There 'Grandad' would be, before every event, telling them they could do it because, in his words, 'they had the little red cells'.

The same cells, the same genealogy that had made him a sporting champion. Surely on occasion the lads would tire from the constant round of cricket, football, tennis, swimming and running?

On occasion, yes. Then they'd play golf.

Their Gymea home was very near to Kareela Golf Course, and

a favourite activity after school was to go to the course to search
for golf balls. Again, it was a competition. Not only who could
find the most golf balls, but also who could find the *best* golf
balls.

On the weekend they would go and play, in a trio.

'If you played golf with Nick,' says Simon, 'you pretty much
counted on going through a putter or a club every round. He'd
slam putters into trees and the putter head would fly off or he'd
bash the driver into the turf and so on.

At least by this time Simon and Peter had begun to learn the
delicate art of getting Nick out of these filthy moods.

'After he did something like smash his putter into a tree,' says
Peter, 'it all depended on whether you talked to him about it
and chastised him. If you did that, then you were history; you
wouldn't get him out of it for a full day. But if you just kept
absolutely silent and let him brew on it, you had a chance of
calming him down within half an hour or so.'

So it went. One little boy pounding his putter into a twisted
lump of metal while the other two boys stood silently by, a quick
look of silent exasperation between them but saying nothing.
Then quietly to the next tee, waiting for the storm to pass.

One of the reasons the lads were so keen to do well at golf
was that it was their father's favourite game. While Max had
neither the time nor the inclination to join them in playing Vince
or racing snails up the wall, he loved to play his sons at golf.
When he got the time.

Throughout most of their childhood Max simply wasn't there,
other than late at night or early in the morning. From running
just one pharmacy he had soon progressed to doing the overall
buying and running of the seven shops that his boss had bought
and was even busier than before.

When the boys looked up to their father they saw an ambitious
man who loved his family, yet worked so hard that for weeks
at a time he was not sighted at the evening dinner table.

It was 'all about working hard for rewards', he explained to
them. Sure, he wanted to come home a lot earlier; sure, he'd
love to come into the backyard to play cricket with them instead
of going back out to one of the shops on a Saturday afternoon;
but he was working hard now, so that he'd be wealthy enough
to spend a lot more time with them later.

Apart from the odd skiing weekends, his one respite from this work usually came at the end of year when for a couple of weeks he and Ro would take the family away for holidays up to Ro's father's holiday house in the Blue Mountains to the west of Sydney. It was here that the three boys and their father would get into their most serious golf.

Left to their own devices the boys would play up to fifty-four holes a day. While the competition between them was hard, they were also there to improve their strokes so that they'd be ready to impress their father when he did play with them. That was the really big occasion.

Simon, who later became so good at the game that he considered turning professional, remembers: 'The first part of the struggle came at the beginning of the round when we'd fight among ourselves to see who could hit off first because we wanted to impress Dad with our shots the most.

'So it was, like, hitting our shots, standing and saying "See that, Dad? That was a great shot, wasn't it?" It was like looking for accolades from your father because you respected him so much in a competitive manner. It was not so much self-satisfaction as showing your father who was the best sportsman.'

Around them, as they continued their golf, their backyard games, their snail races and brotherly brawls . . . Sydney, and the times themselves, were a'changing. This was, after all, the late sixties when the Vietnam war was at its height, when the sexual revolution was in full swing and protesters on the streets of the city were a common sight.

Such goings-on were no more than vague rumblings in the distance, which if they cocked their ear just right and stood on their tippy-toes they could manage to hear, but as it was of no particular interest to them, they rarely bothered.

The boys played on.

CHAPTER THREE

The Playing Fields of Newington

Franklin: *Have you ever thought, Headmaster, that your standards might perhaps be a little out of date?*
Headmaster: *Of course they're out of date. Standards always are out of date. That is what makes them standards.*
Alan Bennett, *Forty Years On*, 1968

Newington College, Stanmore, stands as an island of genteelism amid the proletarian sprawl in the inner west of Sydney Town.

When this famous boys' private school moved to its present site in 1880 (after its founding in 1863), the surrounding area was mostly occupied by the semi-rural bourgeoisie who lived around what was then an undeveloped part of Sydney. The school's raison d'être was as a refuge from what was considered at the time as the horrors of public education, and soon became *the* place to go for 'the sons of Christian gentlemen'.

These pupils were drawn predominantly from the nearby suburbs, together with a smattering of the sons from the far landed gentry. All were boarders initially.

It is an imposing school with the grandeur of its spacious grounds and original sandstone buildings contrasting rather markedly with the 'higgledy-piggledyness' of many of the surrounding terraces. Since the turn of the century waves of haphazard development have washed up to and around the school's boundaries, but left the insides unchanged. The school merely drew its students from ever further afield. The bourgeoisie had for the most part long before moved on, gone to points south, east, and particularly north.

But while the east and north of Sydney had many private schools, and the west had a fair sprinkling, the south had nothing. Max and Rosemary Jones, living in the south, decided to send their sons to Newington because it was very highly regarded and also the southernmost private school of the inner western sprinkling.

This would involve a lot of train travel for the boys—from Gymea station to Redfern to Stanmore and then a five-minute walk—up to three hours a day, round trip. But they felt it would be worth it because they regarded Newington as such a fine school.

For a time, though, it was touch and go whether the Joneses could afford to send them there. Max was again financially strapped, having bought his own pharmacy by borrowing 100,000 dollars, and it was as yet uncertain whether the new business was going to be a success.

While the fees for just one boy at Newington were crippling enough, those fees would triple when the other two boys followed. They decided they could just manage if they tightened their belts and budgeted.

So one day in early February of 1972 the oldest son Peter was dispatched to Newington. Early that morning Simon and Nick watched their brother prepare for school with some trepidation. He was looking more grown up and distant from them with each item of clothing he added—first the shorts, then the grey shirt, the tie, the Newington blazer and, most incredible of all to the two young 'uns, a straw boater.

'It was like our brother had suddenly turned into an adult,' recalls Nick. 'I wanted to rip all that stuff off him and get him out in the backyard for one last game of Vince before he went, but he was way too important for that now; too grown up. He was going off to catch a train.'

And *to* train, as it turned out. After years of battling in the backyard with his brothers, and taking on all-comers around the Cronulla area in a variety of sports, Peter had all the baggage he needed to be an immediate sporting success at Newington. He went right into the As of both the cricket and rugby teams, was immediately a valued swimmer for the school and a particularly good runner.

Halfway through Peter's first year he was picked to run in that most prestigious of events, the Greater Public Schools Athletic Day, which was the same gathering at the famous Sydney

Cricket Ground that his grandfather had been the star of half a century earlier.

Max and Ro decided to take their two younger boys out of Miranda Public for the day to see Peter run. Amid all the carnival atmosphere of the cheering crowds, waving flags and competing schoolboy athletes, at least one little boy stood entranced.

'It was fantastic,' Nick says. 'I couldn't quite believe that my own brother had come this far to be a part of this world and that was the one thing that really made me look forward to going to Newington. To go and compete in the schoolboys' sports and to see if maybe one day I could run in a GPS event like that myself.'

Peter did well that day, breaking the GPS record in the long jump and earning fourth place in the 800 metres. In a school where athletic ability was so highly prized Peter, through such successes, had established a first-class beach-head into Newington, making it easier for the following two brothers.

It was also at this stage that Peter decided to follow what was fast becoming a rather skewiff family tradition. Just as the lads' grandfather had gone from 'Farr-Jones' to 'Jones' and back to 'Farr-Jones' and their father had gone from 'Farr-Jones' to 'Jones', Peter decided to go from 'Jones' to 'Farr-Jones'.

'There were five Joneses in my year at Newington,' says Peter, 'so it was obvious.'

Peter Farr-Jones it was, then, who was playing on the wing for the 14As rugby team the following year against the Shore School while his mother Rosemary watched from the sideline in the company of Newington's affable headmaster, Tony Rae.

'We were just standing there, talking about the game,' recounts Mr Rae, 'when out of the blue these two extraordinarily long-haired fellows came up, demanding money. I said, "Oh God, Rosemary, you're not going to send those two to me too, are you?" And she said, "They will have a haircut before they come, I promise you," and she handed over a few coins to each of them. That was my first meeting with Nicky and Simon.'

With the requisite haircut, Nick arrived at Newington in February of 1974. Immediately he had an identity, not just as little Nicky Farr-Jones, the fair-haired and freckled kid who was one of the smallest in school, but as 'Grot's brother', Peter having picked up the unfortunate nickname very early on in school.

Being 'Grot's brother' was useful, for Nick was feeling lost.

His 'lostness' did not last long though. Mindful of his parents' encouragement to 'have a go at everything', Nick hopped right in. There were countless activities he could turn his hand to and all of them were competitive, which suited him even better.

Academically he was put into class 1B, and immediately applied himself to his studies, being one of the few student commuters to actually hit the books during the train trip.

One of his early teachers from this time, Clive Woosnam, remembers that 'Nick was always a hard worker and very meticulous. Presentation of his homework was always beautifully done. The oddity was that he seemed to be more assiduous in doing his homework than he actually was in class, when his mind might wander. It was only when he was specifically going to get a mark on something that he would really apply himself.'

Nick soon made firm friends with the boys in his class, among them John Roper, also from 1B, who recalls that, 'Nick was the sort of bloke who was fairly shy when the teachers were around but totally at ease and cheeky with us. If you were standing around outside a class and somebody suddenly put licorice down the back of your shirt and started patting you on the back, you knew it was probably Nick.'

Another good friend of that time was the headmaster's son, Stephen Rae. Many was the time that Stephen would go over to stay at the Farr-Jones house, or Nick would stay over at the Headmaster's Residence at the school. At the end of term, one would often go on holidays with the other's family.

It was through his son's friendship with Nick that Headmaster Rae would get an early and intimate look at the lad who would go on to be Newington's most famous graduate.

Two incidents particularly stand out in his mind: There was the time when Nicky had gone up with the Rae family to their holiday house in Avoca and, after a pleasurable afternoon barbecue on the front verandah, Mr and Mrs Rae had retired to the house.

But now there's a funny thing. Nick, alone and unaware he was being watched from the window, twirling the circular plate on the barbecue round and round. What on earth could he be doing, spinning it around like that? Then the penny dropped.

Tony Rae recounts: 'Directly below the verandah a road was running by, and Nicky was listening for the sound of cars coming up the hill. When he had anticipated exactly where the car would be at the right moment, he twirled the hotplate so that a sausage and a tomato were hurled off it to splatter on to the windscreen below.'

The headmaster had just gone out onto the verandah to remonstrate that this was not the behaviour he expected of a Newington boy and certainly not of one who was a guest in his own house, when he heard the sound of a car screeching to a halt, reversing, and he was soon confronted with a furious motorist storming up the drive.

Usually Stephen Rae was sensible enough to keep his distance when Nick was engaged in such nefarious activity, though on one notable occasion he too got caught, when on the way back from Avoca one Sunday evening the two of them were reported to the station master at Gosford because they had been practising golf shots from the train, firing golf balls into the passing tangle of farms.

Back at school there were many extra-curricular activities to be involved in, even before you counted sport.

When his form was asked for volunteers to join the debating team, and no one else would at first volunteer, Nick threw his hand up 'to see what it was all about'.

It was about swaying a lot of people to your point of view, even when you might not really believe it yourself—great groundwork for a future lawyer ('My client is innocent'), and not bad for a future Wallaby captain either ('We *can* beat the All Blacks today by twenty points, I'm telling you!').

In the early days he was predictably terrible. No eye contact. No confidence. No delivery. Slowly it came. If at the end of that first debating season he wasn't exactly a budding Socrates, he was at least writing his own speeches and starting to deliver them with the bare beginnings of confidence.

At its best, Newington was like that. While other schools might concentrate just on turning out people who were well-grounded academically, Newington wanted to go further. Ye olde school prided itself on its ability to turn out good *men*, of gentlemanly disposition, equally capable of knowing how to break down a logarithmic equation to its most basic unit as knowing good manners, as being able to stand and speak confidently in public, in French if necessary. Young students would be exposed to many different experiences that would help to create well-rounded individuals, and in the process hopefully a lad might come across a previously undiscovered talent and make it blossom.

Sport was a large part of this. Not just sport to fill up an afternoon a week, but as a part of teaching boys some of the rudiments of winning and losing, competitiveness and teamwork, camaraderie and a healthy lifestyle. Sports and academics were the two pillars on which the lives of the Newington students were built.

To maximise the possibilities for sporting and other competition, the school was divided up into 'Houses', a tight grouping of students who would compete against each other year-round in intra-school contests to see who was the winning House at the end of the year. Like Peter before him, Nick was put into Johnson House, and the first sport of the year was swimming. Nick, who'd spent a good part of his youth pounding up and down pools, blitzed 'em, winning the under thirteen years fifty metres backstroke and coming second in the fifty metres freestyle.

There was also cricket, where Nick played in the 13As, and athletics, in which he particularly shone, taking second in the hurdles, third in the long jump and first in the 800 metres event.

His success in these events led to his selection to represent the school in the same annual Greater Public Schools athletics carnival at the SCG where he had seen Peter run the year before.

Bliss. Pure bliss. Running for his school at the SCG. On the occasion of each boy's success, there was none more pleased than Rosemary's father, Noel. By now quite elderly, he cherished his grandsons' sporting achievements and never missed an event.

Sometimes, before the race, he'd take them aside to give them last minute bits of advice. 'Make your first ten yards after the gun goes off very fast to get clear of the pack.' 'Whatever happens, don't get trapped on the inside when you come into the final turn.' 'Don't be afraid of pushing yourself too hard, it's only pain.'

For Rosemary, hearing her father talk to her sons this way brought back memories. It was exactly the way he had spoken to her when she was an athlete back at Kambala training for the swimming and athletics.

'Listen to me, Rosemary,' he would say in that very calm but forceful way of his, 'you *can* run another lap. Of course you can. You think you're tired and exhausted but what you must understand is that you've just got to get through that tiredness. It's like there's a valley on the other side that you run into and . . .'

'. . . and he was quite right,' says Rosemary. 'You'd ache and ache and suddenly you'd go a little bit further and your whole body would relax and you'd start to enjoy it, start to go faster.'

If athletics occupied an important part of the school's sporting agenda, there was another sporting pursuit that was the real focus. It was called rugby, and in principle wasn't that different from the games of Vince the Farr-Jones boys had played for so long back home at Gymea.

But this was different. Vince had been purely a boyish game; this was something else again. For the school, rugby was part of its tradition, a game that had been played by boys wearing the school's proud colours, black and white, since the days just after Newington's foundation.

As with so many private schools down Australia's east coast where the game flourishes, Rugby is considered by Newington the ideal sport for forming some of the hard edge that a man requires. Coping with pain and exhaustion. Keeping on going regardless.

It might well have been the Duke of Wellington who said it best, when he made his famous remark that 'the battle of Waterloo was won on the playing fields of Eton.'

The good burghers of Newington wouldn't have been at all surprised and it was compulsory to play rugby at that time unless one had a medical certificate of exemption.

And so it was that on a cold Tuesday afternoon in May of 1974 Nick went down to 'Old Boys' Oval' and the first year rugby selection trials, to see who would go in which team.

Trials were generally a rabble. Kids who had only the most rudimentary understanding of the rules would go back and forth up the field, running into each other, with the ball somewhere in the middle. The teacher-coaches on the sidelines would try to work out who ran into whom with most enthusiasm and graded them from there.

Nick was more than a little put off from the outset that all the other boys had steel studs in their boots, *real* rugby boots, while he still only had his plastic-studded soccer boots from the year before.

It went well for all that. Not knowing much at all about the rules, he simply reverted to his own rules of Vince and knocked over anything that moved with the ball in its hands, and on those occasions when he got the ball, he charged forward and into the fray. At the end of the game he was told by an openly admiring teacher, Peter Hipwell, that he would be in his team, the 12As. Mr Hipwell, or 'Bub' as he was affectionately nicknamed by the boys, was already well known to Nick, as he was the master-in-charge of 1B.

'He was just one of those kids you notice right away, who can do things in sport,' Hipwell says. 'You don't really teach them, it's more a matter of guiding.'

At the first training of the 12As, Nick was keen to get going and full of questions. 'Where do I go?' 'What do I do?' 'When do we get started?' And finally, 'What position do you want me to play, sir?'

Hipwell looked the lad up and down one more time—funny, he seemed even littler out here in the open air—and said, 'Well, you're so small I guess you're a natural half-back.'

One of the great things about rugby for schools was that it automatically catered for all body types. The tall kid became a second rower, the robust kid a prop, the slight and fast kid went to the wing and invariably the smallest kid of all became a half-back. If it was predictable then that 'the smallest kid in school' would end up as half-back, less predictable was how well he would perform from the beginning.

'Right away he knew how to run with the ball,' says Hipwell. 'He could step and kick, he had co-ordination and he really really wanted to win every game we played.'

Passing took a bit longer to master because that was a skill Nick had not already learnt in the games of Vince, though he soon got the hang of it, more or less. And the main thing was he loved it.

Playing Vince in the backyard with your brothers, for the pure pleasure of running into each other, was one thing. Doing much the same with a lot of other players, with lots of people watching, when you were playing for your school, added another dimension of pleasure entirely.

It wasn't a terrifically successful season, with only five wins from thirteen games, but at the end of the year the school magazine, *The Newingtonian*, recorded that, in the 12As, Nick Farr-Jones had been 'among the best three players', and he loved that too. Recognition through rugby.

There was also some academic recognition for him when, at the end of the year, he received a Merit Prize for Effort at the

School Speech Day, and was told that he would be moved up to the 'A' classes the following year.

During the school holidays the favourite day of all for the boys and their father was generally when they would go to the Sydney Cricket Ground to watch a day's play of the Test cricket. When Max himself was a young man his father had always taken him there, and he'd in fact been privileged enough to witness the last test Sir Donald Bradman ever played at the SCG.

The boys could not claim anything so exalted, though they were at least there on the famous occasion during an Ashes series, when English fast bowler John Snow was being pelted with beer cans from the notorious Sydney Hill.

The Farr-Jones lads weren't even fifty metres away from Snow at the time. Saw it all. They'd just put some more zinc cream on their noses after polishing off the last of what their mother had put in the 'Esky,' when it all broke loose. A part of sporting history, and *they were there* when it happened.

Apart from cricket they would also go to soccer matches, and occasionally rugby league matches with their father, but never a rugby Test match.

'I don't know why not,' says Max now, 'it just wasn't something that the boys clamoured to go to, and while I wouldn't have minded, we just never got around to it.'

Back at Newington the school years rattled past—filled as they were with a wide variety of activities. Just as the backyard at Gymea was its own self-contained little world, so too in a way was Newington. It took something important to happen 'outside' before they'd notice.

The man they called 'The King' died on 17 August 1977, on the Australian calendar. Far away, in some of the scrub that grows wild on the east coast of Australia, a small boy in jungle greens was moved enough to carve *Elvis Presley died today 17/8/1977*, in the base of a gum tree.

Nick, who'd always been a great Elvis fan, wasn't the only one in jungle greens that day. Off in the near distance he could see them, hundreds of them, similarly attired. This was 'cadet camp'. Junior soldiery. Just another part of Newington's program to produce well-rounded young men—well tutored, well mannered, accomplished in sport, and even able to take their part in a military organisation.

At least that was the theory. Try as he might, Farr-Jones could never quite get the hang of blindly following orders.

It wasn't so bad when he could see what they were getting at, but if the 'military authorities' (actually older students with higher rank) asked him to do something stupid then he couldn't help but relieve himself of the opinion that it was in fact stupid.

After all, what the hell was the point of standing to attention in a *certain way*, so long as you were standing to attention *more or less*? Who the hell cared in the final wash-up?

Sergeant Dockery cared, for one. Actually it was Mark Dockery, a Newington student two years ahead of Farr-Jones at school, whose unfortunate duty it was to try to beat some sense of military discipline into Nick's recalcitrant head.

'It wasn't easy and I don't know if I can claim victory in the end,' Dockery says now. 'He could never understand why his boots had to be polished and his belt buckle shined, that sort of thing, and he was always a nightmare at the end of year Passing Out Parade, because you wouldn't know how he'd turn up, if he'd come polished or not.

'He had an attitude which meant that he was often down on my list to do fifty push-ups after drill-training was over. Still, it was a good-natured sort of rebelliousness he had, and I thought he was overall a good kid.'

If Nick found it hard to cope with discipline in military life, it was far easier to cope with when it came to rugby. There, discipline had a real point to it, because it often meant the difference between winning and losing, and because as captain he was primarily the fellow imposing the discipline.

As captain of successively the 13As, 14As and now 15As, he had come to be a great believer in discipline as a means to win a rugby game. The discipline not to talk back to the referee if a decision went against you, the discipline to play more or less to the game plan, the discipline to force yourself to keep going even when you might be tired.

And even the discipline not to give in to the temptation to retaliate when provoked. Greg Mottee, who played with Nick in the 15As, remembers a game against another GPS school when Sam Clifton, one of their team-mates, was felled by a wicked blow from behind.

'Nick came into the huddle with tears in his eyes—he was so shocked by what he saw—but he told us just to forget it, not to try and get the guy back; that the best way to even the score was just to play hard and beat them.'

The Newingtonian of 1977 recorded that although the 15As had only marginally more wins than losses to their credit, at least 'Nicholas Farr-Jones never gave up trying in any game. His captaincy was one of setting an example for the rest of his players to follow rather than merely giving orders and cajoling . . . '

Nick's rugby education would continue on an end-of-year Newington rugby tour to Japan, the United Kingdom, Europe and the USA.

The tour was taken away by a teacher who was also a former Wallaby, Herb Barker, and by the school athletics coach, Barry Rex.

It was touch and go whether Nick would initially make the trip because as a fifteen year old among a touring party that was primarily made up of seventeen year olds his parents were a little concerned that he would be out of his depth, but Nick was so keen to be a part of it that his parents eventually conceded and came up with the money. Max Jones at least took Barry Rex aside at the airport and asked him to keep a special eye on the lad, but other than that he was on his own for the first time.

There was only so much Rex could do. With another twenty-nine boys to look after he could not be everywhere at once, and it was inevitable therefore that the tour would provide its fair share of seminal moments for the youngster.

The trip stood then not only as the first rugby tour he had ever been on but also the first time Nick had smoked a cigarette and the first time he got drunk.

On the ferry during the crossing from Dover to Le Havre he and a friend, Simon Stiles (who was later to be tragically killed in a car accident), made the mistake of following some crewmen to a cabin party where the drink of choice was white bacardi.

One thing led to another, led to another drink, led to Nick being so drunk, sitting in a toilet cubicle, that there would be bruises on his thighs for the following five days from the weight of his drunken head pressing his elbows down into the flesh.

Then there was the rugby. On this particular tour Farr-Jones was not the first choice half-back. That distinction belonged to a boy in the form ahead, by the name of Col O'Connor, a good, solid-passing half-back whose major skill was to be able to drill the ball far and accurately.

Halfway through the tour O'Connor noticed that while Farr-Jones was reasonably proficient at passing the ball from right to left, when he passed it from left to right the ball was likely to spray wildly in any direction.

'Listen,' he told the young'un after a game in London, 'you will never be a good half-back until you can pass the ball to both sides with equal accuracy. You've got to practise your passes till you can put out a long flat pass to left or right *every* time you need to.

Farr-Jones listened, as always one part boy and three parts obsessive streak.

Early the following morning in Kensington Gardens Nick was to be spied passing the ball to the left, aiming to hit a thin tree some ten metres away, then retrieving it, then going again. He also took to carrying a squash ball in his pocket, which he would continually squeeze so as to strengthen his left wrist.

And he was yet really to begin. The real work came when he returned to Australia. Happening once to have heard that golfers sometimes practise swinging two clubs together so that just one club will feel light when they approach the first tee, Nick decided that the equivalent in rugby would be to practise passing by using a housebrick.

It was heavy. It was hard to do. It was perfect.

He practised with the brick just as he used to practise with the soccer ball as a much younger lad. Which is to say all day long.

When the time again came for the rugby season, he attacked with new vigour, confident that this season he would be able to fire with both barrels, and not just the right one. And his confidence proved well founded. Passing to the left the captain of the 16As might not have quite been good enough to knock the cigarette out of a passing sparrow's mouth at twenty metres, but he'd go close.

He also brought to his team supreme fitness. Just that year—Nick's second last in school—he'd won the School's Cross Country Championship in the under sixteen age group, on the same day Peter had won the Open and younger brother Simon had won the under fifteen.

Not that there were always to be such rosy successes in running. In August of that year, 1978, Nick was upset. Very upset. It wasn't just that he'd lost in a sporting event, which was always galling enough, but that he'd again lost to Mike Ritchie, the boy from Sydney Grammar. In fact not just 'the boy from Sydney Grammar' but also the boy who lived just over the road from him at the new house his parents had bought in Cronulla (the pharmacy was now doing well). The boy, who had become a good friend of his, the boy he bloody well never beat in the schools' athletic competitions.

What *really* got to him was the way Ritchie had beaten him. Always it was the same thing. Nick'd be leading in the 1500 metres pretty much all the way through, and then with about 100 metres to go Ritchie would 'kick', and with his superior sprinting ability be able to haul Farr-Jones in and pass him at the death to come first.

Barry Rex felt for his young charge. With the big GPS meet at the Sports Ground coming up in a few short weeks, and the rivalry between Newington and Sydney Grammar as keen as ever, he knew that a lot of that ineffable thing called 'school prestige' would be riding on such high-profile events as the 1500 metres, and that Nick felt the responsibility keenly.

'I never thought that Nick was an absolutely fantastic athletic talent,' Rex recalls now, 'but he had something even more important than that—he knew how to work hard over a long period of time. He was the hardest trainer I'd ever come across and I think he was like that because, in terms of athletic talent, he was maybe just that bit in the shadow of his other two brothers.'

Hard worker he might be, but it still wasn't getting him any closer to beating Ritchie in the GPS meet.

Rex decided that Nick had to change his whole strategy. 'I said, "All right, mate, so we've got to go out faster. We've got to run even laps all the way. You've got to go flat out right at the start and burn him off so at the end he's nothing left to kick with. We've got to do him that way."'

In the time left leading up to the race, Nick trained, Rex says, 'as hard as anyone I've ever seen', and he had to shepherd him off the oval for fear he would strain himself.

On the day before the race the two journeyed from Newington to the Sydney Sports Ground, where the venue had been recently moved from the SCG, to familiarise themselves with the territory.

In a scene that might have come from *Chariots of Fire* the two walked around the deserted field. At a point some 200 metres from the finish Rex marked the spot and said, 'Now, Nick, *you're* going to "kick" from here.'

In a last-minute revision the plan was for Farr-Jones to ease off just marginally in the third lap so that with 200 metres to go he could, if necessary, 'kick' himself and kill off whatever hope Ritchie might have of staging his own big finish. But still go out very, very hard.

As always the GPS crowds had turned out in force.

'I was feeling tight, hard, wanting to get on with it,' Farr-Jones remembers. 'I avoided Mike the whole day before the race and right up to the gun because, though I didn't want to snub him, I was in no mood to be friendly or do any palling around. I think he felt the same way.'

He did.

'There was always something about him when it came to sport,' Ritchie recalls now. 'It didn't matter how much you were mucking around, how close a friend you might be to Nick, when it came to sport and someone was keeping a score, or timing you, then he would be deadly, deadly serious. On that particular day I did happen to catch sight of him before the race and he looked as if he was on a mission or something. He was just so set, so determined.'

The gun went off, and as planned Farr-Jones tore out of the blocks to take the early lead. Ritchie sat in behind, thinking that if Nick kept up this pace he'd burn himself out in two laps.

But three laps later, when they rang the bell, Nick was still in the lead and moving along well—although, as he remembers now, 'I knew that Mike was just there behind me, that he'd come at me, and unless I burned him off with those 200 metres to go, as planned, then he'd beat me.'

It all worked to perfection, except that Nick couldn't quite burn him off, as planned. When he made his 'kick' from 200 metres out, Ritchie came with him, so he kicked a little harder and Ritchie came again. Fifty metres from home, Farr-Jones was just barely ahead and could feel Ritchie making one last assault, when he pulled up from somewhere the last bit of energy required to reach the line first.

When he collapsed over the line, just in front of Ritchie, the crowd roared its approval for the great race and Noel Burns murmured to his daughter beside him that 'the little red cells' had come good again. That and a will to win that seemed all but indomitable.

'I think you're born with a certain amount of competitiveness,' Nick says, 'but I attribute most of my competitiveness to the fact that I had a brother either side of me, and whatever we did, whether it was golf, tennis, cricket, Vince Farrar, running races, or whatever it was, I had to try extra hard to beat them.'

His father Max agrees, in slightly more pithy terms.

'Nick always had the killer instinct the other two lacked,' he says. 'He was definitely less athletically gifted than Peter and maybe less than Simon, but of my three sons he was the one that developed the greatest will to win, come what may.'

The odd thing of course is that such an aggressive will to win did not turn Nick into rugby's answer to John McEnroe—a boorish brat who offended people wherever he went. On the contrary, he was later known as very much the Rugby diplomat.

Part of the credit for this—the overlaying of a reasonable human being atop an entirely unreasonable will to win—can be traced to something that began one summer's evening in 1978, on Christmas holidays from Newington.

Nick was with Simon and Mike Ritchie's brother Mal, when he decided they should all go up to the local pizza shop in Caringbah for some dinner. There was also the possibility, as Nick recalls, that they might meet some nice girls.

Bingo. Two blondes, maybe sixteen or eighteen, a little hard to tell.

Hi. Whatcha doin'?

About to go off to the evening service at church. Would you like to come?

Yes.

Simon was aghast. 'Only a very short time after meeting these girls Nick was going off with them to church to attend evening service. Had I not seen it, I wouldn't have believed it.'

Nick's religious background at this stage was pretty much 'standard brand'. The family was Presbyterian, chiefly in the sense that that was the church they currently were not attending.

They were taken to Sunday School as young children, 'to get some moral training', Max says, though that had stopped after a couple of years because they had all been so miserable and hated it. Other than that there'd been attendance to chapel at Newington, and the odd class of divinity during which Nick's mind used to wander 'to whatever sport I'd be playing in the afternoon'.

Somehow, though, Caringbah Baptist was not like other churches. Though physically it was quite normal—red brick and dull—*spiritually* it was something else again.

There was no set format to the way the service would run and almost anything might happen. At the first service Nick attended someone stood and started the congregation singing, before the service started. Then someone else got up and welcomed the visitors. Another gave a testimonial as to why he had become a Christian.

Nick was hooked. A youth service followed the main service and after that some of the young ones went out together for a late-night bite to eat. Nick found the whole thing so enjoyable he started to go back every Sunday after that and his social life was soon enmeshed with this group of young Christians.

The religion had its effect. 'After a month or so I was really touched by Christianity and the people, and after about two months I started to get this warm feeling and *understand* the Gospel and I ended up making a big commitment to Christ.'

For his parents and brothers it was a difficult time. They simply could not understand how Nick, *Nick*, of all people, had been so suddenly converted to such a dramatically different way of life. Instead of being around the house or out with his brothers somewhere on a Sunday, he'd be going to church, a youth service, then fellowship, then out with some of the other Christians afterwards. Often not getting home till 10.30 p.m or even later.

His mother, oddly enough, was the most concerned about the sort of company he was keeping.

'It's not that we didn't like them or anything like that, it's just that they seemed so quickly to be a dominant force in his life. Usually you meet people and gradually warm to them and maybe become friends as time goes by, but these Christians appeared on the scene and right away they were sort of central to him.'

Acceptance also came hard for both of Nick's brothers.

'All at once,' says Simon, 'our own brother was starting to "bag" us for the way we spoke, our attitudes, our lack of Christian belief, things like that . . . going out too late. So you'd say to him, "Hang on, that's not *you* speaking is it, Nick?" and you'd just cop it both barrels—"*Yes* that *is* me, I've CHANGED, Simon, don't you understand?"'

And in many ways he really had changed.

All the family credit Christianity with having helped to curb Nick's explosive temper, just as they credit it with giving him perhaps a more rounded, gentler view of the world. While once he might have tended to explode immediately into a rage over the smallest thing, they could now almost see him mentally consulting the Christian texts before flying off the handle.

Still, there was essentially the same old Nick beneath it all.

A couple of years after his 'conversion to Christ' Simon went with Nick and some friends to the Caringbah local for 'a bit of a drink'.

In Simon's memory it went like this: 'We were all sitting at the table, having a beer, and these guys were sitting next to us, drinking heavily, becoming more and more drunk, and they started sliding their empty beer glasses across the table and smashing them into ours.'

'As soon as this started you could see the look in Nick's eyes— he'd lost it completely—and all of a sudden I thought, "Oh, no, he's going to blow", but it seemed his new Christianity was holding him back. And he just said to one of the guys, "Don't do that again. Please don't do that again."'

'So these guys thought that was great and the next guy finishes his glass and slides it across and it smashes a glass right next to Nick on the table. So Nick jumps out of his seat, grabs the guy, hurls him against the wall and says, "Listen, mate, I'm a Christian first but I'm getting very angry and if you do that again I'll kill you."'

'The guy just got back into his chair like he was scared stiff and we didn't hear a word from them for the rest of the evening.'

The position of the school captain within the private school system is extremely prestigious. While in hindsight it might seem strange that someone like Farr-Jones should not have been viewed as a serious contender for this position, Headmaster Tony Rae says he was in no doubt at the time.

'I didn't even think of the possibility. There is a certain sort of maturity required for someone to be captain of a school like Newington and Nick just didn't have it. Not that he was immature exactly, but he certainly wasn't the right one for such a role. He was too much of a rascal, in the nicest sense of the word.'

After all, the headmaster reasoned, it would be hardly

appropriate to appoint a boy as school captain who had apparently laughed so hard on hearing that the prize his old debating partner Phil Stott was going to receive was a *violin* that he fell off his laboratory stool and hurt his elbow. This was not school captain material at all.

Nick was, at least, 'over the moon' to be made a prefect, and elsewhere had a great leadership record. He captained his rugby team all the way through school, bar the initial year of 12As, captained the athletics team, the swimming team, and having converted to the tennis team in his final year (having been disillusioned with cricket because the brutes had only put him in the thirds), he was also made captain of that, even though he ranked only third out of four players.

Surprisingly, the greatest disappointment in Nick's school career came in rugby.

The First XV is the most prestigious sporting team in any GPS school, and never having played a single game for anyone other than the 'A' team Nick of course had his eye on the First XV half-back position.

After all the pre-season trials had been completed it was announced that one Murray McGain would be the First XV halfback and Nick would have to be content with captaining the Second XV.

With a view to what Farr-Jones has since achieved in rugby, it would be tempting to regard this as a colossal error.

Then again, maybe not. Perhaps Farr-Jones had a better pass, but McGain was much bigger and faster and in the opinion of the First's coach, Ray Hill, 'seemed to have a better combination with the five-eighth'.

Headmaster Tony Rae concurs that however good Farr-Jones was to become, he simply wasn't up to it at the time.

'Quite simply Murray McGain was clearly the better half-back, I've no doubt.'

Indeed, McGain must have been doing something right. Not only was Newington's First XV of 1979 remembered as one of the finest the school has produced—remaining unbeaten for the entire year, including a handsome win over the legendary, almost unbeatable, St Joseph's College—but at the end of it all McGain was named in one of the prestigious GPS combined representative sides.

In the end, while the whole thing might have been a great

disappointment to Nick, the rest of the school barely noticed. A little crew-cutted kid in first form at the time, Phillip Kearns, didn't care for one.

'As far we were concerned all the players in the Firsts and Seconds were legends. We were aware that Nick was one of the famous Farr-Joneses but it didn't particularly strike us that he only made Seconds.'

With the rugby season fading and still no sign of his breaking into the prestigious Firsts, Nick reluctantly turned his attention to his studies.

At that time in New South Wales (1979) the Higher School Certificate exam was designed to give you a number out of 500. This number then determined which university courses would admit you. So naturally the number you left with was all-important in shaping your career.

While Farr-Jones had been diligent in his studies for his first four years at Newington, he had slackened off somewhat in the last two as he got progressively more involved with school sport.

There was only one thing for it. Close everything else off and hit the books. He even took to sleeping on one or other of his boarding friends' floors, so as not to waste time journeying back and forth to Cronulla every day.

On the nights he did spend at home his family could be sure that the light would be creeping out from under his door at all hours.

'My enduring memory of that time,' Nick says, 'is continually studying until one or two in the morning, and panicking that I was going to make a mess of it. That's what gave me the energy to study so hard, I suppose. Fear of failure rather than a real desire to excel academically.'

Come the actual exams he was nervous enough to throw up several times immediately beforehand but equally determined to just tough it out, come what may.

In a student's life there are surely few greater moments for reflection than when you walk out of the school gates for the last time. For Nick, there was relief that the exams were over, hope that he'd done well, and of course regret that he hadn't studied harder earlier. He recalls also feeling a little sad that the whole school thing was over.

Over the ensuing months, while waiting for his results to be annnounced, his thoughts turned to which course he should apply for at university. Although slightly tempted to follow his father into pharmacy, 'Mum said she didn't want me to do that because she thought it was such an atrocious lifestyle, so that was out. I had always greatly admired my grandfather, and he was a gun corporate lawyer, so I thought I'd follow him into law.'

So it was law. And where else but at the alma mater of his mother, father and grandfather, Sydney University?

His mark, when it came, was just enough to scrape in.

CHAPTER FOUR

Sydney University

'There are . . . two educations.
One should teach us how to make a living and the other
how to live.'
James Trustlow Adams.

S ydney University lies some three kilometres away from Newington in the Camperdown of Sydney's inner west. The ties between the two educational institutions date back to 1869 when the first game of schoolboy rugby ever played in Australia was between Newington and Sydney University (won predictably enough by Uni), and their campuses are also similar, with 'Uni' also boasting historic sandstone buildings and beautiful sporting ovals.

Sydney University Law School, where Farr-Jones was to attend, is set off-campus in the heart of the city on Phillip Street. A tall, somewhat characterless building placed right beside the New South Wales Supreme Court, the law school has none of the historic soul of the main campus but all of its slightly haughty attitude. And then some.

Into this august place of learning then did the young Farr-Jones arrive in February of 1980 . . .

The two, institution and lad, were never properly to hit it off.

Farr-Jones was an outdoor sort of person. The law school offered the quintessence of an indoor existence—small windows, miles upon miles of dusty legal books and, for good measure, *underground* lecture halls. Farr-Jones preferred his study to come in well-rationed and easily consumed dollops. The law school demanded of its adherents a constant diet of quiet study.

One who remembers Farr-Jones from that time is John Oxland, his lecturer in criminal law.

'He was not a great student in terms of academic excellence, so much as a great person to teach. I took an immediate liking to him because he was so "in balance" in terms of Juvenal's famous aphorism: *mens sano in corpore sano* (healthy mind in healthy body). I thought he would make a far better lawyer from society's point of view than a student who was just brilliant academically. I still think so.'

For Nick, it was always a relief to finish the lectures at the end of the day and head back up George Street on the #106 bus towards the Sydney University campus proper where there was at least grass and trees, colour and movement, air and ovals.

Particularly ovals. During his first days at the University, Nick had signed on the dotted line to join the Sydney University Football Club and found himself a few weeks later training with the Sydney Uni Colts side—the under twenty-ones. Soon afterwards he would be trying his very best to make it into the Firsts of the three Colts sides.

The moment came, one wet Tuesday night, when the Firsts' coach Lindsay MacCaughan gathered the entire Colts squad on Uni's number two oval and read out the lucky players who had made it into Firsts.

'Second-rowers: Jordy Clapham and Peter FitzSimons.

'Breakaways: Andrew Dunlop and Richard Vaughan.

'Lock: Matt Playfair.

'Half-back: Nick Farr-Jones.'

Nick was delighted.

'When I didn't make the Firsts at school I had to start wondering if maybe I was already turning into one of those schoolboy athletes who never do anything once they get older, so I was just delighted that I'd climbed back into a Firsts side.'

Even playing for a team so comparatively lowly as a Colts Firsts side has a certain kudos attached to it in a place with such strong traditions of rugby as Sydney University. Back at the law school in Phillip Street Farr-Jones was already walking a good foot taller.

Yo, Nick! What are you up to this weekend?

Oh, I'm playing for University.

What team do you play for?

I play for Firsts Colts.

'I was just so proud to tell people,' he recalls. 'To walk around law school and be able to say that I was playing for Firsts Colts was just *fantastic*. That was probably why I was prepared to go from law school in the city to training at Uni, walk to Redfern Station, take a one-hour train trip home and then walk home, which was another fifteen minutes.'

The side announced by coach Lindsay MacCaughan that first night stayed together substantially throughout the year and was in the happy situation of finding that not only did they have a strong player in each position but more importantly a chemistry existed among them which almost always ensured they could do what was required to win. And without overwhelming effort. They did not train particularly hard or long; they did not introduce any stunning new tactical ploys; they did not even go through any massive psyche-up sessions before going out to play. They simply didn't need to.

While Farr-Jones was integral to the success of the side, and was a popular enough team member, he was not captain or vice-captain, and certainly not 'one of the boys', in the classic sense. His contribution on the field was robust—the same lad who had been one of the smallest half-backs Newington had seen in his first year there was arguably the biggest half-back Uni Colts had ever boasted—but off the field he was rarely seen. Too busy attending his various Christian functions.

'It was just one of those things,' he says. 'Pursuing Christianity was really my top priority.'

When at the very end of the season the Uni Firsts beat Manly up at Eastwood's T.G. Milner Field in the Colts grand final, nearly all the team then went out 'on the plonk'. Bar Nick. He went to a Christian function that was being held that night in Miranda.

'I was delighted that we'd won,' he says, 'but given the choice between going drinking with the boys, or going to a Christian function, at that time I would automatically choose the Christian function every time.'

After getting through three of his four subjects in his final exams, for his second year at University Farr-Jones decided finally to call a halt to the daily travelling to and fro from Gymea to the university, and instead live on campus in one of the male residential colleges, St Andrews. He was joined by younger brother

Simon, who was starting university that year in the Arts faculty, and older brother Peter, returning for his third year of Economics.

The amazingly synchronised decision was encouraged by the fact that at the beginning of that year their parents had headed to Europe for an extended trip—meaning that the Hotel Farr-Jones was now reduced to a mere barracks.

The three arrived at St Andrews in February of 1981 and settled into the marvellous old building situated just next to Prince Alfred's Hospital on the south-western edge of the campus.

Like Newington, St Andrews was an exclusively male establishment, not a little sports and rugby mad, populated almost entirely by lads from a similar social background to that of the Farr-Jones boys. And it was all part of a wider college world that was to Sydney University what the boarding house had been to Newington—the backbone—though infinitely more wild and varied in character.

Each of Uni's residential colleges has a different ethos, attracting different sort of people. Sancta Sophia and St Johns, for example, are both Catholic colleges, the former for women, the latter for men. In college parlance the residents of these two colleges are known as the 'Choppers', local slang for the seriously Catholic. St Pauls, on the other hand (where the 'Paulines' play croquet on the manicured lawns), seems to attract a preponderance of landed gentry lads, while Wesley as the only co-educational institution is far more laid back and free wheeling—less in need of contact with the other colleges as it is so much more self-contained. They are known as the 'Wowsers'.

The residents of Women's College have no particular nickname, though the institution is substantially made up of women from the non-Catholic private schools.

Then came St Andrews college. Nominally Presbyterian, the Andrewsmen were known in the time of the brothers Farr-Jones as 'Andrews Animals'.

The St Andrews College song says at least something about their ethos, a song all of the new St Andrews students are obliged to learn in their first days at the college.

All together, sing . . .

For Andrews men are we, and proud indeed to be,
Not Anglican Pauls, nor Roman John, nor Wowser Wes-er-ley,

Nie Sancta Dyke nor the Prince Alfred Nursery,
Where else can man, in life's short span,
Find life and love so free?

On the first night, Nicholas Farr-Jones was assigned to Room 86 in Top Floor Main, a tenement of rather monastic austerity— a small window and a mattress placed on milk crates on the floor being the only real concession to the more traditional creature comforts.

The hierarchical system in residential colleges is notorious and Andrews was no exception. As a new student, he had to expect that his room would be a little short of glamorous. There was, too, within the college a basic pecking order, whereby the longer you had been in the college the more respect you were automatically accorded. First-year students were known as 'freshers', second-years as 'Sophomores', third-years as 'Heavies', fourth-years as 'Gentlemen', and those very few who remained five years were generally too revered to even speak to, let alone have a pet name for.

There wasn't a hazing system as such, à la the old English way, where older students would systematically bastardise the younger ones, but the bare remnants of that system were still in place when Farr-Jones got there.

In some ways an anachronistic sort of institution for the 1980s, St Andrews had a sense of history which was part of its charm. In some places the sandstone walls have been worn smooth from the brushing arms of countless generations of 'Andrewsmen'.

The first evening of every year begins with the Annual General Meeting, a high falutin' name for an invariably bawdy and rollicking event. It is the time when the freshers are subjected by the older students to a variety of experiences, all designed to inculcate them with the spirit of the place, to make them know not only that they reside on the lowest spot on the totem pole, but also that it is a very venerable totem pole to be on.

And there is Nick. He's the athletic-looking kid with the nervous grin, dressed in the academic gown of flowing black material that all the other freshers around him are also wearing as they all are sitting down on the ground in front of the older students, who are sprawled over the more comfortable seats. And now a crooked finger is calling him up to his feet to stand in front of the entire college—180 males strong.

'What's your name, fresher?'

'Nick Farr-Jones.'
'WRONG! What's your name, fresher?'
'Nick Farr-Jones.'
'WRONG! What's your name, fresh?'
'Uh . . . fresher Nick Farr-Jones?'
'Right. Spell your name, fresh.'
'N . . . i . . . '
'WRONG! Spell your name, fresh!'
'N . . . i . . . '
'WRONG! *Small* "n", fresh.'
'Uh, small "n", small "i", small "c", small "k" . . . '
And so on.

Others in this unfortunate group of college neophytes would
be obliged to perform any number of humiliating tasks, from
singing their school song while standing on their head, to pushing
a peanut across the floor with their nose, to feigning physical
love with a pizza box . . .

To outsiders, admittedly, such activities can sound a little close
to the aforementioned 'systematic bastardisation', but those who
have been through the process generally have a far more benign
view.

'Basically,' says Farr-Jones, 'it's just the Andrews way of putting
a guy fresh from school—the fellow who's the big fish in the
small pond—into his place. You're no longer the big fish, son.
You're a part of this Andrews community and you're a *fresher*.'

While Nick's experience on that first night was fairly typical
in terms of the mild humiliation he underwent, later that same
evening something happened that right away set him apart from
the other freshers.

As the AGM went on, one of the older students, a 'Gentleman'
by the nickname of Splurge, asked Nick to walk up to Newtown
to get him a Four Seasons pizza, hold the anchovies. And on
the double.

In such an environment, when an older student asks a younger
student to get him a pizza it is not asked as a favour, but as
a command. It is just one more way of gently rubbing the younger
one's nose in the fact that he is the junior member.

Under the circumstances, Farr-Jones didn't really mind going
to get the pizza. He knew the way the system worked and thought
he might as well go along with it just for the hell of it. At least
this once.

Having ordered it, and feeling a bit peckish himself, he saw a couple of mates from the law school and ended up joining them for an hour or so.

When he eventually got back to college, complete with the stone-cold pizza, he half suspected that Splurge would be a bit annoyed at his tardiness. But Splurge had in fact left 'annoyance' behind a long time ago, as he had 'anger' and even 'rage'. Hello apoplexy.

Didn't Farr-Jones know he was only a FRESHER!?! Didn't he know that when a Gentleman sends a fresher out to get a pizza he means RIGHT F---- NOW?

It was something of a seminal moment, with the college taking a moment's pause to measure the new boy's response.

'Next time,' Farr-Jones hissed, 'get your own f---- pizza.'

And walked off.

It was heresy, pure and simple, for a mere fresher to speak to a Gentleman this way—and on the first night of college yet. But this was no ordinary fresher. Already he was rumoured to be closing in on the Sydney Uni First Grade side, and in sporting terms there is hardly a more revered team in the whole university.

Despite this initial public confrontation with a senior member of college, it was not held against him and even secretly admired by many of those who had thought the great Splurge was in need of publicly being taken down a peg or two.

Glenn Kable, one of the students who witnessed the scene, says: 'The word went round pretty soon after the pizza incident that with this particular fresher, it was probably a good idea not to ride him too hard.'

To say that Nick soon settled down to the routine of college life is to imply a certain measure of boredom—'routine' and 'boredom' usually being fairly close cousins. But Andrews for Nick wasn't like that at all.

Nick's 'routine' was filled with sport, sport, and more sport, mixed in with attending legal lectures, going on late-night drinking sessions (where he soon found he could 'skol' a schooner of beer in 1.4 seconds), consorting with the young ladies from nearby Women's College, occasionally studying, and more often playing cards till dawn. His continuing Christianity was, in such an environment as this, not going to be allowed to get in the way of having a good time, and he soon acquired a reputation as a 'stayer'— someone who at midnight was just starting to switch into high gear.

If late night was the time of greatest revelry, though, the most important social hour of all in college life was dinner time. To attend, one had to be attired in black academic gown and tie, and once inside the great hall of the dining room (freshers filing in last of course), all the students would have to bow their heads as the principal said a Latin grace—once at the beginning of the meal and once at the end, signalling that the students could now take their leave if they so desired.

In many ways it was a crazy collision of an anachronistic way of living and a modern, slightly-out-of-control one . . .

After the principal had said that first grace (in Latin), appropriate form was for the students to yell 'YEE-HAH!' in reply. Beneath their black academic gowns and ties they were just as likely to be wearing a torn shirt and jeans. They were waited on hand and foot at the long wooden tables by older waiters wearing black ties—who came into the college via the Tradesmen's Entrance—but it still wasn't out of the question to throw food at each other on certain celebratory occasions.

The contradictions notwithstanding, Farr-Jones loved it all—the whole sense of tradition he'd known at Newington, mixed with the good dose of wildness that is the common condition of suddenly liberated schoolboys.

The college calendar was filled with rituals and traditions which each generation of Andrewsmen interpreted in their own way.

On the day of the winter solstice, reckoned by the heavies to be the coldest day of the year, the freshers were taken on the traditional 'fresher walkabout'. This involved the older students dividing themselves up into groups of three or four and then bidding at auction for the rights to take pairs of 'cattle' (what the freshers were known as on this night) out on the walkabout.

Once the group had secured the rights to take a pair out, the freshers were then blindfolded, put in the back of a car or utility truck, together with some of their more precious and bulky belongings from their room, and then dropped in the middle of nowhere in the middle of the night, with their belongings and no money, having been told to get home the best way they could.

The Heavies and Gentlemen were particularly keen to take them to the most inaccessible places as possible because when it was all over prizes were awarded for the team whose freshers had taken the longest time to get back.

In this venture Farr-Jones was paired with Brenden Miller, a slight lad from Gilgandra in the state's far west, and after a four-hour blindfolded drive they were dropped on a fire trail about twenty-five kilometres outside of Jenolan Caves—situated over one hundred kilometres inland from Sydney in fairly wild and forbidding country.

Not that they had any idea at the time where they were. Once the blindfolds were removed all they could reckon on was that they were on some sort of a rough track. For the next ten minutes all they could hear was a *clang, clang, clang,* followed by ever fainter manic laughter, as the guys who had dropped them went to the trouble of removing every small signpost for the next three kilometres.

And then nothing.

Two a.m. Freezing cold. No traffic. Nick with his tennis racquet, a beanbag, his bar heater, and a lot of his legal textbooks. Brenden with a cricket bat, some bulky personal effects and most of his legal textbooks too. What to do?

Why not, Brenden wondered out loud, empty the beanbag of all its beans and fill it with all their luggage?

It is not only in the fields of famous endeavour that genius strikes, and the system worked. Walking like that, each of them taking one corner of the heavy beanbag over their shoulders, they found that after ten minutes or so they were soon warm enough in the crippling cold to attend to another of their needs—sleep.

An extremely powerful infrared satellite above the Jenolan area that night might just have been able to pick out their forms beside the winding track: two small red blobs of body heat huddled together for warmth, beneath a large bag containing objects unknown.

Like this, they managed to get as much as twenty minutes' sleep at a time before the cold would again wake them. It would take another couple of kilometres' walking before they would again be warm enough to get more sleep . . . and so on. At dawn they finally discovered they were fifteen kilometres from 'JC', and after hours of intermittent walking and resting they finally made Jenolan Caves at three o'clock in the afternoon.

When they got back to Andrews at ten o'clock the following evening, bumming rides on trucks and trains, Farr-Jones was sure to kick in the door of the Heavy he judged as most responsible for leaving them there. A joke was a joke, fresher walkabout was fresher walkabout, but *fair dinkum*, the guy had it coming.

In the meantime Simon and Peter Farr-Jones were paired to go on their own walkabout the following morning. Nick just happened to be passing when they were about to leave.

They were in the back of a ute, with the tarpaulin just being pulled down over their prone bodies and blindfolded faces. Which would have been fine, except that, as Nick well knew, Simon on occasion suffered from claustrophobia.

Nick was not happy, not by a long shot.

Knowing Simon would be uptight under the tarp, he simply stopped the ute by standing in front of it.

'Guys, you're not going anywhere while my brother's panicky.'

'Bullshit, fresher. Get out of the way.'

'I promise you, you're not going anywhere.'

It was no match. Farr-Jones's steely protectiveness against the Heavy's quavering bravado. The tarp was pulled back.

'You all right, Simon?'

A relieved nod of the head.

'Now you can go guys.'

Which they did. With the tarp pulled back.

The reason, perhaps, that Farr-Jones was able to get away with such nakedly disrespectful behaviour was because he already had a small legend going in his favour concerning his contribution to the college's sporting life.

Nick and his brothers were in every team for the college— the swimming, the athletics, the tennis, the rugby. More often than not helping Andrews to win.

And in the meantime the rugby for the University club continued. On the strength of guiding the Colts to a win the year before, Lindsay MacCaughan had now taken over the University First Grade side and one of his first jobs had been to appoint his victorious half-back of the previous year as the new First Grade half-back, together with another three Colts.

The first game of the season was at Uni against Randwick— an opposition replete with the three famous Ella brothers and Simon Poidevin—and although Nick had the pleasure of making his debut with his own brother Peter on television, Uni ended, in Farr-Jones's words, 'getting flogged like a convict caught with the governor's wife'. (They lost by thirty points.)

A loss the following week, followed by another loss the week after that, and the tension within the club grew. MacCaughan had come in at the expense of Rupert Rosenblum and Johnny Rouen, a couple of the club stalwarts who had been co-coaches the year before, and both men now started to agitate to get their jobs back.

Four weeks into the season, with Uni yet to record a win, occurred an event euphemistically known in Uni rugby history as the 'Night of the Long Knives'.

In an extraordinary meeting held in the rooms that overlook the main rugby oval, the old guard launched a coup against MacCaughan, passed a vote of no confidence, and had themselves reinstated as the new coaches.

Farr-Jones, himself at the meeting, saw for the first time what a little bit of rugby politicking was about. It proved to be a valuable part of his rugby education.

'I was a bit shocked by it all, seeing how our coach could be shafted after so short a time just through politics, but there was nothing I could do. I definitely voted and I voted in favour of MacCaughan, but I probably was too shy and too timid to speak in favour of him. It was a sad night.'

Sadder still the following Tuesday when he found himself dropped from First Grade in favour of Tom Jenkins, the man he had replaced at the beginning of the season.

With MacCaughan now banished and, even more galling, First Grade starting to win again without him, it seemed for a time as if his baptism into the Big Time was to be just that—a brief dip. He never considered for a moment giving up mid season, but then again . . . if not disgruntled he was still far from gruntled at the manner of his dropping.

Fortunately his reserve grade stint only lasted three weeks.

One Tuesday night in early May he was up in the Andrews dining room, pushing some food round on the plate to pass the time before reserve grade training started, and the hell with it if he was a bit late, when 'someone came racing up to me and said, "Nick, you've got to get down to training. You've been reinstated into First Grade!"'.

Down in the Uni changing rooms he met briefly with Rupert and Johnny, then raced on to the field to catch up with the others.

This happened to be the very night that Rosenblum and Rouen had decided to put the side into the hands of the one and only David Brockhoff. A former Australian coach who had also been

Sydney University's most successful coach, 'Brock' would often make guest coaching appearances with various teams in the club. As Farr-Jones would find out, the great man's love of rugby in general, and Sydney University rugby in particular, was only marginally greater than his capacity to turn wondrous phrases.

In his tracksuit, his old towel around his neck and gumboots going clear to the knee despite the warm autumn evening, Brock was in full cry, stabbing the air with his finger as he expounded with great ferocity to the Firsts . . . something Farr-Jones knew not what.

Drawing himself up like Churchill on D-Day he got to the point: 'Let's face it, men, it hasn't been a good year. We're second last, and now we play Parramatta, who are on the bottom of the ladder. Fellas, you must have been looking forward to this for a while. But . . . no, rubbish! We know how Parra will play and we take none of it! First five minutes, men, we lock the bully out of the gate . . . and then for the rest of the afternoon we play in the field.'

So *that's* the general game plan, Farr-Jones thought. 'Lock the bully out of the gate.' Fine.

Enough of the generalities. Brock was ready to get specific. First the instructions to the forwards: 'You have to be everywhere, breakaways. *Everywhere*! No excuses . . . Cause havoc at the breakdown like sharks in a school of mullet. As for the tight-five, all day like wind through wheat. Not scattered rocks here and there, but like *wind through wheat*. And when you're through the other side we're like crowbars through the Opera House window. We get in, loot the joint and get out.

'And remember, no height in the lineout is no excuse, we must have the fruit, so every lineout dockyard brawl. Except our 22— row of ministers—no easy penalties.'

To Farr-Jones it sounded a lot like gibberish, though it was perfectly clear to those who knew Brock well.

So to the training proper, and the team-run had been going only for about ten minutes when Brock again blew his whistle.

Not happening to know Nick's name at the time, he came up with the instant and logical appellation of 'half-back', as in: 'Oh no, no, *no*! Half-back, listen to me! Listen. No Harbour Bridges! [meaning no high-parabola passes.] For Christ's sake, no Harbour Bridges or the pigs [the forwards] will slit your throat!'

The redoubtable Brock underlined the last threat by a swift

movement of his forefinger across his windpipe, and Farr-Jones got the message.

This was no ordinary man.

Twelve years down the track Farr-Jones names Dave Brockhoff as 'if not the greatest technical influence on my career, at least the greatest spiritual influence'.

While Nick enjoyed being back in First Grade and for the rest of the year performed, in the estimation of Rupert Rosenblum, 'solidly if not spectacularly', it still didn't stand as the most important or hard-fought rugby he would play that year.

That honour belonged to the games he would play with St Andrews College.

The sporting event of the year in the college calendar was Rawson Cup Inter-college Rugby, where teams from the all-male colleges plus Wesley would play in a round-robin tournament over several weeks to determine who was college champion.

The importance with which these games were taken is hard to overstate. The University five-eighth Michael Hawker, who was both a Pauline and veteran Wallaby with many games against the All Blacks to his credit, is reputed to have said that two of the three hardest games he has ever played were college games. In the testosterone-charged world that was the male residential colleges, the right to call yourself the very best footballers on the campus was worth a lot more than mere bragging rights at the local bar. The honour of your whole college was at stake.

When Farr-Jones played in his first game for St Andrews in June 1981, he could not believe the pomp and ceremony with which the game was attended.

On the day of the game, none of the players attended lectures. It was a matter of priorities, and if you thought that your studies were more important than your football on this day then you didn't have the right attitude. It was a day to give everything to college and nothing to self. The team would have breakfast together and then an early lunch, all the time building for the big game.

Then it was time. The fifteen selected players would file out of the portals of the college's sandstone archways and walk, still in single file, towards number one oval, some three hundred metres away—the noise from the crowd at the oval getting louder with every step.

Leading them at the head, as has always been the tradition

at Andrews, was a lone Scots piper playing 'Scotland the Brave' as they walked across the green grass of St Andrews oval, down past the end of Prince Alfred's Hospital, through what is known as the 'Lucky Crack', a break in the wall just near the Medical Library. No talking now, all quiet, just the sound of the bagpipes and the approaching roar of the crowd. Then out on to the field to play.

Up in the stands the Andrewsmen, the Paulines, the Choppers, the Wowsers, and the women from Sancta Sophia and Women's College would yell themselves hoarse for the duration of the game.

'For me at the time,' says Farr-Jones now, 'I guess those college games were the first time I had any hint of what really big-time rugby could be all about. It wasn't like a normal First Grade game for Uni at all—club rugby was just about being the best in Sydney. But the college system was its own little world, and those games were like real Test matches to see which was the best country in the world, and it really felt like what I imagined a Test match to be.'

Speaking of which . . .

Though he was playing good rugby for Sydney University First Grade at the time, there appeared to be no thought in anyone's mind to give Farr-Jones a run in even the lowliest of representative teams. Not that he was particularly upset about this: 'Put simply, it had never been a particularly great ambition of mine,' he says. 'I couldn't even make the Firsts at school, so it would have been fairly forlorn to develop an ambition in that area.'

He did, however, harbour at least enough ambition to attend a selection trial in the middle of 1981 for the NSW under twenty-one team, with a man by the name of Norm Tasker as coach and chief selector. Even then his attitude was all wrong.

Arriving a bit late, his opening line to Tasker, as they both remember it, was something like, 'Look, Norm, I can only play one half for you and then I've got to race back and do some study.'

'Mind you,' says Farr-Jones, 'even though he never picked me, I remember playing an absolute blinder.'

'He played all right,' says Tasker. 'I remember it well because he was somehow such a cocky kid, and people had been telling me to look out for him because he was good. But basically on the half-game I saw he seemed only a little above average.

'The thing about Farr-Jones, see, is all those marvellous skills he has he really acquired only *after* he'd reached full maturity. He certainly didn't have them in 1981 from what I could see.'

If Nick wasn't thought of as a genuine representative contender at that time, however, he at least had contact with some of those who were, and remembers being deeply impressed by the association.

One of the more established players in the Uni side at the time was the talented hooker Patrick Allaway, who had a limited association with both the Sydney and New South Wales sides.

On an evening soon after the Night of the Long Knives, Farr-Jones remembers going to Allaway's room at St Pauls college to talk to him about an upcoming game, only to be told by someone that he wasn't there because he'd had to go to training with the Sydney side, for which he'd been called in as a reserve.

'A *reserve* for the *Sydney* side? I just thought that was unbelievably impressive. Here I was in his room in college and he's a reserve and probably putting on the Sydney jersey right now.'

Always it was the same thing. The rugby season over, exam time would loom and you'd suddenly be jolted back to remembering why you had come to university in the first place.

There is a magnificent spreading jacaranda tree in the southeastern corner of Sydney University's historic quadrangle, and local lore has it that if you haven't started serious studying for your final exams when the jacaranda tree first starts to bloom in the middle of spring then you are in all likelihood going to fail.

Needless to say, between all the sporting, social and college activities that Farr-Jones was engaged in it was not at all uncommon for him to only be hitting his books when the jacaranda tree was in full bloom. A particular problem when so many of his law exams were 100 per cent—meaning that his entire year would stand or fall on the result of his final performance.

Usually it would come upon him suddenly, the realisation that if he didn't get to work absolutely immediately and stick to it, he was going to fail.

Then it was on. Study. A total blocking out of all the nonessentials so he could pore over the books in the hope that he would cobble together just enough information to scrape by on the day of the exam. There were only two problems: there was not enough time; and he was too obsessive. In the time he did have it was just like when he took his HSC—his perfectionist streak would kick in and he would spend an inordinate amount of time on the first third of the course, till he got it *absolutely right*, then he'd move on to the next third, till he got it right, and then he'd suddenly realise he had no time left for the last third.

The same problem showed up in the exam itself and if asked to write six essays in three hours he would always spend fifty minutes on the first question till he got it right, forty minutes on the second . . . and five minutes maximum on the last. But somehow he managed. From knowing, by his own estimation, 'not that much' six weeks before the exam, he recovered enough to pass three out of five subjects in his second year.

Returning the following year to Andrews, things had changed in some measure (he was no longer a fresher, for starters), but the rhythm of his life was constant. Lots of late nights, law lectures, lazing around on the front steps of the college chatting, lots of YEE-HAH!s, and most particularly a lot of sport for the college and rugby for the university.

If there was one guy Farr-Jones saw more of than most it was probably Brenden Miller, whom he had originally got to know quite well when they had gone on the fresher walkabout together. What Farr-Jones saw in Brenden was a happy-go-lucky sort of guy from the west, come to the Big Smoke for his studies, who retained an engaging naiveté.

What Brenden saw in Farr-Jones was generally a very odd sort of fellow indeed. He liked him a lot, there was no doubt about that, it was just that he never really knew quite what to make of him. There was his Christianity, for example. Nick had long been known as the college's most curious Christian, but Brenden saw it at closer quarters than most. And he just couldn't figure it. The same guy who played cards for money till his nose bled, drank beer with the best of them, and was not an infrequent visitor to nearby Women's College late at night, also had biblical quotes with pictures on his college room wall. However late he had been carousing the previous night, every morning he would set the alarm so as to be able to get in at least half an hour of bible study before lectures. If he didn't wake, then sometimes Brenden would have to suffer the supreme embarrassment of having other bus passengers look at *him* because he was sitting beside someone who was reading the bible on the bus.

Sometimes, too, they would be on the bus, and Brenden would know for a sure and certain fact that Nick's hangover was every bit as bad as his own after the previous night's session, and Farr-Jones would nudge Brenden in the ribs and pass him a card on which was simply written 'The Meek Shall Inherit the Earth.'

The feeling in college was that Nick's Christianity could only be reconciled with his nocturnal passions on the understanding that between the ten commandments there was still an awful lot of leeway for action. And that in the face of his own transgressions he could always show himself some Christian forgiveness.

But other things were even more difficult to understand. Like his sudden inexplicable bursts of anger.

In Brenden's eyes, no one dug deeper to put money in an obviously hungry busker's basket, no matter how atrocious the music; no one had such an innate sense of justice, to take down a peg or two those in the college who might have been throwing their weight around and lift up a peg or two those who were not quite making it; no one he knew reacted so immediately if one of his friends was in any sort of trouble.

And yet no one he knew had ever hit him so hard. One night they were just walking along together, going back to Nick's room to study, when, for the pure hell of it, Brenden gave Nick's hair a playful tug. Nick dropped him, just like that. One punch. 'Don't *ever* pull my hair,' he said, and walked away.

A couple of weeks after the hair incident, Brenden flicked a bottle top at Nick, which to Brenden's horror hit Nick's eye with such force he had to be taken briefly to the eye hospital. Was there anger? Annoyance? Incriminations? Nothing. No one could understand how Nick could be taking it so well, but Brenden knew.

'I hadn't pulled his hair,' he says.

But in a tight spot Farr-Jones was the guy to have on your side. On one occasion, through the alcoholic mist of a 4 a.m. morning, they decided to go over to St Pauls to spray a Pauline's room with a fire hose, just to pass the time. They found the room they were looking for on the ground floor, with voices coming from behind the door. Farr-Jones unravelled the hose, Brenden manned the tap.

'Okay, Brenden, when I give the signal you knock on the door and then get ready to turn it on as soon as he opens it.'

Knock, knock.

'Who is it?'

'We just want to talk to you for a sec.'

'Okay. Just a moment.'

As soon as the door was opened, Nick yelled, 'Now, Brenden!' and let the guy have it. The first guy, anyway. Neither he nor Brenden had any idea that there were six of them in there and through the torrent of high pressure water hurling them back inside, the Andrews boys gained about five seconds to make good their getaway. But the particularly drunken Brenden made a wrong turn, and instead of heading to the exit and the safety of Andrews territory he led them to a corridor cul-de-sac with only a toilet to hide in.

It was when they heard running outside and voices yelling 'They're in there!' that they knew they were in trouble. At least Butch Cassidy and the Sundance Kid had died a fairly quick and clean death. Brenden knew that he and Nick would be lucky if they'd got the tar and feathers off themselves come a week Tuesday.

The thought momentarily crossed Brenden's mind to be really noble about it and tell Nick to 'run and save yourself. I am weak and you are strong and you'll have a better chance without me,' when Nick hit on the solution.

'Grab my belt, Brenden, with both hands, and keep your head down. When I open the door we run like hell, got it? I'll start swinging and you keep pushing me through.'

Got it.

A Pauline by the name of George Blunt was the unfortunate man in the 'point' position on the other side of the door. He was also the first to fall. What could he have told a police officer? 'Sir, I was hit by a runaway train with fists flailing out the front and Brenden Miller's little legs pounding away at the back, pushing it through.'

If Farr-Jones wasn't averse to raising a little havoc in the male colleges now and then, he usually drew the line at doing the same thing at either of the colleges for women. One of the most celebrated activities for young Andrewsmen at that time was to go on 'Boal Runs', apparently named after a former student who invented it back in the early 1970s. This involved:

1 Stripping naked.
2 Putting on your sandshoes.
3 Putting on your loose black academic gown.
4 Running like a mad mongrel dog across St Andrews Oval
   and into Women's College, with your gown flapping behind
   you in the wind, and then up and down the corridors generally
   raising hell.

Harmless fun, mostly, and regarded as such, but still not quite
Nick's cup of tea. When he went to Women's College he liked
to be neatly dressed, looking good and smelling fine.

In his whole college career, Nick only went on one Boal Run,
and in the memory of fellow student Glenn Kable he ended up
being listed as 'Missing in Action'. Five of them left the college
late that night—they were counted out—but at the end of the
mission only four returned.

According to Kable they had been running up a corridor, having
one helluva time and the last they knew of Nick was when they
heard a female voice behind them saying, 'Nick! Hi!'

And when they looked around he was gone.

Real romance for Farr-Jones would only come the following
year.

While Farr-Jones was entering his third year of St Andrews
college, a seventeen year old by the name of Angela Benness was
arriving at Women's College.

Daughter of a noted professor of radiology and his wife, who
were soon to move to Sydney from Adelaide, Miss Benness (who
was firmly a 'Miss' and not a 'Ms') had come to Sydney Uni to
secure an Arts degree and just as Nick had done two years earlier
at St Andrews, Angela soon found herself immersed in the
university's inner sanctum of residential colleges.

Which is why, as part of her own fresher initiation on the
night before lectures were to begin, Angela happened to be
standing with all the other new girls just outside the entrance
to Women's College. They were gazing up at some of the more
senior students on the first floor who had told them they wished
to make an important announcement to them.

And that announcement would be . . . ?

Buckets of water. More buckets of water, and yet more, as
the girls ran screaming every which way in high hilarity, trying
to escape the sudden downpour.

Welcome to Women's College. From there, they all went without changing, straight to the Student Prince Hotel where as always it was the busiest night of the year. Full of friends who hadn't seen each other for three months mixed in with all the new arrivals.

As the group of young wet women arrived, the hordes of male students from St Johns, St Andrews and St Pauls moved back to make room for them . . . and just as instinctively closed back in upon them as soon as they were securely within the pub's maw.

While the beer flowed and the volume increased, still more people came, and some more beer and more wine and 'where-ya-from?'s and yet more people kept coming as the volume and the alcohol flow were turned up. At about 9 p.m. it was no longer possible for an errant mouse to squeeze into the pub let alone another person and what about this for a good game? If we push here, they're all packed in so tightly that those people on the other side of the room will feel it and then they'll get the whole room going and . . .

. . . and soon it was going just like that. With the exception of a few people sitting on the outer fringes most of the room was on its feet, all alcohol and hormones, surging back and forth. In the middle of it all Angela Benness was not exactly panicky, but she had not drunk enough to enjoy this game as much as the others and as every surge passed through her she gradually worked her way to the edges. It was a propitious final surge then that pushed her from the mass and almost into the lap of someone sitting on the edges.

It was Nicholas Farr-Jones, not quite sober himself, but not yet in the mood for those sorts of fun and games.

Hello.

Hello.

A few more minutes chatting, whereby Farr-Jones managed to tell Angela that in his opinion she was 'the prettiest girl in the room', and Angela had to take her leave, together with the group she had come with. Not back to Women's College, of course, for it was still way too early, but to another student pub up the road, the White Horse.

Which was where, some two hours later, Angela saw that nice boy who had told her she was the prettiest girl in the room coming up to ask if he could buy her a drink. And it went from there.

A small chat then, and when he ran into her a week later in the same pub, Farr-Jones ended up walking Angela back to Women's College and their relationship was really off and running. So much so that the following morning Angela phoned her mother to tell her that she had met the man she was going to marry.

Halfway through the first academic term, Angela's mother, while on a visit up from Adelaide, was to get her own close-up look at the man her daughter kept talking about. They were just sitting down for a nice cup of tea in Angela's ground-floor room at Women's College when there came some frantic tap-tap-tapping at the window and a voice from outside: 'Ange . . . Ange . . . let me in . . . let me in hon. Are you there?'

Sprung.

Not the best way to meet one's future mother-in-law, but Mrs Benness was nevertheless happy to see that in the flesh, when he eventually came in via the door, he was a very polite boy. Well dressed, clean shaven, minded his 'ps' and 'qs', and was very respectful and deferential to her. In short, he seemed a well brought-up young man.

Her opinion of him was confirmed when soon afterwards Nick came down to stay with the family in Adelaide over Easter, just before the Bennesses were to move back to Sydney for good. The consensus of the Bennesses, according to Mrs Benness, was that he was 'A delightful boy, self-assured, though perhaps a little shy on a one-to-one basis.'

They were also pleased to learn that he was a Christian.

Back at college, Angie found that Nick's fellow Andrewsmen now treated her with a certain respect—a respect that was not always obvious in their treatment of other women undergraduates.

It wasn't that Andrews was misogynist *per se*, but then again it wasn't at all uncommon for females walking across St Andrews Oval of an evening, on their way back from lectures or perhaps medical rounds at the hospital, to have obscenities yelled at them from one or other of the St Andrews rooms that overlooked the oval.

But it never happened to Angela.

Farr-Jones: 'I didn't like that sort of stuff going on in the first place, and I'm proud to say I never participated. But if I'd ever heard that someone had been disrespectful to Angie I would have been very very unhappy with whoever had done it.'

In fact Farr-Jones was something of a pioneer in the opposite direction, and when he would invite Angela to dinner she often found herself the only female in a dining room full of Andrewsmen. On such occasions Nick always went to great pains to be affectionate, which wasn't strictly speaking the Andrews way, not in public at least.

For her part, Angie made a point of getting interested in this game called rugby that Nick seemed so absorbed in. Having been raised and educated in Adelaide she had only the vaguest idea what the game was all about. But she'd learn soon enough, as during much of that wet winter she would find herself on Saturdays at one far-off rugby oval or other, somewhere in Sydney, trying to work out which one of the mud-men was Nick.

More often than not he was the guy barking directions at the bunch of particularly big mud-men, who were apparently known as the 'forwards'. Then, she noticed, he would get the ball from them and pass it to someone and then bark at them some more till they all got to wherever the ball was next.

Despite his Uni rugby career, college football also remained important to Farr-Jones. Not that all the memories were good. In fact if Nick could name the most upsetting moment of all in his University career, it happened on a football field.

Andrews were playing Johns on a stinking wet day in 1983. 'Stinking' being the operative word because the mud that lies beneath the university ovals is the sort that stinks if someone even spits on it. On this day the rain had been so heavy that the stench was almost unbearable.

Which was the least of Farr-Jones's worries. Up ahead of him, about twenty metres from the goal mouth, Rob McEwan was shaping to take a kick for goal that would win the game, and the entire competition, for St Johns. The whistle had already blown so this was the original shot of No Redemption. If McEwan missed it, then St Andrews would win.

'I was so hyped up, and wanted him to miss the shot so badly,' Farr-Jones says, 'that when he started his run-up to kick the goal, I not only ran out at him, which you're allowed to do, but I also called out something, which is against the rules.'

The ball went wide, which normally would mean that Andrews had won it all, and Farr-Jones threw his arms into the air in victory. But the referee would have none of it. Citing Farr-Jones's cry of distraction as a breach of the rules, he awarded McEwan another kick. This time McEwan kicked it straight through.

The St Johns students streamed on to the field in jubilation and, walking back to college, Farr-Jones, as Brenden Miller remembers it, 'just wept'.

'Not great big sobs or anything, just sort of walking along, on his own, trying to stay away from everyone, and crying quietly.'

If a good deal of his rugby education came on the field with St Andrews, it was still Uni rugby that was providing him with the week-in, week-out experience of playing the game at a high level. The fact that he was not in a strong team helped stretch his talents to the utmost. In the whole year, University only tallied up five wins, and finally the truth became apparent. Uni was going to finish bottom of the table and, under the rules at that time, they were headed for the obscurity of Second Division.

It was a major disaster for the club, and a minor disaster for Farr-Jones personally. Whatever small hopes he might have harboured of playing representative rugby seemed dashed for at least a year. Even if he were to play terrifically well there would be no one there to see him and certainly none of the representative selectors.

There was yet one way out of it.

One of his team-mates, Peter FitzSimons, put the suggestion to him. Why not ditch Uni and come with him to Manly, where this new guy Alan Jones was taking over? Or go somewhere else, so long as he could keep playing in First Division? Otherwise he'd be spending all of 1983 looking at his *Gregory's* street directory trying to find out how to get to obscure clubs he'd never heard of. One thing was for sure, if he didn't go to Manly or some other club, his chances of cracking the Big Time were nil.

Farr-Jones remained unmoved. He might have, in the distant past, left Cronulla RSL under sixes to go to the Lilli Pilli under sevens, but he'd be damned if he'd leave Uni to go anywhere else.

FitzSimons moved on. Farr-Jones, ever the loyalist, maintained the faith and stayed.

CHAPTER FIVE

A Whiff of the Green
and Gold

*'In sport you either get tremendous fulfillment or
tremendous disappointment.
Nothing else in life is so cut and dried.'*
Richard Meade, British Showjumper 1972.

I t was one of those September days where the sun shines hot
and the wind blows cold. In the final two minutes of the Sydney
Rugby Union grand final of 1983 out at the old Sydney Sports
Ground, Manly—who had last won a Sydney premiership thirty-
two years before—were holding on to a 12-10 lead against Randwick.

A great triumph was at hand, but there remained for Randwick
just one last chance of victory. Awarded a scrum deep in Manly's
territory, the ball came back Randwick's side to Wallaby five-
eighth Mark Ella, who shaped to kick a three-point field goal
that would have won the game for Randwick.

Perhaps Ella's most distinguishing feature as a player was that
he always seemed to have time—'time to read the defence and
write a review about it', as the cliché runs. Not on this occasion.
With three Manly backrowers charging hard at him, he was forced
to hurry the kick slightly. At first blush it seemed to have been
launched straight and true between the goalposts some thirty-
five metres distant.

Just as the entire sportsground picked up a bead on that small
rotating piece of leather and began to follow its path, it started
to drift . . . drift . . . drift out to the right, over the dead-ball
line and out.

With it went the last chance of a Randwick victory and, as it turned out, something far more significant indeed.

In the crowded Manly dressing room afterwards, the man who stood tallest was one Alan Jones, practically unknown in Australian rugby to that point. But for the first time Jones really had something solid on his rugby resumé with which to launch himself. In this, his first year of first grade coaching, he had taken what was only a mediocre Manly side and shaped them—cajoled them, *bullied* them—into a side capable of taking on and beating the mighty Randwick side.

After such a victory Jones might have been expected to simply bask in the glory and set about doing the same next year—with one eye on a representative coaching job a few years down the track.

Not 'the Jones boy'. Although this former prime ministerial speechwriter has many undoubted attributes, patiently waiting his turn is not one of them. And the man whom he desired to replace, Bob Dwyer, was becoming increasingly vulnerable.

Then in his second year of coaching the Wallabies, the Randwick-bred Dwyer had only a mediocre record to that point. Dwyer's real undoing, however, was the Wallabies' performance on their tour to France, which took place in the month following Manly's victory. The Wallabies stumbled at the precise moment Dwyer could least afford it.

Again, things might have turned out very differently if the same Mark Ella who had narrowly missed a final field goal in the grand final had put an even more crucial field goal over in the last minutes of this Wallaby tour.

After holding the French to a draw in the First Test in Clermont Ferrand, the Wallabies were down 9–6 with only minutes remaining in the Second Test in Paris. When the ball came to Mark Ella he shaped for the field goal that would have evened the scores at 9–9.

This time the ball was not even allowed to be caught by a stray puff of wind. Just as the ball left his boot it came into contact with the outstretched palms of the charging French captain Jean-Pierre Rives, and the moment was lost. France scored a converted try soon after that and the Australians had gone down by the score of 15–6.

That loss tipped the tally of Dwyer's record into the negative figures of five wins, six losses and one draw. The stage was set for a coup.

In early 1984 Jones announced his intention of standing against Dwyer for the position of Australian coach. The 1 February edition of the *Sydney Morning Herald* records the very clever stance taken by Jones over his nomination when he said that it was 'representations from players and officials in New South Wales and Queensland' that particularly influenced him to nominate for the position. He continued: 'What else influenced me to make up my mind is rugby being the big game it is, with a large international following, the team needs credibility and I'd be providing that.

'We're entitled to expect of the national team that it should win. That is justifiable on the strength of the personnel we have. I also would want to bring a professional approach to the position. With all that in mind, I have decided to put my name forward.'

Jones's nomination was met with only a brief public reaction from Dwyer: 'He's entitled to stand, but I'll definitely be nominating.' And although Dwyer fought a valiant rearguard action against the Jones candidacy, and received great support in the press for so doing, it was 'all over, Red Rover', as they say in the rugby ranks.

Jones was to say privately to his Manly players at a training session at Narrabeen Fitness Camp in mid February, 'Dwyer can say whatever he likes to the press, *I've* got the numbers.'

And he did. On 24 February it was announced that Jones was the new Australian coach and a new era in Australian rugby had begun.

As a little-known Second Division player, Farr-Jones was so far removed from these top echelon machinations of Australian rugby that the thought he might be involved with one or other of these coaches as a Wallaby himself before the end of the year would have been presumptuous at best.

Yet the watershed mark was there—Jones, the man who would first select him for Australia and shape his early rugby representative career, had just taken over from Dwyer, the man who would eventually make him captain and with whom he would find his greatest success.

Jones was like no other man Australian rugby has seen, before or since. The sort of man with the energy to move King Cheops's pyramid ten paces to the right if its aspect was not quite to his satisfaction, he immediately set about finding the people he would need to take Australian rugby to the summit of international success.

And with none of the deposed Dwyer's in-built loyalty to the incumbents of the current Test team, the environment was right for a large number of new players to be introduced. Just as he had done at Manly a year earlier, Jones examined in minute detail the strengths and weaknesses of the personnel he had available, and more particularly the sort of talent that was on hand outside of the immediate team: talent that could be brought in and moulded to his specifications.

What he saw in the Wallaby half-back position was not overwhelming. The two half-backs who had gone on the Wallaby tour to France, Dominic Vaughan and Tony Parker, had acquitted themselves competently but not brilliantly. The other candidate was Phillip Cox, who had been both the Test halfback and Jones's halfback at Manly the year before until a serious injury had put him out for the rest of the year. He would be available for the 1984 season but it was as yet unclear how well he would recover from his knee injury.

In just such circumstances, Farr-Jones' good fortune was to be given a chance to display his diverse array of rugby talents, at the precise time that Jones was on the look-out. This 'chance' came from a most unexpected direction . . .

Amazingly, the selectors of the Sydney side of 1984 decided, despite the fact that Farr-Jones was nominally the sixth- or seventh-ranked half-back in Sydney, to pick him to go on the Sydney tour to Europe. The credit for this goes to the chairman of the Sydney selectors, Bob Urquhart, who had seen Farr-Jones playing in the combined Second Division side the previous year and told his fellow selectors, Barry Want and coach Peter Fenton, to go 'and have a look at this kid play'.

The beginning of 1984 found Farr-Jones, oddly enough, working with a jackhammer.

Now good friends with the man whom he had previously been so honoured merely to know, Pat Allaway, he was living with Allaway in Sydney's fashionable suburb of Clontarf. The two were working every day labouring with jackhammers so as to make a few extra dollars in their holidays for the upcoming Australian Universities' tour to Britain they had both been selected for.

The only good thing about working on the jackhammer was that every now and then you got to stop, and it was during one morning break that the younger man saw an extraordinary thing in the newspaper.

A 'Farr-Jones, N.' had been selected to go on the Sydney tour to Europe later on in the year. No mistake. The selectors had decided, in their words, 'to give the kid a chance'.

It was a fortunate beginning to what would prove to be a whirlwind year for him. No sooner had he returned from the Australian Universities' tour—a five-week jaunt through Europe, which stands at least as the first time he wore the green and gold colours—than he immediately had to attend training for the Sydney side which was about to depart for Europe.

The other Sydney players had been training for some time while Farr-Jones had been away in Europe, and his introduction to them came down at Balmoral Beach, where the Sydney side had a final training and barbecue before leaving in two days' time.

'I remember just feeling so out of it,' Farr-Jones recalls. 'I knew a couple of the young guys, but everyone else was pretty much unknown to me. That was the first time I went down there and I just thought "Well jeez. How do I approach these guys? What do I do?"'

He needn't have worried. If there is anything Farr-Jones had an instinctive feel for after two decades of playing all-male sport, attending an all-male school, living in an aggressively all-male residential college, it was how to quickly make friends with a lot of males he'd never met before.

And he had plenty of time to do that before the team actually touched down on European soil. The team took off the following Tuesday, flying what the players called the Air Garuda 'milk run' to Europe, and going to almost as many places as their luggage in seemingly every small town between Sydney and Zurich.

In the thirty-six hours that the flight took there was little else to do but drink and 'pal around', and Farr-Jones did plenty of both.

By the time the team had landed in Zurich and taken the bus to Livorno, Italy, for the first game, Nick had so obviously risen in the affections of the team that the coach Peter Fenton decided to make him vice-captain.

This was indeed 'giving the kid a chance', and then some. To make a young kid on his first tour captain of a backline which included such luminaries as Brett Papworth and Gary Ella seemed bizarre at the time—even if Fenton might now argue it was a stroke of genius given what that kid would go on to do.

The custom before games on tour is for the backs and forwards to divide up and have meetings in the rooms of their respective captains. So it was on this occasion, with all the backs gathering in Nick's room at 3 p.m. in preparation for the night game which was to start at seven o'clock.

There was just one problem. The captain of the backs, Farr-Jones, had never before attended such a meeting and had no idea what to do.

'Okay, Nick, we're all here.' Gary Ella said.

'Well, that's wonderful. What do we do now?".

'You're supposed to chair this meeting, to run it.'

'What do you want to do, what do you want me to say?'

'Well, talk about what we're going to do today.'

Farr-Jones recalls now: 'Then I suppose I kicked off and somehow managed to pass the buck. But it was a worry all right.'

Again he needn't have worried. Simon Poidevin was captain of the entire team and so took on all the real burden. As for Farr-Jones, he just settled down and played his usual game, which on this night went very well. The Sydney side won handsomely and followed Standard Touring Procedure by celebrating in a variety of Livorno bars throughout the night.

At one of these bars, in the wee hours, Farr-Jones found himself with 'Butch' Walker and Mark Harding, two of the front-row Wallabies on the tour, and, though merry himself, Walker was eventually able to get out that he thought Farr-Jones had played a first-class game, that he was most impressed, and that he had no doubt that 'one day, Nick, you're going to be a Wallaby'.

That day would prove to be less than two months away. The local Italian paper reported the following day that the young 'Fa-Jones [sic] ha giocato bennissimo', played very well indeed, and his representative career was off and running. For the rest of the tour he continued to shine.

His report card from the tour was not totally positive, however.

Writing in his book, For Love Not Money, Simon Poidevin would say of Farr-Jones's efforts that 'having played alongside him on that tour I couldn't help but be impressed with his tremendous talent. But I thought he was a tremendously un-disciplined player; that he didn't want to do what the rest of the team was doing. It frustrated me at the time and at the end of the tour I had a very long talk to Nick and told him that if he wanted to have a part in any future international teams then he couldn't just go off and do whatever he wanted to do.'

Your witness, counsellor . . .

'I knew what Simon was talking about,' says Farr-Jones, 'but as I remember it, it was more off the field where he thought I was undisciplined, rather than on. On it, I think I was as disciplined as the next player.'

Poidevin's criticism aside, Farr-Jones's performance on the field had been impressive enough that for the opening games of the Australian domestic season, he was picked ahead of Test incumbent Vaughan as the reserve halfback for Sydney's matches against Queensland, Fiji, and NSW country, and when Cox was briefly injured managed to play two top-line games against Auckland and Queensland.

In the middle of all this, of course, he still had to try to get some legal studies done. Back in Sydney all the other law students were putting in long days and nights, wrapping their minds around 'Boilermakers' cases and the classic 'Carbolic Smoke-ball Company', while Farr-Jones was obliged to spend seemingly every night of the week at one training session or another for either Sydney, Sydney University, or St Andrews College, where he was still resident.

But needs must; the legal studies had to wait behind rugby in the queue of his life's priorities at that time.

As 'top-line' as playing for the prestigious Sydney team was, however, the real dream was to play for Australia. Having met Jones briefly at a trial match in Singleton soon after returning from the Sydney tour to Europe he at least knew that the Wallaby coach knew of his existence, but apart from that there had been no contact between them.

But Jones was watching all right. As he was later to divulge, what he apparently saw in Farr-Jones was a very big halfback who was as strong as an ox, just the sort of halfback he could use as a fourth backrower behind the monster pack he was assembling.

So it was that at western Sydney's Concord Oval one cold and blustery afternoon in mid May 1984 the NSW side had taken on Queensland in the afternoon, got thrashed in the at-times bitter clash, and the survivors of both sides huddled in the tent to find out who would be on the forthcoming Wallaby tour to Fiji.

The crowd caroused and drank as they waited for Alan Jones and the two other Australian selectors to appear. When they finally did so the tent went into a sudden hush, as tents are wont to do on such occasions, and Alan Jones stepped to the microphone.

It was right away a break with precedent, and significant of what was to follow in the Jones era. The usual form on such occasions is for the manager of the Wallaby side, in this instance Charles 'Chilla' Wilson, to make such announcements. But Jones would have none of that.

He did, however, at least observe the tradition of preceding the reading of the list with a few preliminary comments bearing the usual sentiments about the difficulty of selecting a touring squad of only thirty players when there were so many wonderful players available, blah, blah, blah. But the *list*, Alan. Get to the list. Ahem.

'Black, James,' he began . . .

Right away a ripple of surprise moved through the crowd. As his first official announcement as national coach Jones had named as a new Wallaby a close friend who had not even been a regular of the Sydney Firsts side.

In so doing Jones laid himself wide open to accusations of bias. Yet, as was to be a hallmark of his era, Jones for the most part was a dominant enough personality that he got the team he wanted.

But back to the list . . .

Coolican, John.

Farr-Jones, Nick.

FitzSimons, Peter.

They were off! Firm friends for the past five years, Farr-Jones and FitzSimons had now both been selected for the Wallabies. As they picked up their kit to head for the gate and their cars out in the street, FitzSimons noticed something more than passing strange . . . What on earth could be wrong with Farr-Jones? Not only was he not doing cartwheels, not singing, not doing anything much at all, but he actually seemed rather subdued.

What on earth could be wrong with the man? Nick, is it not a marvellous, marvellous thing that we have just been named in the Wallaby side together?

'Yes, but we still lost to Queensland,' replied Farr-Jones—which struck FitzSimons at the time, and does still now, as something of the mark of the man. No matter that he had just fulfilled one of his greatest ambitions to become a Wallaby, he still couldn't get over the recent disappointment of having lost a game where he knew he could have played better.

The irony in Farr-Jones's selection for the Wallabies, only five years after being considered too small to play for Newington Firsts, was that again it was his size that was a factor in his selection; but this time it was because he was so *big*. While the number one half-back, Phillip Cox, was 170cm and 70kg, Farr-Jones dwarfed him at 180cm and 82kg, and was in fact even heavier and taller than the breakaway vice-captain of the tour, Chris Roche.

So this was Fiji. Hot. Humid. Friendly black faces. An undercurrent of widespread religious belief which nevertheless seemed to have little effect on the men and women who populated their late-night bars. An enthusiasm for rugby union bordering on the fanatical. But *hot*. And humid.

And this was the Wallabies. A group of young Australian males imbued with a sense of privilege in wearing the green and gold; a sense of history in being but the latest generation of a tribe of Wallabies with a long and glorious past; and of course a sense of fun and adventure.

And this was Alan Jones. Everywhere. Always. The constant centre of attention. Telling stories at the dinner table. Consulting his senior players. Nurturing confidence in his younger players. Exhorting all to have a 'commitment to excellence'. Talking. Talking. All the time talking. Introducing a kind of 'Jones-Speak' that would also become synonymous with his era. A typical Jones speech of the time would run thus: 'We must deny these people time and space. Out on the paddock, we will yield to no one. We must have the skills and the discipline and be totally ruthless in our determination to win. We must be unapologetic in the pursuit of victory and have a total commitment to excellence.'

An odd sort of bloke, Jones, right from the beginning of his tenure with the Wallabies. Jones around young people was like a master builder walking along a shabby street, who with every step, could see a hundred different ways to make improvements. The difference being that while the builder would have asked money to do it, Jones simply did it for the satisfaction, and much of his adult life seemed to revolve around getting young men to fulfil their potential in a variety of ways, be they academic, sporting or even social.

At The Kings School in Parramatta where Jones had worked in his twenties as a school teacher he had quickly formed a coterie of eager young students around him and achieved extraordinary success. Mediocre students suddenly started performing well, and previously so-so sportsmen were seen forcing their way into the First XV and First XI. Along the way he also caused a great ruckus in the school, as it was divided between those who swore by him and those who swore behind him. He had that sort of personality which seemed to often arouse either great loyalty or fierce antipathy.

Nevertheless, whatever the principles are of making young men achieve, Jones had great experience in applying them, well before he took over the Wallabies. A lot of it was simply hard work.

In those first training sessions in Fiji many of the senior Wallabies were heard to complain that never in their lives had they worked as hard as they were now, and while that was also true of the younger Wallabies they kept their mouths firmly shut. Nick, particularly, was probably one of the Wallabies who minded the least how hard Jones pushed them.

A large part of the Jones message was *urgency*, running from drill to lineout to scrum to drill, not wasting any time, and that suited Farr-Jones fine. The new coach was a perfectionist who wanted to work his players hard—and the new reserve halfback was a perfectionist who not only didn't mind being worked hard but on occasion enjoyed it. Perfect.

Among footballers there is an innate sense of who in the team does the genuine hard work, both in training and during the game, and this was perhaps where Farr-Jones earned much of his initial respect from his fellow players. That and the fact that when the regular training session was finally over he didn't take part in the 'extra sprints session' that Jones would always cast such an admiring eye over. Farr-Jones was a hard worker by nature, not in a self-conscious, ostentatious fashion.

For the good impression he made on the training field though, in his first couple of days with the Wallabies Farr-Jones was just a fraction withdrawn socially.

On the way to that first training in Fiji, Alan Jones had addressed the Wallabies from the front of the bus. 'Yes, and if I could have a bit of attention for a moment,' he began, 'I'd like you to meet the man who will be our bus driver for the tour, Boogie . . . '

'BOOGIE!' immediately yelled Simon Poidevin. 'GET DOWN!'

The bus roared with laughter. Farr-Jones, however, only tittered nervously. It was his lot to find himself sitting up the back of the bus next to the captain of the tour, Andrew Slack, who had been playing Test rugby while Farr-Jones had still been playing in the Second XV at Newington.

'I was really nervous,' Farr-Jones recalls now. 'Just being on the bus alongside Slacky, because he was a guy I admired greatly. I was a lot younger than him and just starting out and not really sure if I belonged in such esteemed company and here I was with a guy who definitely belonged, the captain of the whole shooting match, and of course you've got to try and make conversation like it's the most normal thing in the world for you to be sitting next to the Australian captain up the back of the bus as one of his team-mates. Slacky was terrific, of course, and put me totally at ease right from the beginning, but I really did wonder there for a while if I wasn't an unintentional gate-crasher at a Wallaby party.'

Yet again Farr-Jones needn't have worried. Just as it had been on the Sydney tour, it would take him a remarkably short time to get close to the beating heart of the team, and he was aided immeasurably in this by his performance on the field—always a good way to move up the social pecking order on tours—and on the field, right from the beginning, he was excellent.

Though he hadn't played in the first game of the tour, when the Wallabies had beaten the 'Western XV' 19-3 at Churchill Park in Lautoka at a minuscule ground with Fijians dripping from the branches of every tree within sight of the field, he had at least got some idea of what would be awaiting him on the field in his own debut.

Farr-Jones made his debut for the Wallabies in the second game of the tour against the Eastern Selection at the National Stadium in Suva.

It was extremely wet. And the Fijian crowd, normally a congenitally friendly people off the field, were on this occasion solidly against the Wallabies after it had become known that Alan Jones had insisted that the Isa-Lei Hotel, where the Wallabies had been lodged up in the hills outside Suva, was 'not good enough for an international team' and demanded that they move down into Suva proper to the Suva Travelodge. The Fijians felt offended at this uppityness and would have loved nothing better than to see the Wallabies brought down a peg or two.

Under which circumstances it was impressive that Farr-Jones played as well as he did. In the midst of flying mud, fists, feet and Fijians, he still managed to get the ball right on the money and into the hands of his five-eighth time after time. In the first half Farr-Jones secured the ball from Bill Calcraft from a short lineout and barged over for a try with two Fijians hitching a ride into the in-goal as he went. In the second half he was hit very hard and very late by a Fijian prop—who was sent off for his trouble—but recovered enough soon afterwards to play a crucial role in a late try for winger Brendan Moon. Australia got through to a hard-fought 15-4 win, Farr-Jones was named man-of-the-match, and as they came off the field captain-for-the-day Chris Roche made a special point of coming up and congratulating him for his efforts under such difficult conditions. An auspicious beginning.

Farr-Jones remembers it mainly for the pleasure he felt at making his debut than for the game itself, but the senior Wallabies were impressed. Andrew Slack, for one, recalls the 'amazingly cool authority' with which Farr-Jones played.

That evening, as a Wallaby debutante, it was Farr-Jones duty to pour the drinks at the team Happy Hour. The last is a Wallaby tradition after games where the players—still dressed in full regalia, with blazers on and ties done up—gather in a private room usually well furnished with beer. For the next hour at the command of one of the senior Wallabies designated 'The Judge' they drink, sing, tell yarns and génerally carry on. This evening as Nick moved around filling glasses he was gratified at how many of his new team-mates congratulated him on his performance.

The buzz among the team that night as they celebrated, was that Nick must indeed be very close to forcing his way into the side for the Test.

But no. Jones began on this tour what was to become established custom over the next four years of his reign—to call in those players who might have thought themselves possible Test selections and explain to them, just prior to the announcement, why they hadn't made it.

The day after the game Farr-Jones received a call to go and see Alan Jones in his room.

Ah yes, Nicholas. Thank you for coming. Sit down.

Jones, in Farr-Jones's memory, began to launch into a congrat-

ulatory prologue on Farr-Jones's tour so far and the beginning
of a long explanation of why, nevertheless, he wasn't going to
pick him in the Test side.

Farr-Jones interrupted.

It's all right, Alan. It's all right. I'm just delighted to be part
of this squad. I'm privileged to be here. You don't have to tell
me why Phillip Cox got the spot in front of me. He's the right
man.

Sure enough, when the team was announced Farr-Jones was
listed only as a reserve, a fact that caused a minor stir among
the players and travelling press. Jim Webster of the *Sydney
Morning Herald*—who had in his previous day's match report
gone so far as to liken Farr-Jones to the 'great John Hipwell'—
wrote of the Test team that 'the chief surprise was the preference
of Phillip Cox at half-back instead of Nick Farr-Jones, who gave
such an exceptional display against the Eastern Selection
yesterday'.

In the same article Alan Jones was quoted as saying: 'It was
very hard to leave Farr-Jones out, after an absolutely outstanding
performance by him yesterday. I just feel that to ask the young
man to play that well twice in a week is a lot.

'But he has now proved he is right up among the best of them
and I've told him that and his turn will come.'

Australia won the test against Fiji on the Saturday by 16–3,
with Farr-Jones sitting safely in the stands as a reserve while Phillip
Cox did the deed out on the field. The game itself was not
outstanding for any particular feature other than a good Australian
win—though as a small historical quirk it is worth noting that
for the third time in six months Mark Ella had a failed attempt
at field goal, the result of which went clearly in Alan Jones's
favour. Again he kicked, again it missed, but in this instance
the referee must have judged it to be 'close enough' for he awarded
it anyway.

Whatever, the Jones-led Wallaby side had begun 1984 in a solid,
if not spectacular fashion. The Wallabies celebrated that night
in the bars around Suva, and then back to Farr-Jones and Fitz-
Simons' room at the hotel.

In the final wash-up to the tour, the players checked out of
the hotel on the following morning and were just about to leave
for the airport when Alan Jones got on the bus and, pointing
to Farr-Jones and FitzSimons, said, 'I want to see you and you.'

Feeling just a little like two boys who had been called before the headmaster, the two left the bus to be confronted by an almost apoplectic Alan Jones, who proceeded to berate them in front of the entire watching busload.

Hear me, and hear me well, Jones began, the room you two have been 'living' in is a pigsty, a shambles, a shocker, a disgrace. It might be good enough when you're living at Wesley or Andrews College but it's NOT GOOD ENOUGH WHEN YOU'RE REPRESENTING AUSTRALIA!

These proved to be just his opening remarks. The Jones tirade continued for at least another three minutes and the upshot of it was that if Farr-Jones and FitzSimons wanted to be considered to play for Australia again then they had better 'lift their game', as he for one was quite prepared to leave them behind rather than take them on future tours.

After the obligatory replies of 'yes, sir, no, sir, three bags full of sorry, sir', the two eventually got back on the bus and settled down quietly in the vain hope that their ears might eventually stop ringing.

Things had changed for Farr-Jones on his return to St Andrews College. Already a BMIC (Big Man In College) for his sporting prowess before he left, he re-entered the portals of Andrews as a certified, card-carrying Wallaby. In the all-male, old-school-tie world of St Andrews there was little that could be more prestigious.

'The difference was immediate,' Brenden Miller recalls. 'Nick didn't go round seeking for anyone to treat him differently, but I think you could say that when he was walking into the dining room or along a crowded corridor, the way seemed to part just that little bit easier for him.'

His law professors were not moved by the same spirit, however, at least when it came to allowing him extra time to prepare for his mid-year exams, and again the inevitable cramming followed.

The challenge for the Wallabies now was to play a full series against the All Blacks, an entirely different sort of challenge to the one presented by the Fijians. In the entire rugby landscape two features generally stand out as summits of intensity and toughness—Test matches and local derbies. When put together as in local derby Test matches between two such countries as

Australia and New Zealand it becomes perhaps the toughest brand of rugby on earth.

And Jones, as he told his Wallaby charges straight after they assembled for the First Test, had no intention of coming anywhere but FIRST in such a contest as this. Can you feel it, men, can you FEEL it? Everybody is writing us off, they don't think we can win. Not even our own people think we can win. Someone just rated us 100–1. But we're going to show them all. This is an historic opportunity to beat these people, to send them home with their tails between their legs. For too long Australian rugby has suffered at the hands of these arrogant New Zealanders and now it is for us to seize the opportunity, to be arrogant ourselves, to be totally unapologetic in the pursuit of victory, to out-physical them, out-muscle them, out-manoeuvre them, and out-play them. To be part of the renaissance of Australian rugby. What I ask of you all is simply this: a total commitment to excellence.

It was a brand of rhetoric that the players were fast becoming used to, but it was still inspiring in its own way to most of them. Whatever else, there was something about the coach's amazing passion and intensity that proved infectious to the majority of the players—and those few who were turned off by it would fall by the wayside soon enough.

For the First Test against the All Blacks at the SCG, Farr-Jones was again announced as reserve for the Test team. Even though he had already achieved this honour while in Fiji, there is something altogether more special when wearing your national colours on home territory.

'Funnily enough it's one of my most enduring rugby memories, even though I was only a reserve,' Farr-Jones says. 'We went out to warm up on that old number two ground that used to stand next to the SCG and I suppose a couple of hundred people assembled to watch us. It was while I was doing all the exercises that I saw my Dad as part of the crowd, just watching me, sort of quietly *beaming* . . . and, I don't know, I guess it was just that I was there in my Wallaby tracksuit with my No. 16 Wallaby jersey and I was his son and I could just tell he was so proud, and I kept glancing at him and he just kept on beaming back at me and . . . '

And with ten minutes to kick-off it was back to the dressing room.

The tradition at that time was for the coach and the reserves of both teams to sit up in the Member's Stand on the north-western edge of the grand old ground, and it was from here that Farr-Jones sweated out the next eighty minutes of the game.

It might seem odd that one who was so proud to wear the Wallaby jersey even as a reserve should be almost actively praying that he didn't take the field, but that is the way it was. Part of it was the mysticism of the moment.

Players closing in on finally achieving their goal of playing a Test feel almost as if they're about to cross a bridge into a mythical, magical land that they've long heard about and always hoped to enter. When they do cross that bridge it is not unnatural for them to want it to be attended with appropriate ceremony. In short they don't want their first Test to come about because of injury to another player. Farr-Jones felt that exactly.

'I was nervous the whole time, just hoping that Coxy would play the full eighty minutes.'

There was, however, another sentiment coursing through him. Fear. Pure and simple.

'You've got to picture the scene. The place, this wonderful historical ground where Bradman had scored so many centuries, where so many generations of Wallabies had previously played—and for me the place where my own grandfather used to run and win the GPS championships—was packed to the rafters with people that included all of my own family and most of my friends, and out on the field the All Blacks themselves were going hard at it. I was thinking that if Phillip does get injured this is the place where I could really embarrass myself and my family and friends badly. I was wondering if I was up to this level of rugby. What if I knock the first ball on? What if I throw a wild pass that gets intercepted and they score? What if, what if, what if? That sort of thing.'

Cox did complete the full eighty minutes and Australia won well that day by 16–9, scoring two tries to nil.

The Jones era was off to a good start with now two out of two Test wins. But more of the Jones signature to the times was added on the Monday after the Saturday test, when eight of the Sydney-based test players announced to the press that they would not play in that weekend's upcoming Sydney vs All Black match, despite having been selected. The man behind it was of course Alan Jones, who told the eight players he did not want them to play for fear that they would injure themselves before

ABOVE Nick Farr-Jones being held by his grandfather, with *(from left)* Rosemary, brother Peter, and Rosemary's late sister, Belinda

BELOW The terrible trio: Nick, aged three, at the front, with Simon and Peter bringing up the rear

LEFT First day at Miranda Primary School

BELOW A big night out for the Farr-Jones family

RIGHT The young
soccer player

BELOW Winning the
1500m at the 1978 GPS
competition – Michael
Ritchie comes second

ABOVE In action in a match at Trinity College, Dublin – part of the University of Sydney tour of the United Kingdom and France in 1982

LEFT 1984 – the young Nick Farr-Jones under the guidance of Alan Jones, and 'trying not to put a foot wrong' *John Fairfax Group*

ABOVE Winning the Team of the Year Award in 1991. *From left to right:* Nick Farr-Jones, Stephen Cutler, Phil Kearns, Rob Egerton, Ewen McKenzie, Tony Daly, Simon Poidevin and Bob Dwyer

BELOW Campese and Farr-Jones *John Fairfax Group*

LEFT Angela Benness was in Auckland, New Zealand, when the Wallabies won the Third Test and the Bledisloe Cup in 1986

BELOW Some say Nick talks too much to referees – here's a classic example of getting his point across *John Fairfax Group*

ABOVE With Mark Ella – in 1984, on the Grand Slam Tour *Colorsport*

BELOW The British press called them 'The Holy Trinity': David Campese, Nick Farr-Jones and Michael Lynagh *John Fairfax Group*

ABOVE Nick with his parents on his return from Monaco in 1988, having just been made captain of the Wallabies

LEFT The wedding day

the Second Test. It was not bad sportsmanship *per se*, but certainly not the way rugby had been played to that point. It was all part of the 'new professionalism' of the Jones era, which didn't involve money but did involve a total commitment to winning.

The upshot of it for Nick was that because Phillip Cox had withdrawn he, Nick, was now in the Sydney team to play the All Blacks that Saturday.

Without the frontline Test players the Sydney side was gutted both of its experience and much of its venom, but Farr-Jones acquitted himself well. So much so that Bob Howitt, the doyen of the New Zealand rugby writers, who was present that day, would later say of it, 'Perhaps three or four times in your life you'll see a performance like that where even though the player is an unknown you'll just know he's destined for great things, and that was one of them. He played a wonderful game and what particularly impressed me was how, even though he was on a losing side, he was able to *control* his part of the game so well. He seemed to always take the right option.'

And Alan Jones, who as always studied in minute detail the video of the game, would at least have been impressed with Farr-Jones's display of the same 'cool authority' against the best team in the world that he had previously displayed in very difficult conditions against the Fiji side in Suva.

Nevertheless, for the Second Test up at Ballymore in Brisbane the following week, Farr-Jones again took up his increasingly familiar spot as reserve on the bench behind Phillip Cox.

After the Wallabies were leading the game by 12–0 at one point, the All Blacks staged a famous comeback to win the game 19–15.

In Test rugby, as in all team sports, losses tend to presage changes in team selections, and there was some minimal speculation in the press and in rugby clubs around the land as to whether Alan Jones might be tempted to give Farr-Jones the halfback position. Phillip Cox had not exactly played a bad game, but nor had he impressed particularly. But Cox retained his position for the Third Test and with the series now locked at one-all there was no surprise when a crowd of some 50,000 turned up for the decider back at the SCG.

In one of the most celebrated games of Test rugby to that date, Mark Ella, in the final minute of the match, had yet another attempt at field goal, which missed, and the Wallabies lost by the remarkable score of 25–24.

The Bledisloe Cup, which the Wallabies had thought was theirs for the taking after the First Test, was to remain with the New Zealanders after all. The atmosphere in the dressing room afterwards, all agree, was heavy. Jones didn't particularly blame anyone publicly but what was certain was that with the Wallabies now having had two Test losses in a row the way had been made a lot clearer for those seeking entrance to the land of Australian Test rugby.

Their chance would come in the upcoming Wallaby tour of the British Isles.

CHAPTER SIX

Grand Slam

*'Some people think football is a matter of life and death.
I don't like that attitude. I can assure them it is much
more serious than that.'*
Bill Shankley, English soccer manager

While rugby had started off the year as just one of the many things in the orbit of Nick's life, by July it had been reversed—he was in orbit around rugby. His studies, his life at Andrews College, his relationship with Angela Benness, all had to fit in now with the demands of the game.

'When you make the Wallabies,' he says, 'you suddenly find that a large part of your own identity gets wrapped up in it. It's not like your life is just as before with the exception that there's more rugby in it. It's that everything, but *everything*, changes for you.'

Now it would change more, as the VIIIth Wallaby tour to Great Britain and Ireland approached. Eighteen matches, more than two and a half months away.

In a column headlined 'THREE BABES GOING PLACES', written in the *Sun-Herald* three days before the Wallabies' departure, journalist Jim Webster named 'centre-winger Matt Burke, 19, halfback Nick Farr-Jones, 22, and lock Stephen Tuynman, 21' as three who, if they 'do not make the test team while away, will all go agonisingly close to it'.

'The claims of Farr-Jones,' Webster finished, 'can probably not be ignored much longer.'

Alan Jones was of the same mind. In an article by Terry Smith in the *Sun* a day later, he was quoted as saying: 'Nick has a marvellous pass. He's very tough, highly intelligent, and will be suited by British conditions. Along with Matt Burke, Michael Lynagh and Stephen Tuynman, he's one of the players future Australian teams will be built around.'

Nice stuff to read about yourself before going away on tour, though Farr-Jones claims not to have been too excited.

'Of course it was a pleasure to read that sort of stuff, but I knew I still had a lot of work ahead of me before I'd get the position.'

And work they all did.

In those days, before going away on a major tour the Wallabies would gather for a few days at the Camperdown Travelodge, just 400 metres down the road from St Andrews College and across from the spectacularly gothic St Johns College. It was on St Johns Oval that the Wallabies trained morning and afternoon—harangued, harassed and howled at by the ever-intense Alan Jones. If the Wallabies didn't succeed on this tour it certainly wouldn't be for want of energy put in by the coach.

In the evenings the exhausted Wallabies would return to the Travelodge for more team meetings, video-watching sessions and endless Jones-led analyses of the English provincial teams and the probable English personnel whom they would come up against on the first leg of the tour. Typical of Jones—but new to Australian rugby—the national coach had put a great deal of time into amassing information on the likely composition of each national team they would be playing: their strengths, weaknesses and likely tactics. Through the help of contacts he had in Britain, he had videos of many of their most recent games, which he had studied endlessly. So thorough had been his study that some of the Wallabies reckoned Jones probably knew more about the English team than the team knew about themselves.

Likely half-back? Nigel Melville. Strengths? If anything, their backline. Weaknesses? A certain susceptibility to be rattled if the opposition attacked them early.

The aim of the game was to become the first Wallaby touring side to win all four of the Test matches: to make a vast improvement on the one win, three loss record of the 1980–81 Wallabies. And if that required days with up to eight hours of trainings and meetings, etc, then so be it.

Jones was helped in all his analysis and coaching by his great friend, the affable Queenslander Alec Evans. A man of enormous rugby experience, Evans helped fill in the gaps in Jones's own knowledge, and they could be seen talking together at all hours of the night and day, working out precisely what the next training should consist of, what areas of the Wallaby game needed to be worked on; who was in form and who wasn't; the tactics to be pursued in any given game.

Evans was the first 'Assistant Coach' in Australian rugby history, and if that is now something of an institution, it is because the Jones/Evans combination worked so well. The heart of their combined coaching was to break the rugby game down into its hundred different parts—scrums, lineouts, tackles, passes, side-steps, putting the ball down, picking the ball up and so on—and have the players endlessly polish each separate part before putting it all back together again. No matter that they were already Wallabies and already knew how to pass the ball . . . the basics were always worked as hard as the more sophisticated techniques.

Not that it was all solid work before they left. The Wallabies were now in Farr-Jones's own stamping ground around Sydney University and he'd be damned if they wouldn't sample at least some of the pleasures available.

On the second night of the camp he took a few of the Wallabies—among them Tom Lawton, Andy McIntyre and the legendary Roger Gould—to the nearby White Horse pub. On this night, as on most nights, it was packed with Andrewsmen who upon their entry paused . . . for the barest moment . . . before resuming.

Farr-Jones was on his own turf, and walking tall.

When Alan Jones announced one evening that he had decided the whole team would have professional singing lessons before departure, so as to be better prepared for the tour singalongs (a very thorough man was Alan), Nick knew he had just the place: the chapel in St Andrews, a mere 400 metres away, where they would also have access to a piano.

Jones gratefully accepted, and two nights later the amazing news shot round the college that the Wallabies were in the chapel . . . singing.

Sure enough, as a small crowd gathered at the closed chapel door they could hear the Wallabies warbling away on the other side, singing such favourites as 'I Still Call Australia Home' and

'Waltzing Matilda'. Had they pressed their ears to the door, they just might have been able to make out Alan Jones himself, exhorting the players: 'Lads, we're not only going to be good rugby players, we're going to be good ambassadors, and we're going to know how to sing.'

It was a small and bizarre interlude in what would prove to be an historical three months, but the players went along with it if only to gain respite from the constant round of trainings and meetings.

They boarded the plane two days later with relief because they knew that, try as he might, Jones wouldn't be able to get at them to do any gut-busting exercise for at least the next twenty-four hours.

'Now remember, lads,' Jones told them when approaching Heathrow Airport, 'when you're marking your arrival cards and they ask "purpose of visit?", I want you to mark "business", because that's what we're here on.'

No joke. The team had no sooner arrived at St Ermin's Hotel in London than Jones announced that, seeing as their rooms weren't prepared, they would fill in the time with a solid training session.

It was at this session that the team for the first game was announced and with Phillip Cox still suffering from an injured shoulder, Farr-Jones was in the side. For him, the crucial first chance to impress on tour.

In the week's build-up to that first game, against London Division, the players coined a name for their training sessions— 'Rollerball', after a particularly violent film of the time involving heavy physical contact. Jones was of the opinion that the only way to get match fit was to have the players train 'full on', meaning full tackling, and as they were all competing for positions they set to with a will.

In the afternoons and evenings there was either sightseeing to be done or Wallaby welcoming dinners to be attended. One of the more memorable of these dinners was at the famed East India Club, where at the top of the old four-storey building with its grand old wooden stairs the players saw the famous pink room— the room in which, traditionally, the British Lions team is always selected.

Farr-Jones had already been in London twice that year on rugby tours, once with the Australian Universities side and soon afterwards with the Sydney side. It is not surprising therefore that he was less interested in going sightseeing than some of the other players. Whatever he managed to see from the bus as they went to and from training was fine, but there were other leisure activities that interested him far more.

Such as playing cards.

On the way back from one training session captain Andrew Slack enquired whether Farr-Jones felt like playing cards that afternoon. It was as a man dropping the chequered flag on what would be almost ten years of Farr-Jones card games on Wallaby tours.

That afternoon, and on into the night, he and Slack, together with the Queensland prop Stan Pilecki and some of the touring journalists, Jim Webster, Howard Northey and Terry Smith, played poker for keeps.

The AAP correspondent, Northey, remembers a good portion of his wallet transferring to Farr-Jones's throughout the long game and was also struck by 'the obvious pleasure with which he took our money'.

'Not in a nasty way or anything. He just so much loved playing and winning, I thought, "Well, the Wallabies have not only got themselves a good card player here, but also a first-class competitor."'

Not a bad rugby player either. When the first game against London Division finally arrived Farr-Jones scored a try, acquitted himself well in tackling and made many crucial breaks darting upfield from the base of the scrums, rucks and mauls, as was to become his trademark.

Despite having been with the Wallabies now for the last four months this was only his second game for them and he had done nothing to alter the favourable impression he had made when he had played his first game in Fiji.

The Wallabies won against London Division by 22–3, and it was a jubilant Alan Jones who congratulated them in the dressing room.

In the two weeks leading up to this game the Wallabies had been like a buzzing chainsaw, vibrating endlessly under the strain of Jones's constant harangues, with nothing solid to bite into. With this game, the chainsaw had now hummed satisfyingly through its first major obstacle and the tour proper had begun.

Cox's shoulder still had not healed by the time of the next game so Farr-Jones was again picked. This time the chainsaw faltered slightly against much harder wood and the Wallabies could only manage a 12–12 draw against the spirited Exeter side. Farr-Jones was very happy with his own game though and felt justified in going out that night until the wee hours with many of the other Wallabies.

And why not? Nick was always a more than willing participant on these nocturnal excursions, partly because it was his natural bent, and also because 'going out with the boys at night was also a really big part of me getting to know my fellow Wallabies'.

'When you're the new boy on the block, part of feeling integrated with the team is going out and mixing with the Roger Goulds, the Andrew Slacks and the Stephen Williamses. It was a great honour to go to a nightclub with these guys, and that was a large part of how I got to know them.'

Alan Jones did not see it like that at all.

The evening after the Exeter game Farr-Jones got a call from the coach that he would like to see him in his room at his earliest convenience.

Knock. Knock.

Who's there?

Nick.

Come in, Nick.

As always, Farr-Jones noticed, Jones's room was pristine in its neatness, with everything in its place and a place for everything. The tracksuit he'd worn at training that day neatly folded over the chair, his sandshoes placed precisely beside his leather shoes at the foot of the bed, English rugby magazines—which he'd been perusing for yet more information about coming opponents— neatly opened on the study desk.

Then he started. Both barrels blazing and barely a pause for breath. When Alan was angry the tips of his ears became red first and it seemed to spread from there.

Who the HELL did Farr-Jones think he was, going out every night drinking? Did he think this was some two-bit Sydney University tour, where you could do whatever you liked? Did he think that a rugby tour was no more than just one big party? Did he want to be over here just as a back-up or did he have some ambition to play Test rugby and, if so, didn't he think it would be a good idea to start focusing a bit more on football and a lot less on partying? Well, *didn't he*?

So heated was the Jones attack, and so crushed was Farr-Jones at this sudden anger—he knew he'd been both training and playing well, however busy he'd been at night—that all remonstrations of innocence were useless. 'But I . . .'s were no sooner out of his mouth than they were ruthlessly terminated. The young halfback ended up staring glazedly at a point just over the coach's right shoulder.

The curtains were drawn, they were pink and flowery, and just a little threadbare. Through a crack where the curtains didn't quite meet he could see a lone streetlight as Jones continued.

Twenty minutes later, when the coach's fury was fully spent, Farr-Jones left.

As unfair as it seemed, this vintage Jones attack was probably judiciously timed.

'Jones knew that people react to different things,' Farr-Jones says. 'He believed, and was probably right, that what I needed was a good kick in the derrière. Whereas someone like Michael Lynagh might need a bit of encouragement. Jones knew then how to deal with people to get the best out of them. After that I started to focus more on the possibility that I might play in the First Test at Twickenham.'

While Jones really was adept at these one-on-one sessions, having a constant round of meetings with individual players throughout the tour, he also loved trying to motivate the entire team through stories. On one famous occasion, when he had been putting them through a particularly gruelling training session down at Swansea in the lead-up to the First Test against England, Jones became aware that there was a certain lack of enthusiasm.

So . . . *hold it*! Everyone bring it in tight over here. Gather round, lads. In the memory of one of his more exhausted charges, (Farr-Jones,) the story went like this:

I want to tell you a story about a seventeen-year-old Italian boy by the name of Gucci. One evening his father came up to him and said, 'My son, you're getting to that age when you've got to work out what you're going to do with your life.'

'Well, my father,' his son replies, 'as a matter of fact I've been thinking about that and what I'm going to do is to go into the clothing business.'

'That's wonderful, my son. I'm really happy that you have been giving this some thought, but unfortunately here in Italy everyone's in clothing and you're not going to be able to compete.'

'Well, my father, I've thought about that too. What I'm going to do is use only the best products, the best designs, the best tailors. I'll be able to compete because I'll have a really wonderful product to sell.'

To which his father replied, 'Well, again I'm happy, son, because you've obviously been thinking a great deal, but unfortunately there is a small problem—if you use only the best of everything, you're going to have to charge the top price and no one will be able to afford your gear.'

And his son's answer is the one which can carry you all the way through life. His son replied, 'Yes, my father, *but long after the price is forgotten, the quality will remain.*'

And so what was ever-after known as the 'Gucci factor' was born. Do the hard work now and you'll have long forgotten the pain but the rewards of the work will stay with you. It was a message designed specifically for a bunch of heaving, muddy footballers, wondering if anything could really be worth this much mud and sweat.

Farr-Jones admired the parable and names it as the Jones story he remembers with most affection. It wasn't necessarily something you could draw on for extra energy when nearing the end of an exhausting training session, but it helped create an ambience where hard work was more likely to be done.

Others were less motivated by stories with such simplistic messages. Prop Stan Pilecki remembers wondering how come it was that Jones could be telling a bunch of grown men such a fable and that they were actually listening, rapt.

The tour continued apace.

From the first four games the Wallabies had recorded three wins and one draw and were now approaching the First Test against England. There remained only the game against Swansea on the Tuesday night before playing England in the First Test on the Saturday, 3 November. The collective mind of the Wallabies turned more assiduously than before to the likely selections for the First Test team.

The odd thing at this stage was that there was no strain in the relationship between Farr-Jones and Phillip Cox. Pockets of tension on Wallaby tours between players competing for the same position are as traditional as the green and gold colours they wear. If one player is to play 'a blinder' there is no surer source of a precise recounting of the few mistakes that he might have made than the player whose own selection has been threatened because of it.

The usual rule did not apply in this instance, as Farr-Jones and Cox were quite close and frequently went out together at night. While there was a consciousness between them that two into one doesn't go, Farr-Jones recalls that 'we simply liked each other a lot, which made the situation a lot easier'.

Cox remembers being impressed, in spite of himself, at how well Farr-Jones had been playing to that point.

'What struck me,' he says, 'as one halfback watching another, was that he always seemed to take the right option with the ball. And even if he took the wrong option he was fast enough and strong enough that he could make it work.'

Farr-Jones recalls only being 'hopeful' that he would be selected for the First Test. But surely the tea leaves of the time were reading a far stronger likelihood than that. He had played three of the first four games on tour, and played well. When it was announced that Cox had been selected for the Tuesday game against Swansea, before the Saturday Test, it was obvious he was close—Wallaby practice traditionally being that the Test side is rested for the Saturday game.

The sealer was perhaps during the Swansea game, when Cox made a rare mistake and threw a loose pass, which was intercepted by Swansea for a try. Farr-Jones still took nothing for granted.

So, on the morning after the game the team bussed back to St Ermin's Hotel in London and in a small room on the first floor the Wallaby side for the First Test against England on the Saturday was announced. Again Alan Jones did the honours.

'. . . backrowers, Simon Poidevin and David Codey.'

'Number eight, Steve Tuynman.'

'Half-back [*Farr-Jones's stomach muscles clench involuntarily*], Nick Farr-Jones.' [*And he breathes again.*]

There had been four changes to the team that played the Third Test against the All Blacks—with Steve Tuynman, Michael Lynagh and David Codey all coming into the side as well as Farr-Jones—but the player all the press wanted to talk to was Farr-Jones.

By this time the AAP correspondent Howard Northey had forgiven and forgotten the hammering he had taken from Farr-Jones at the poker table and knew a good story when he saw one . . .

'I think all of us in the press had some sense that Farr-Jones would go on to become one of the game's greats,' he says. 'I don't really know why we felt that so particularly, but there was just something *about* the guy.'

Jim Webster, the *Sydney Morning Herald* correspondent, concurred. In his article that appeared in Sydney the following day he wrote that, 'Australia has a big, powerful, driving halfback in Nick Farr-Jones [now weighing 85kg], who, I feel, is destined to become one of the greatest we have had.'

For Farr-Jones training that morning seemed to pass by in a blur, not only because he was now training with the full Test side for the first time (and he was going to be playing A TEST!), but, as they all knew, as soon as it was over they would be going to Buckingham Palace to meet the Queen. The prospect was made even more agreeable by the fact that the precisely timed meeting at high noon would oblige Alan Jones to cut short what would surely have been a very long session.

The only member of the Wallabies not thrilled by the prospect of meeting Queen Elizabeth II was the Argentinian-born 'Topo' Rodriguez, who still harboured rancour towards England for what it had done two years earlier to Argentina during the Falklands War or, as he insisted on calling it, the war of the Malvinas. That was certainly not a problem when taking on the English on the rugby field, but it was definitely a problem when asked to shake hands and be totally respectful to the Sovereign of that nation.

Nevertheless Rodriguez was eventually persuaded to go with the rest of the team and, dressed in their very best uniform, the Wallabies made ready to depart. But first the briefing. One of the officials from the Australian Embassy had come over to the hotel to read them the riot act about how to behave when in the presence of Her Majesty. The instructions were very specific. *Do* address her as 'Your Majesty' upon meeting and 'Ma'am' thereafter. *Don't* speak to her unless she first addresses you. *Don't* crush her hand with your big paws. *Don't* keep together in one large and intimidating mass. *Do* keep in small discreet groups around the room so that the Queen may move easily from one group to the other.

It was a strange sight, then, for the tourists outside Buckingham Palace that day. Who on earth could those fellows be in that huge bus with the big 'Foster's' logo painted on the side going round and round the statue that stands in front of the palace?

Six times round, seven times, eight times . . . then, as Big Ben struck the twelfth chime in the distance, the gates suddenly swung open, the bus darted through, and it was as if it had all been a mirage.

The Wallabies were greeted in the Palace courtyard and then led up some stairs, down some hallways and into a large sitting room. Spacious. Everything was so incredibly spacious. Ceilings so high they could fit the height of at least another three ordinary rooms. Corridors so wide they were almost rooms in themselves.

The paintings on the wall looked as if they'd been painted back when the palace was built and the carpets had the same marvellously old-world feel. In a vast sitting room the Wallabies were asked to stand in single file in preparation for meeting the Queen.

What would she be wearing? Farr-Jones wondered idly as they all waited. Somehow, subconsciously, he half-suspected she would look like she did in the portrait that used to hang in the schoolroom back at Miranda Primary—with a golden crown and a beautiful long flowing yellow dress. Then suddenly the doors rolled back to an adjoining room and there she was at the other end.

The Queen of England. (Wearing neither the crown nor the shimmering dress, just a dress and hat, and, surprisingly, no gloves.)

The Wallabies all moved forward in single file to meet her. After the initial soft handshake and a 'pleased to meet you, Your Majesty', the players formed small groups of three and four, as they had been instructed, and the Queen started to move around among them.

First impressions are often the longest remembered of fleeting acquaintances, and Farr-Jones's first impression as the Queen finally approached his group was how incredibly small she was. Somehow she looked as small as someone you'd grown up seeing only on postage stamps. He'd rather thought in the flesh she'd be a lot bigger.

'Hello. Are you enjoying your stay in Britain?'

'Yes, Ma'am,' they replied a little nervously, in chorus, nodding their heads perhaps a fraction more than was necessary.

From there the conversation ambled every which way, until interrupted by a terrible splintering sound. Behind them, Wallaby breakaway Chris Roche had leant on an antique table which in its last 300 years or so had never known such treatment, and it had screamed loudly all the way to the ground.

'Don't worry,' the Queen's Equerry called out in the middle of the stunned silence, 'there's plenty more in the storeroom.'

A little laugh from the Queen and she resumed her conversation with the group. Charmed by her, and fascinated by what they had been hearing, the Wallabies became a fraction more emboldened and felt freer to pursue the conversation on their own account.

Before she moved off to the next group, which had been waiting patiently, Farr-Jones tried his luck with one last question. If Ma'am thought it was a good idea, perhaps Prince Edward—who the Wallabies knew was a keen rugby follower—would like to come down and train with them?

Ma'am didn't think it was a good idea actually, but politely thanked him for the kind offer on Edward's behalf.

In all, the Queen's chat to the group had lasted for some fifteen to twenty minutes, and she had left behind her in Farr-Jones something of a devoted royalist.

'She was just so warm and natural, it amazed me. We all thought that meeting the Queen would probably involve sort of shaking hands and her unloading a few pleasantries before we were ordered out, but it wasn't like that at all. She really gave the impression of someone who really cared, somehow, beyond just observing the formalities.'

The phone call pulled Angela Benness up and out of her sleep at about seven o'clock that morning. He knew she'd still be asleep then but couldn't wait to tell her.

His day? Well, . . . he'd met the Queen, chatted to her for a while in fact, and he'd been selected to play his first Test match for Australia.

Standard practice in the Wallabies before Test matches is for the Test players who will be working closely together during the match to room together. So it was that he had just put the phone down after talking to Angela when his room-mate, and the man most often touted as 'the most extravagantly talented player Australian rugby has ever produced', Mark Ella, came back from wherever it was he had been.

A curious sort of fellow, Ella: very laid back and friendly if you got to know him, though not particularly gregarious if left to his own devices. But he was now in a difficult position. While the Jones way of doing things had worked wonders with some, it left Mark entirely unmoved at best, and seriously annoyed at worst.

The Jones/Ella relationship was never going to be a strong one from the moment the new coach had deposed Mark in favour of Andrew Slack as captain; but while there might have been some tension between Ella and Jones on that tour, there was no problem between Ella and the other players, and he was the perfect room-mate for Farr-Jones leading into his first Test.

Though the team management no doubt had in mind that in their four days rooming together Ella would be able to pass on many of the nuances of Test Rugby, Ella took an entirely different approach.

The extent of his specific instructions to Farr-Jones stopped at, 'Mate, whether it's good ball or bad ball just chuck it to me. Fling it over your shoulder and I'll be there.'

Perfect. Simple. And to the point.

'I mean, I was nervous enough already,' Farr-Jones says, 'and if Mark Ella had been really nervous, or tried to give me a hundred different instructions, I know I would have been driven batty. My logic would have been, *he's* Mark Ella and he's climbing the walls, so how should *I* be feeling?'

But it was fine. The morning of the Test Ella barely even mentioned that afternoon's game before they went to breakfast. It was for all the world as if he had some picnic races that he thought maybe he might mosey along to and Nick could come too, if he was of a mind.

'Okay, let's go!' Jones had just given the first of what would be three motivational speeches that afternoon and the players were in a suitably serious frame of mind. As they got on the bus, Farr-Jones deliberately chose a seat on his own so he could be totally quiet and think on what lay ahead of him, what he had to do, how he had to do it, how he would react when . . . *plonk* . . . Alan Jones sat down beside him. Obviously thinking the best way to settle Farr-Jones down was to talk to him, he began to go over what he expected.

Farr-Jones nodded here and there, made the odd 'uh-huh' and 'yup', but his mind kept drifting.

Back at St Andrews College it was in the wee hours of the morning and he knew Angie had been paid the supreme honour of being invited to sit in the beanbag of honour at the front of the television room and that not only would she and all of the Andrewsmen be watching, together with his brothers and just about everybody else he knew, but also his parents would be watching in the stands, together with Angela's father, Professor Benness. He not only knew how proud they would all be, but more importantly how embarrassed both he and they would be if somehow he blew it.

Which he knew he might.

'Frankly I still wasn't sure if someone hadn't made a terrible mistake,' he recalls. 'Remember, only a year before this I was playing Second Division rugby out around the backblocks of Sydney, in front of audiences of three men and a lost dog. Now here I was playing for Australia at Twickenham against the best that England could throw at us.'

Again the old questions returned. What if I throw an intercept pass? What if I knock it on or give away a penalty in front of the posts and they score and win the game because of it? What if I can't get the pass right to Mark? What if . . . ?

Knocks on dressing room doors signalling that the Test players are now required out on the field always reverberate more loudly than the people knocking could possibly imagine.

A few last handshakes, a few last nervous jumps up and down, a bit of a last solemn look around at all the vastly experienced players he was going out there with, and Farr-Jones took his place with the others and filed out the door. It was when he first started walking down the darkened tunnel that led to the pitch that he suddenly felt his first rush of real confidence.

'I have done the work, so I bloody well should be all right. I really should be able to drill Mark with the ball from anywhere.'

And so into the daylight proper as the Wallabies ran out on to Twickenham and into the almighty roar from the crowd, a roar similar to the one unleashed in the TV room of St Andrews, where it had previously been almost silent in anticipation . . . until the first vision of Nick came on the screen. 'YO! GO! NICKO! YOU LITTLE BEAUTY!'

Amid all the tumult Angela Benness sat in the beanbag as she recalls 'quietly praying both that he'd play a good game and that he wouldn't be injured'. In the stands Nick's parents were feeling 'very anxious and very proud', Rosemary claiming she hadn't slept a wink.

The rendition of the national anthems and then it was on. Test Match rugby.

From the first Australian scrum two minutes into the game, Farr-Jones fed the ball in, it came out the back between the number eight Steve Tuynman's feet and then came the moment . . . Farr-Jones's principal role in this, his first game, was simply to ensure that the ball came cleanly and quickly into the hands of five-eighth Mark Ella, who was standing six metres back, ten metres across, and accelerating forwards. A half-back ever since he'd pulled on a boot, Farr-Jones had accomplished this feat thousands of times before, but this was a Test match; it was different. Never before had there been so much pressure on him, never before had the opposition wanted to win quite so much.

When he retrieved the ball from between Tuynman's feet the opposition half Nigel Melville was right upon him. He had just a split second to get the ball away and on its flight to Ella.

So down. Crouch. Scoop. Pass, and away . . .The ball went spiralling on its flight right into the hands of Mark Ella on the burst. With that, Nick's confidence soared and he was going fine. Passing, tackling, yapping at the forwards, darting upfield, doing it all—though most of the time, he says, 'my mind was just on auto-pilot'.

'You don't know why you do what you do, you just do it because it *feels* right.'

At halftime the Wallabies were leading by just 3–0 but soon after resuming came the try of the match. Twenty-five metres from the English line, Farr-Jones arrowed the ball out to Ella. In an attempt to execute a backline move by the name of 'Froggy', rehearsed many times at training, Ella started to drift across field with the ball still in hand.

As he went the English defence appeared mesmerised by the various angles Michael Lynagh, Roger Gould and David Campese were running off him, not knowing which one would receive the ball. In fact none of them would, because Ella sensed the defence's confusion, changed pace and slid through the tiniest of openings, which perhaps only he could have known of, for a try under the posts. It was not the rehearsed move but the net result was the same—six points to the Australians.

Another two tries followed and Australia was leading 19–3 with five minutes to go when Farr-Jones saw at close quarters some of the underside of international rugby. From a kick-off to restart play, the famed English prop Gareth Chilcott—a carpenter by trade, who has been described as having the build of 'a ripe watermelon'— clubbed Farr-Jones to the ground with an overhand right. Welcome to Test Match rugby, sonny.

Slack was to claim to the press when the game was over that when the New Zealand referee Bob Francis had penalised Chilcott, he had commented to Slack that 'he should have been sent off for that'.

'Then why wasn't he?' Slack wanted to know.

The reply of Francis has gone unrecorded, but no matter . . .

Amid the jubilation in the dressing room afterwards Farr-Jones nursed a slightly sore jaw, but that was the extent of the damage. For the rest he felt no pain, and received many personal congratulations on what had been a solid performance.

In the middle of the throng a joyous Alan Jones held court with the press. If Jones's comments about Farr-Jones on that day were a touch restrained—perhaps for fear of having the youngster think he'd already made it—in an interview seven years later with the *Sydney Morning Herald* he gave a succinct summing up of what the new boy had brought to the team as well as his estimation of the lad's performance that day.

'He was destined to be the best in the world,' Jones said. 'He had everything that was needed. He was tough, physically courageous in defence, he had a wonderful boot, he was a running athlete and an instinctive footballer who always went forward. I put him in the team against England and he was outstanding.'

The Farr-Jones Test career was launched.

All touring Wallaby sides are divided up into two informal groups—those who are in the Test side and those who want to be in the Test side. It is not that the latter are second-class citizens, so much as that the former are first-class. After his first Test match and his passing from one group to the other, Farr-Jones was aware that things moved even more easily than before— nothing definite, more a conciousness from all that you are a *Test* player.

After Farr-Jones's performance in that first Test his selection for the second Test against the Irish was all but a formality, but still he was exceptionally glad to hear his name read out, as he would be for every one of the next twenty or so Tests until he started taking it as given that he would be selected.

Of all the countries visited on this tour it was perhaps in Ireland that the spirit of the locals and the spirit of the Wallabies most completely gelled. There was something about the Irish lack of pretence and stuffiness, their own innate sense of 'mateship', that made the Irish sojourn the most pleasurable of the tour.

The locals, men and women, extended their hospitality towards the touring Wallabies in many different and delightful ways. From offering a drink to accepting the offer of one, from agreeing to accompany a Wallaby on a visit to a nightclub to whatever followed from there, it was the most social of times. Nick, like all the Wallabies, had to be careful that Alan Jones wouldn't gain the impression that he was always going out, but with a little discretion this was achievable.

The older, married Wallabies took a more laid-back approach to meeting with the locals, and chief among these was the much-loved prop, Stan Pilecki. A gruff bear of a man, Pilecki was, at thirty-seven, the oldest of the touring Wallabies, and while he was little into nightclubbing he loved nothing better than 'having a yarn and a beer'—as often as not with young Wallabies—about something that happened on a previous tour, or of what the great Wallaby captain Mark Loane had really been like, or of the time they'd found the Wallaby prop Declan Curran asleep in the bath, or the time that . . .

Stan's charm was particularly bountiful when it came to the natives of whatever country they were visiting, and it was part of team folklore that it only took two beers before whomever Stan was drinking with had become his lifelong friend. It was while they were in Dublin that he made a particularly propitious contact: an Irish horse-trainer had become so enamoured of the big Australian after a few beers that he promised to provide Stan, and through him the Wallabies, with 'inside tips' on which horses were likely to win.

For the rest of the tour Stan became the much-respected source of all racing knowledge as he was consulted on all occasions before anyone laid a bet—and together or separately they laid plenty, Nick usually at the head of the queue.

'I don't know if I loved Stan more for his stories or his tips,' Farr-Jones says now.

Cometh the hour, cometh the Test match. The famous Lansdowne Road football field was only five minutes from the Wallabies' hotel, making the agony of the bus trip that much more bearable, and it was to be Nick's first real taste of the Irish. Although the Wallabies were losing the game 6–9 with seventeen minutes to go, they finally came good to win by the tidy score of 16–9. Two down, two to go, and they were on course for the Grand Slam.

Yet there was a lot of work to do before what was judged to be the hardest game to win of the entire tour—the Test against Wales. And there would be some particularly hard provincial games in the lead up.

Arguably the hardest of these was the game against the famed Irish side Munster, and although the Wallabies went on to win it Farr-Jones recalls not being at all happy with his own game. One of the problems, he surmised, had been his longish hair getting in his eyes and that night he decided to have 'one of the boys' cut it.

Back home in Australia there would probably be few things to interest Steve Tuynman and Phillip Cox less than the cutting of Farr-Jones's hair, but in a Munster hotel room, on tour, with a bit of beer in them, there seemed nothing more enjoyable. The project was undertaken with predictable high hilarity and an equally predictable result. So dreadful a result that eventually journo Howard Northey was called in with a handheld razor to try to even it up. Northey might have been a little drunk himself, as he recalls.

This would merely have stood as a mildly amusing episode to break up the threat of tour tedium, but for a curious postscript . . .

During the journey through the green and hilly country to get to Llanelli in Wales, Alan Jones noticed the mutilation atop his star halfback's head and was apparently in no doubt at all what had caused it. Taking second-rower Stephen Cutler aside on their arrival, he gave his theory some air. It had all been Cutler's fault.

'Look at what you've gone and made Farr-Jones do to himself!' Cutler recalls the coach exploding. 'It's all that rubbish lineout ball you gave him against Munster. You've finally made him snap!'

Jonesy was just like that—he said some strange things, no doubt about that, but the players for the most just accepted it. The guy was a winner, they were winning, and you just had to go with the Jones flow, whatever he said.

The Wallaby caravan moved on. Together with Farr-Jones and his atrocious haircut.

To prepare for the Test against Wales the team moved to the picturesque sea town of Porthcawl on the Welsh south coast. At least it was probably picturesque—they could barely see it through the rain that fell the entire time they were there. A tourist destination in summer, it was all but empty now in the middle of winter and the Wallabies felt they had the run of the town. They settled down to hard training, while elsewhere the Welsh papers of Cardiff trumpeted the arrival of a worthy foe for their own boyos.

Jones's story of choice going into the Welsh Test was about Nadia Comaneci, the Romanian gymnast who had won the gold medal at the Montreal Olympics, eight years earlier. She had done this at the age of thirteen and after she'd come off the bars, having achieved the world's first ever perfect scores, the journalists had crowded around her to ask what was it that enabled her to achieve something no one in the history of the sport had been able to do.

And do you know what she said, men? Do you know what she said? She said, '*My mind was full of getting it exactly right.*'

For this Test against Wales Jones wanted them not just to win, not just to play well, he wanted them to concentrate on getting it exactly right.

Some relief from the build up to the Test was provided by Stan Pilecki. His Irish horse-training friend, who had to this point proved to be amazingly accurate in his tips, had phoned through with news of an outsider that was in fact 'practically a certainty'.

'A Sure Row', the name this 'streak of lightning posing as a horse' ran under, was going to be running the Thursday before the Test, with the handsome odds of 7–1, and the Wallabies dug deep to get on every last pound they could with Stan. And how they wished they'd dug even deeper when it actually got up and won. Farr-Jones, for one, won a tidy 700 pounds and began to hang round Stan all the more.

The screaming police escort that took them from Porthcawl to Cardiff gave them some indication of how seriously the Welsh regarded their rugby Tests and they were ushered into the world's most famous rugby temple without the slightest delay. Nothing was too good for the men who were going to serve as choice fodder for their boyos that afternoon.

In the rugby experience, standing with your team out on the field before the game as 67,000 Welsh supporters sing 'Land of My Fathers' stands as one of the most moving. Actually, the Welsh didn't seem to sing it so much as all resonate together as one, with the anthem simply coming out of them . . .

It was while standing there, though, that Farr-Jones couldn't help but notice that already his football boots were a centimetre deep in the heavy muddy ground, and he knew more than ever that the sort of game he would play this day would have to be entirely different from the preceding two.

A wet and slow field meant that the ball would be difficult to handle and move in the backs. From being just a link man, as he had been in the first two games, between the forwards and the backs, Farr-Jones was suddenly one of the trumps—the one to keep the ball close to the forwards and make constant darting runs himself.

Which he did, with many probing runs from the base of the scrum creating havoc in the Welsh defences. Two of the tries for Australia came from just such a Farr-Jones probing run up the blindside, the first to Tommy Lawton and the second to Michael Lynagh.

But to the highlight of the afternoon and one of the most famous tries of the decade. Halfway through the second half a Wallaby scrum was set up five metres out from the Welsh line, and just before Farr-Jones put the ball in he heard the forward call of 'Samson' go up, signalling that the pack was about to put on an 'eight-man shove'. This is a process whereby the forwards, instead of just trying to stabilise their own scrum, essay to all push together and push the opposing side backwards.

The most humiliating fate for any pack is to be pushed backwards in such a fashion, but amazingly, centimetre by centimetre, it happened before Farr-Jones's eyes—the Welsh pack giving way as the Australians advanced. It was a moment when half of Wales sat stunned, refusing to believe that a Welsh pack could ever be so humiliated, but there was no denying it.

Eventually the Wallaby pack had pushed the Welsh pack behind their own line, and with the ball still securely beneath the feet of the Australian second-row, Wallaby number eight Steve Tuynman was able to fall on it for a try. Victory to the Wallabies by the score of 28–9. Dawn the following day found many of the triumphant Wallabies still out celebrating.

There was, understandably, a lot of pressure on the side leading up to the Test against Scotland. After the final game at Murrayfield they would either be known as the Grand Slam Wallabies or 'the side that did really well in Britain, winning three out of four Tests'.

Jones as always had a motivating verbal flourish: 'Never forget, boys, you can be a rooster one week and a feather duster the next.' And in an effort to ensure that the Wallabies did in fact remain roosters, Jones ran them very hard indeed. So hard it was inevitable that there would be some sort of blow-up somewhere. It turned out to be with Farr-Jones.

Now with three Test selections under his belt, Farr-Jones felt much surer of his ground—less the shy new boy and more his old self. The one with a short fuse if the occasion warranted it, and sometimes when it didn't; the one who was rarely inclined to back down whatever the circumstances.

After a long bus trip from Porthcawl the Wallabies arrived late in the day to Southport to be greeted with the news that Jones wanted them to complete a brief training session, 'just to get some of the cobwebs out of our system'.

Which is the way it started, but long after the cobwebs had been brushed away the Wallabies were still at it, driving hard and continuing well after the sun had fallen away. Jones for some reason was in a particularly foul mood that afternoon and lived on the whistle, constantly exhorting them to new agonies in the name of being ready for the Scots in a fortnight's time. Farr-Jones took it all on board quietly enough, though, as he says, 'Hating every moment of it and the Gucci factor be damned.'

However, at last the blessed whistle to signal the end of training sounded. Jonesy had just one more announcement to make.

'Okay, these people will do some extra work: Farr-Jones, Grigg, Reynolds . . . ' Surely he couldn't be serious. Okay, so Jones had a policy that if you hadn't played in the last three or four days you had to do extra work to maintain your fitness, but this in Farr-Jones's mind was ridiculous—he was totally exhausted.

He intended to invoke the only let-out clause he could think of. Jones had often said to them that, 'Common sense prevails.

So if you feel that your body is a little tight and you'll be risking injury by doing extra work, let me know.' Surely, if he reminded Alan of that, he would be let off from doing the extra work, as he was tired and his hamstrings did feel particularly tight. Somehow, though, the words came out wrong. Instead of saying, 'Excuse me, Alan, would you mind terribly if . . . ' what came out, in a voice tinged with insolence, was, 'Alan, I'm *not* going to do this.'

Very quietly Jones turned to the other six players he had named and said, 'Okay, you other six, go off and start some fifty-metre sprints,' and then turned fully towards Farr-Jones.

'How DARE you talk to me like that! *I'll* be the judge of what work you can and can't do! I am the *coach* and my function is to decide such things, otherwise the whole structure of our team endeavour would fall to the ground. DON'T YOU EVER speak to me like that and . . . .'

And so on. In a similar situation, in fully 999 times out of a thousand, the castigated player, in the face of an angry coach who held all power over selections and his future rugby career, would have backed off, apologised and gone off to do his sprints with added vigour, albeit head bowed. But on this occasion something inside of Farr-Jones reacted angrily and decided to take Jones on. And worse still, Farr-Jones burst forth with what he now refers to as a 'non-intellectual response'.

Basically he swore at Jones and stormed off.

And still Farr-Jones wasn't done. After slamming the door behind him as he charged into the changing room he proceeded to amaze Michael Hawker, Chris Roche and Andrew Slack, among others, by kicking bags around and slamming his fist into the wall as he publicly vented his spleen.

Slack and all were watching this display in stunned silence. But Farr-Jones was past caring, almost—until the focus of their gaze shifted from him to a point over his left shoulder, and he realised that someone else had come into the changing room. The man himself—Alan Jones. Even then Farr-Jones refused to be cowed into submission, and continued to mutter under his breath, even as he threw his things into his bag and harrumphed onto the bus.

By now the entire squad knew what was afoot, and the busload of Wallabies went very quietly back to the hotel with the two focal points of their attention, a darkly thunderous Alan Jones

ABOVE Farr-Jones passes the ball to Tim Horan in what would be a historic win for the Wallabies against France at Strasbourg in 1989

BELOW Nick Farr-Jones and Simon Poidevin against the All Blacks in the Second Test in 1986 *John Fairfax Group*

ABOVE Bloodied but unbowed, versus the British Lions at Ballymore in 1989 – with Robert Jones in pursuit *John Fairfax Group*

BELOW The Four Musketeers: David Campese, Peter FitzSimons, Nick Farr-Jones and Michael Lynagh, the way *Sydney Morning Herald* artist Bill Leak saw them prior to the Wallabies' departure for France in 1989

ABOVE The biography was in the future... Peter FitzSimons and Nick Farr-Jones in 1989 (after the First Test versus France) toasting the future victory in the World Cup, 1991

BELOW Nick Farr-Jones and Bob Dwyer in Wellington, 1990 – after the All Blacks 23 Test match-winning run ended *John Fairfax Group*

David Campese, with only five minutes to go, scored the final try in New Zealand to win the Bledisloe Cup in 1986 at Eden Park – pictured here with a delighted Farr-Jones
Dominion and New Zealand Times

At the time it seemed the end of Farr-Jones' involvement in the 1991 World Cup
Photopacific

ABOVE Victorious –
Nick Farr-Jones and
David Campese hold
aloft the World Cup
John Fairfax Group

LEFT Mid-November
1991. Home from the
Wallabies' triumph at
the World Cup

ABOVE The young lawyer. At the Garland Hawthorn Brahe offices – with his grandfather's photo at far left

BELOW Lunch in Adelaide with the Bradmans

ABOVE With Australian Test cricketer, Mike Whitney *John Fairfax Group*

BELOW With Nelson Mandela *John Fairfax Group*

up the front of the bus, and a carpet-biting mad Nick Farr-Jones down the back.

It was a confrontation, however, that Farr-Jones could never win, and by the time the bus arrived back at the hotel he began to reflect on the probable consequences of his actions. He'd be lucky to escape with just missing out on selection for the Scottish Test, and a listing of NTA (Never to Tour Again) seemed at least a possibility. Maybe his Wallaby career had finished before it had properly begun.

It was a slightly calmer, more rational Nick, then, whom the manager of the Wallabies, 'Chilla' Wilson, collared in the foyer of the hotel as soon as they arrived. Chilla told him he wanted to see him with Stan Pilecki for a 'discipline meeting' in his room. (Unbeknown to Nick at the time, Stan had also had a run-in with the coach after Nick had stormed off, when he had told Jones that he, Stan, was quite prepared to play halfback if Nick didn't want to. Alan didn't take it in quite the right humour.) As always with the affable Chilla this 'discipline meeting' involved a bit of a drink of whisky, a bit of a chat, a bit of discussion on how the guilty one could get out of 'trouble'. Basically, Chilla told both Nick and Stan they had to apologise.

Half an hour later, and now genuinely remorseful, Nick was at Alan Jones's door. He had drawn the short straw and had to apologise first. He knocked twice, but there was no answer.

Farr-Jones knew Jones was in there because he had heard the sound of running water being turned off as he approached the door, but he could hardly barge in there or yell out, 'I know you're in there, Alan, and I'm coming in to apologise ready or not!'

There was nothing for it but to write a letter of apology and slip it under his door.

It worked, after a fashion. Farr-Jones again went to see Jones after dinner and again the coach let him have it, but this time with none of those annoying interruptions from the recipient.

The gist of it was that never in Jones's life had *anyone* ever spoken to him like that, never could he believe that Farr-Jones of all people would be so insolent, and if Farr-Jones were playing at Manly he would find himself playing fifth grade next week.

Sorry. Sorry. Sorry.

They left it at that, with Jones having firmly re-established his supremacy over the recalcitrant player and Farr-Jones still not at all sure he would be named in the final Test side to play Scotland that weekend.

Before getting onto the bus for that Test, Jones gave the Wallabies just one more thing to think over.

'Just remember, there are four things that don't come back: the spent arrow, the spoken word, lost time, and the missed opportunity.'

The air was drizzly, the ground wet, and the stands packed with 65,000 rugby afficionados. While the Wallabies were playing for the Grand Slam, the Scots were playing for the huge honour of being the nation to deny them the pleasure.

Often in Test matches something will happen in the first minute of the game that is indicative of the whole game to come. But not this time . . .

Nick had been chosen for the Test after all and, after he had fed the ball into the first Australian scrum, the Scots were treated to the rare sight of Mark Ella dropping a ball coming straight to him, but it proved to be only a slight aberration in what was to be a masterly game from him. Not only did Ella throw a cut-out pass fifteen minutes into the game which led to a Campese try but, more importantly, in the second half he was the lynchpin of a move which went: Farr-Jones to Ella, inside to Gould, back to Ella and over for Ella's fourth try in as many test matches, his personal grand slam.

However, it was Nick's own try that sticks most firmly in his memory. With fifteen minutes to go, from a planned move off a two-man lineout, Farr-Jones darted into the lineout himself, got the ball, scurried down the touchline and, although he had to fight off two Scottish tackles, ended up scoring in the corner.

Australia ran out eventual winners by 37–12 and the Grand Slam was theirs. In the wild scenes in the dressing room afterwards, the primary feeling was of both jubilation and relief. Relief that they hadn't blown it, relief that they wouldn't have to face the wrath of Jones, relief that they wouldn't spend the rest of their lives ruing the lost opportunity.

The official black-tie dinner that night started soberly enough, but somewhere near the end it involved prop Andy McIntyre, Steve Tuynman and Farr-Jones dancing a highland fling while they tried to keep the world from seeing what was beneath their kilts, but not too hard. And the band played on.

There were many many emotional moments in the days immediately after the Grand Slam. None more so than at the final team dinner in London, before flying home.

Jones, who genuinely deserved much of the credit for the achievement, was at his eloquent and oft grandiloquent best and made a speech bringing home just what they had all had the honour to be a part of.

His chosen theme was that the team must stay together spiritually, if not in fact, must never forget what they had achieved and how they had done it, and must never forget each other. Always, he said, we will be known as the 'Grand Slam Wallabies', and in years to come when we see each other at Grand Slam reunions I will be honoured to see each and every one of you because I will know that you have all played your part in our great victory.

Thunderous applause, and not a few misty eyes.

So the Wallabies flew back to Australia triumphantly. Up to that point an uneasy peace had reigned between Farr-Jones and Jones, and nothing further had been said about the unpleasantness at Southport. Things had calmed between them. Forgive and forget.

There was, though, just one more major blow-up to get through.

When the Wallabies arrived at Sydney's Kingsford-Smith Airport there was a large media contingent waiting to report the happy news of the 'heroes' homecoming'. For them, few of the returning players provided as much of a 'story' as the new halfback Farr-Jones, who had played so well on tour after being unknown only a few months before.

The most obvious of all journalistic questions begged. 'What was it like? How do you feel about being a Test star now?'

Farr-Jones's reply, reported in the papers the following day, was that: 'The Tests weren't hard enough.'

The essence of Farr-Jones's comments was that while he, like all rugby players, had been steeped in all the mysticism of *Test* matches, making them entirely different from just hard rugby matches, he had found the whole thing a lot less demanding than he had imagined.

Jones's rang his halfback the following morning, after he'd read the papers.

'How *dare* you try and belittle what we achieved over there by saying it was easy? Don't you know that if you found it was easy it was only because of the tremendous amount of work we did? Perhaps you think you're so *good* that you didn't find it very demanding? Well, let me tell you . . . '

If Farr-Jones had learnt one thing in the past year in his dealings with Jones it was to pick his moments to take him on and this was definitely not one of them.

Yes Alan. No Alan. Sorry Alan.

With the benefit of hindsight Farr-Jones can see that Jones really did have a point. 'There's no doubt I got a good ride for my entry into Test rugby. I was damn lucky to play in a wonderful team behind a great forward pack to protect me and give me good ball, with Mark Ella outside me and a wonderful backline outside him. Had I been in a different team I would have probably come off thinking "Jeez, so *that's* what Test match rugby is all about".'

None of which changed the essential point. Farr-Jones had breezed through his first four Tests and was yet to be really tested.

While Farr-Jones had previously noticed the difference in the way people treated him as soon as he had become a Wallaby, it was as nothing to the way they regarded him now that he was a fully fledged Test player in a victorious team. The phone seemed never to stop ringing, there was a constant round of celebratory dinners to attend and people even held the lift for him.

Glory alone though did not pay the bills or get him through his impending law exams. Although he'd taken the precaution of bringing his law books with him on the tour to Britain, he'd done no study at all.

Worse still, the law school would not let him do late exams for the ones he'd missed while away, and he was told he would have to come back to school the following year to re-do a couple of subjects.

The irony of it all was that while it was his rugby that had made his legal studies suffer immeasurably, it was also his rugby that had led to his being offered an extremely handsome scholarship to Cambridge University. Soon after the Wallabies had completed the final leg of the slam against Scotland, Farr-Jones received a phone call from Ian Robertson, the former Scottish international who helped coach the Cambridge backs, and was asked if he'd like to come and play with Cambridge for a couple of years.

In return for his services to the rugby team the famous university would offer him not only entry but also full board and tuition fees. Farr-Jones declined, knowing that such an option would preclude continuing to play for Australia; but if nothing else it gave him an inkling of the opportunities that would be open to him in the future by remaining a Wallaby.

Even without a law degree from Sydney Uni, though, Farr-Jones decided the time had come to take a job with a law firm while he completed his remaining studies. And where better to go than to the law firm his grandfather had been a partner in for so many years, Garland, Seaborn & Abbott? In mid-December he called Stephen Martin, one of the partners of the firm whom he had come to know a little when Martin had coached one of the lower-grade teams at Sydney University.

Martin asked him to come in for an interview, which Nick did. The senior partner asked him a lot of questions about the Grand Slam tour and before the week was out he had a job, due to start in early January.

CHAPTER SEVEN

The Beat Goes On

'There is something about the very blackness of the All Black jersey that turns the marrow cold, and strikes fear into your heart like no other jersey can.'
J.P.R. Williams, Welsh rugby legend

All dressed up with nowhere to go. After all the hoopla of the Grand Slam victory, all the laurels and thundering applause, the Wallabies came on to their leanest year of Test matches in modern times.

A one-off Test against the All Blacks in New Zealand was the only highlight, sandwiched between two home Tests apiece against Canada and Fiji. Solid meat, sure, but a very thin sandwich.

'It was like having a Maserati during a petrol strike,' says Farr-Jones.

The presence of Alan Jones did not diminish in any of the Wallabies' lives because of it. When you were in 'my team', as Jones referred to it, there was always a fair-to-middling chance that when the phone rang it would be him. Mail-call, and a letter from Alan setting out the goals of this month, this season, and this year, were not at all unusual. There were frequent dinners at his stylish home, meetings in his office at Sydney radio station 2UE (where Jones had begun work in what would prove to be an extraordinarily successful career as a broadcaster), and private training sessions where the coach would put his charges through sprints.

The rugby calendar might have been freed up that year compared to last, but the 'commitment to excellence' that Jones demanded from his players would not be allowed to waver a fraction.

Farr-Jones juggled the heavy requirements of being a Wallaby around the demands of now working in a big-city law firm. He would often be obliged to leave his colleagues early in the evening to their legal briefs so as to go to a Jones training session. And if not a training session for Jones, then one for Sydney University, Sydney or New South Wales.

There were also social requirements. As if to underline his new status as the Test halfback, early in the year he and Angela received an invitation to go to 'meet the Queen and Prince Phillip' at a reception at the Sheraton Wentworth. There were 400 people there and they never actually met the royals but it was a nice invitation to receive all the same.

On the legal front, Farr-Jones settled down to work.

If his employment by the law firm had in some measure been smoothed by his status as a card-carrying test Wallaby, there were no special favours granted him once he'd 'bundied on' for the day. Together again with his old St Andrews friend Brenden Miller, who'd joined the firm not long after Farr-Jones, the two were initially obliged to share an 'office' that had been used as the firm's cloakroom cum telex room prior to their arrival. As Dorothy Parker once said in the late 1950s: 'He and I shared an office so tiny that an inch smaller and it would have been adultery.'

The room would have perhaps sufficed as a functionable office if the partners had stopped using it to hang up their coats and brollies, but it seemingly never occurred to the brutes to do so. On a wet day the scene might have been titled Office From Hell. The two juniors were seated on opposite sides of a small desk, divided by a wafer-thin partition to give them some semblance of privacy. One after the other the partners would enter the room, shaking the last drops of water off their umbrellas before hanging them up, the telex clattering all the while, the phone ringing, and yet another partner coming in to drop off his coat and have a bit of a chat on the way.

Every word of every phone call made by one could be heard by the other, which was manageable when it was a legal call but more difficult when it was personal.

Somehow they coped, and in the process learnt a lot of what a life in law would involve for them. They quickly understood that most of what they had been learning in law school for the past five years had only very limited relevance to what was required of them here.

At the law school they had been learning a lot of high-minded legal principles—together with exceptions to those principles, exceptions to the exceptions, exceptions to the exceptions to the exceptions . . . and so on, nearly all of it theoretical in nature.

But like all law firms, Garland, Seaborn & Abbott required their junior solicitors to be primarily legal mechanics. In the same manner that an apprentice at the local service station would learn how to replace a carburettor and tune it to the beat of the engine, Nick and Brenden learnt the legal process of such things as conveyancing, with all the 't's crossed and the 'i's dotted absolutely correctly.

For Nick it was a genuine pleasure to be working in the same law firm that his grandfather, Noel Burns, had devoted his whole legal career to. The most potent reminder of his relative was a portrait that hung in the firm's boardroom, gazing down austere and distinguished. With his uncle Neil also having worked there for many years before becoming a barrister, Nick was now the third generation of the family to have the honour, even though he still had to punctuate his time in the office by regular visits to the law school to continue studying the final two subjects.

Embarking on a legal career would prove to be an astute move by Farr-Jones in terms of advancing a professional career, if not strictly in terms of nourishing his spirit. While the Central Business District of Sydney Town is often accused of operating on an 'old school tie' principle, it is in fact more complex than that. There is an old school tie network that those with the right stripes can tap into ('I'm from Newington, you're from Riverview, I think we're on the same wave length'), but there is also quite a powerful Sydney University connection ('Didn't I used to see you in lectures in 1982?') and a thriving rugby union underground ('You're not the same Smith that used to play on the wing for Australia are you? I've always wanted to meet you'), to name but three of the aces that could be laid on the table when it came to getting ahead.

A lot of legal work could be done just as well by one firm as another but as an ex-Newingtonian, ex-Sydney University and, most particularly, an increasingly distinguished test Wallaby, Farr-Jones had an excellent chance of succeeding.

In the words of Michael Holden, the chairman of Farr-Jones's law firm, and one of the partners who employed him, 'In law there are finders, minders, binders and grinders . . . and Nick has always been a first-class finder.'

And as one of the firm's 'finders' through his rugby fame, there was no question that when the time came for Test rugby Nick would be granted as much time off as he needed. Come June, when the Tests were looming, a lot of the firm's partners would dally a long time over dropping their coats off in order to chat with Farr-Jones over the likely fortunes of the Wallabies.

Nick naturally thought the Wallabies would go well. There had been two notable drop-outs from the previous year's team— the star of the show, Mark Ella, together with the captain Andrew Slack—but the rest of the Test team remained substantially intact.

The loss of Ella aroused the greatest media attention. Still disappointed at the loss of his captaincy and deciding he no longer wanted to chafe under the strict discipline of the Jones regime, Ella had announced his retirement soon after returning from the Grand Slam tour. In the process he fired a bitter Parthian Shot to the effect that Jones had made the Wallabies altogether 'too serious about winning at all costs'.

If Jones had one strength in such matters it was a very thick hide, and whatever hurt he felt at Ella's criticism remained well hidden. Nothing was to be allowed to interfere with the preparation for this year's challenges, however thin on the ground they might be.

It was like he so often said, 'Well, you know, men, the dogs bark and the caravan moves on.' It was sad that Ella had decided to leave the caravan but if that was the way he wanted it, then so be it. The training sessions continued unabated.

When the Canadians arrived in June it was very much in the manner of pigeons stepping into a cage with battle-hardened and hungry eagles. While the players were enthusiastic enough, they lost both Tests by a total margin of almost 100 points, causing many people to question the purpose of playing matches against such weak rugby nations.

Farr-Jones at least had had the pleasure of playing his first Tests on home soil, scoring two tries in the first one. The second of these was scored on much the same spot where Noel Burns had finished first in the 100 metres over sixty years earlier.

The new captain of the side, Steve Williams, remembers being impressed at how far Nick had come from the previous year when he had made his debut. 'In '84 he really was just a young kid who they were giving a chance to and he took it,' Williams recalls. 'With Ella and Slack in the backline, Nick was called on very little to give his opinion on which way they should play the game, but in '85 they were gone, replaced by far less experienced players, and Nick was pretty much calling the shots for the inside backs. It seemed to come to him naturally.'

The Canadian visit had provided a very tepid warm-up for the Wallabies before playing the main game of the year, the Bledisloe Cup game against the All Blacks in Auckland. They might have lost to the New Zealanders by a single point last year, but this year, by God, they were determined to redress the balance.

Despite now having played six straight tests without a loss, Nick still had a nagging doubt that he had just been lucky thus far, knocking over what was essentially a bunch of wood ducks, and was yet to be really tested.

The rest of the team were also feeling the tension. To begin with, Alan Jones was pretty much as intense as they'd ever seen him. This was the big one, the game after the Grand Slam victory, which would prove that in the space of only two years he had taken the Wallabies to the very summit of world rugby.

While the Wallabies were now becoming used to Jones's eccentrically intense ways, most of the New Zealanders had never seen anything like it, and after the Wallabies' first training sessions word spread of the extraordinary spectacle that was on offer. For every training run thereafter more and more of the locals and media crews came down to watch.

Jones at full throttle in the days leading up to this particular test was indeed something to behold. Usually at a Wallaby training session the cameras would be pointed at the players, but so bizarre was the figure of Jones to the New Zealanders that there was only one focal point of attention, the man himself. A newspaper photo from the time shows Jones in archetypal pose—almost bent double in his effort to get the maximum sound out of his whistle. He was a constant hive of activity—all of it noisy. Blowing his whistle. Yelling to the physiotherapist to get some attention to this man on the double and TWEEEEEEET! for Rodriguez to *get lower* when he hits those rucks, and TWEEEEEEET! for Nick to NEVER, EVER, attempt a chip-kick when you've got men outside you like that! and TWEEEEEET! bellowing at the forwards to DO THAT DRILL AGAIN until you bloody well get it RIGHT!

As Farr-Jones recalls, 'Alan would be blowing his whistle and screaming about ten things at once—most of them sensible things, but never just in a normal voice, always screaming and blowing his whistle, then more screaming and more whistle blowing, all the time.'

The final reason things were particularly tense leading up to this Test match was because of the situation in New Zealand rugby vis à vis South Africa.

Just before the Wallabies arrived in New Zealand it had been announced by the NZRU that they would be accepting an invitation by the South African Rugby Union for the All Blacks to go on a tour soon after the Wallabies had left. This was greatly opposed by the large New Zealand anti-apartheid lobby.

The real pump-primer for the nasty scene that the Wallabies had flown into, however, was when two lawyers from Auckland, of strong anti-apartheid persuasion, had taken the New Zealand Rugby Football Union to the High Court to obtain an injunction to prevent them sending the All Blacks to South Africa. Their case was that by sending the All Blacks to South Africa the Union would be exceeding the charter of their constitution, which stated that they 'must always act in the best interests of New Zealand rugby'.

It all made for a predictably tense atmosphere in the days leading up to the Test, one tinged with the threat of the same violence that had occurred during the Springboks' 1981 tour to New Zealand. The fear was that the anti-apartheid protesters might well choose to underline their opposition to the proposed tour to South Africa by doing something to disrupt the coming Test match. As a safety measure, a police guard was put on all the entrances to the Wallabies' hotel.

Before the game the Wallabies went out to warm up on the Eden Park number two ground and as always when he warmed up before a Test, Nick looked to the surrounding people to see if his father, who was now amply making up for his absence during Nick's childhood, was there. Sure enough he was, just on the edge of the pack, beaming proudly as always. But what was that plume of smoke coming up from just over his left shoulder? It turned out that someone, presumably from the anti-apartheid group, had let off a smoke bomb in one of the stands, and although no one was hurt it reinforced the tension surrounding the game.

The game turned on one basic movement from the All Blacks.

Late in the second half, with the All Blacks behind on points and looking more than a little wobbly on their pins, the New Zealanders were awarded a penalty from well inside their own half.

The Wallabies were just trotting back their ten metres to prepare to face whatever the All Blacks were going to do when they realised that, quite out of character, the All Blacks had already tapped the ball and were away. In a movement half as wide as it was long the All Black winger Craig Green had scored in the corner before any of the Wallabies quite knew what was happening, and the All Blacks were taken to a 10–9 lead, which was the way the game finished. For the second Test in a row the New Zealanders had come out winners by a single point.

Jones was upset after the game, as any coach would be who had worked so hard, done everything possible, come so close, only to fail by such a narrow margin—for the second time in successive Tests. What particularly galled him, as he told the players, was that he thought he had covered every possible angle in preparing the Wallabies to beat the New Zealanders; he hadn't in his wildest dreams thought the All Blacks, who are normally predictable (albeit excellent in their predictability), would beat them by scoring from a tap move, of all things, *from sixty metres out.*

Live and learn. The thrust of the Australian press coverage was that Australia had played generally well but had let an historic opportunity pass. Farr-Jones emerged from the game with his reputation enhanced, Australian Associated Press reporting that: 'Big halfback Nick Farr-Jones, often playing like a ninth forward, but also showing he's as nimble as any scrum base player, had a superb game.'

One interested observer, in particular, agreed. Brian Lochore, the All Black coach, had already seen something of Farr-Jones's prowess in provincial teams, but this was of course the first time he'd seen him in action in a Test match as a direct threat to his own team.

'Nowadays I'd have no hesitation in naming Farr-Jones as simply the best halfback of his era,' says Lochore, 'but even so early in his career as 1985 he was very, very good.

'He was so complete. Great running from the base of the scrum, great kicking and tackling, and most impressive of all was his passing. Equally as good with a left or right pass, the thing was when he was bent down low at the base of the scrum, he had absolutely no backswing before he passed and so didn't give our halfback any time to take action. He was usually so low down over the ball that our halfback would be lucky if he could even *see* him let alone try and read his game.'

There was still some Test rugby left in that year, and a month after the Wallabies returned to Australian shores the Fijians arrived . . .

Just as it had been a year earlier, theirs was a very happy-go-lucky style of play with a rough underside, relying as little on the Book of Rugby Orthodoxy as it did on the Marquess of Queensberry rules on how to have a gentlemanly fight in rugby. So, if a player felt like twirling the ball around his fingertip and behind his back as he ran directly across field before stopping and hurling the ball in completely the opposite direction, then he did so and more power to him, just as, the way the Wallabies tell it, they were none too particular about which part of the body they rucked and what they grabbed for in the middle of the ruck.

All up though, it was a spectacular brand of high-risk rugby that spectators loved and opposition teams feared, because when everything worked well the Fijians were quite capable of upsets.

In this instance the Wallabies were quite right to be wary of the Fijians too, because right from the First Test the Islanders showed their mettle by scoring an impressive twenty-eight points against the Australians, almost as many as all the Wallabies' opponents had clocked up on the recent Grand Slam tour. The only problem was that in reply Australia had scored fifty-two points, including two tries by Farr-Jones, so their game was lost. The Wallabies ran out equally easy winners in the Second Test, on the scoreboards if not in the fights, ending the thin year.

At least Farr-Jones emerged from the year a better player than when he started. He had consolidated his position in the Test team, deepened his understanding of what was required of him at the international level, and garnered valuable experience against three other national teams.

Farr-Jones's relationship with Alan Jones during the year saw the consolidation of an emerging pattern—hot and cold, hot and cold—cold and professional during the rugby season, much warmer in the off-season. The coldness during the rugby season would occur partly because when it came to half-back play both Jones and Farr-Jones felt they knew for a sure and certain fact the way things should be done. Which was terrific when they agreed, but a definite problem when their strongly held opinions would differ.

To take for example their differing views on the correct defensive pattern a half-back and a back-row should employ to protect against opposition attacks . . .

After playing in the halfback position for the past fifteen years of his life, Farr-Jones figured he had more of an idea than Jones on which pattern was correct, and he didn't mind saying so, albeit in polite terms. As for Jones, having been studying just such things as a coach for at least that long, he too had set ideas and told Nick things would be done his way, with no 'albeit's at all.

Often Farr-Jones would have to publicly defer to Jones on the training field, only to breathe to the backrow after he'd gone that 'we'll do it my way'. The curious thing is that even though it would invariably be done the Farr-Jones way during the actual match, Jones never blew up the way the backrow and Nick often feared he would. They never knew quite why at the time and still don't.

There were also the same philosophical differences between them that had first shown up during the previous year's Grand Slam tour. At all times, on the field or off, Jones had an overwhelmingly serious and professional approach to the game and there simply weren't enough hours in the day for him to do all the things he wanted to do in preparation for victory.

Farr-Jones was different. If all there was going to be was rugby and no enjoyment for enjoyment's sake then there was simply no point to it. And even while hard at it in the middle of training or playing, he saw no harm in having a little joke here or there, or in being out and about carousing after training was over, and this difference in attitude was a continuing source of friction between them.

In the off-season, however, Jones and Farr-Jones would become close, and their differences would fade. Outside of rugby, Jones had a diverse background and could be charming and interesting company at the dinner table. As a former speechwriter to a prime minister, an Oxford graduate, and a man who had travelled extensively around the world with great experience in many fields, the twenty-three-year-old Farr-Jones felt there were many things he could learn from him.

As often as twice a week then during the summer months Nick would receive an invitation from Jones to go to dinner at his home in Chippendale. Most often it was just the two of them, chatting late into the night over a bottle of wine, perhaps listening to classical music as they talked (rugby, as often as not, only being discussed in passing).

Nick enjoyed such evenings immensely, but regretted that Angela was rarely invited and then only when he would say to Jones he could only make it if she could come too. Fortunately Angela understood the exigencies of attending when the national coach beckoned, and it was okay . . . for the most part.

Then, as the rugby season loomed, the warmth between coach and player would dissipate and the tension start to increase as their whole relationship would once again be channelled through the difficult medium of rugby. Though the two might still dine together during the season from time to time, it was just not quite the same.

Jones's relationship with many of his players was similarly close, though less inclined to blow so hot and cold as it did with Farr-Jones. A lot of the Wallabies owed him on a personal level. A scholarship? Jones could organise it for you, and frequently did. A job? Ditto. Need the coach to help organise credit to buy that house? Alan again. And when Jones couldn't organise credit, as happened on one occasion, he dipped into his own pocket to buy the house anyway and the player concerned would pay him back when he could.

It was kindnesses such as these that helped make Jones the undisputed 'boss' of the side. He was an entirely different sort of coach from any that the players had known before, and most of them at that stage *believed* in him.

'There was just something about him,' Nick says now, 'that was almost like an irresistible force. Alan could make things happen.'

In 1986, the challenges facing the Wallabies were satisfyingly difficult. Apart from one-off Tests against Italy and France and a two-Test home-series at home against Argentina, the important thing was that there was a full, three-Test Bledisloe Cup series to be played in New Zealand against the All Blacks, and rugby offered few greater challenges than this. Hopefully this time the mantle of unofficial world champions would finally be theirs, after having been denied it twice in the previous two years. Again they would have substantially the same team (with Andrew Slack making a comeback to replace the retired Steve Williams as captain), but they would be two years' harder, more experienced and cohesive than the last time they had played the All Blacks in a full 3-Test series.

Although Farr-Jones had only been a part of international rugby for the relatively short time of two years, already his reputation around the international rugby traps had grown to the point where he was considered among the best half-backs in the world, if not already the best. So much so that in early 1986 when the International Rugby Board held two Test matches to celebrate their centenary—the first at Cardiff Arms Park between the British Lions and the Rest of the World, and the second at Twickenham between a combined Five Nations side and the best the Southern Hemisphere could put together—Farr-Jones received an automatic invitation to play.

The two games stand not only as one of the highlights of his rugby career but also as the first time he came into contact with the South African rugby players who had also been invited to play in the Rest of the World side, and the first time he really got to know on a personal level some of the All Blacks.

While one of the more celebrated clichés of the rugby game is that players who have been going at each other hammer and tongs throughout a game are often seen having a beer together afterwards, the truth behind the cliché is enduring. Together with the Australians in the first Rest of the World side, for example, there were such legendarily tough All Blacks as Andy Haden, Mark Shaw, and Murray Mexted—players with whom the Wallabies in the side had had many fiercesome encounters over previous years—and though the uninitiated might have thought such a history as that would prevent any real warmth growing between the Wallabies and the All Black sections of the team, the opposite was true. Out of the Test matches, respect for each other's ability had grown and it was a rare pleasure to be playing with each other instead of against each other.

This nascent friendship was encouraged in its growth by Brian

Lochore, the same All Black coach from the year before, who was now in charge of the Southern Hemisphere/Rest of the World teams and who the Australians would now come to know as one of the true gentleman of international rugby.

And all put together, with some South Africans and the two Frenchmen, Serge Blanco and Patrick Esteve, helping out, the Rest of the World indeed made a formidable side for the first game—ripping into the British Lions and beating them by 15-6. For Farr-Jones it brought back memories of the Grand Slam, two years before, when on an equally wet day at Cardiff Arms Park he had played his part in a great victory.

For the next Test the side changed slightly as the Frenchmen dropped out to join the combined Five Nations team and were replaced by more Wallabies, Springboks and All Blacks. Nick ceded his place in the side to Dave Loveridge, the former All Black halfback, and took Loveridge's spot on the bench.

The coming Test took on the aspect thus of Southern Hemisphere vs Northern Hemisphere for the Heavyweight Champeen Championship of the World, and that suited the South fine. It is one of the curiosities of the rugby world that the majority of rugby power lies south of the equator, and put together in one side they were formidable to the point of being unbeatable. So much so that on the morning of the match Nick decided to break his golden rule about not betting on the outcome of his own game. Having heard the local consensus that the Five Nations side might really give the southerners a shake this time, he set out to find the nearest Ladbroke's betting shop, to find out what the 'points start' was.

A simple phone call to head office and the answer came back quickly. The wise-heads at Ladbroke's were prepared to bet that the Five Nations side would finish at least within 8.5 points of the Southerners.

Too easy really. A look in his wallet revealed that he had exactly 220 pounds, and although Farr-Jones knew he'd need about three pounds for the taxi fare back to the hotel, he decided he'd rather walk and put every last brass razoo on his side to win. Two hundred and twenty pounds down on the South to rise again.

In fact the South got the requisite 8.5 points ahead after only ten minutes, and finished the game with a 33–12 victory. Not the easiest money Farr-Jones had ever made, but among the most satisfying.

As the Happy Hour after the game was among the most enjoyable. Over the preceding two weeks the players had become very close, and if they'd come into this venture a little wary of each other, all that had now been left behind entirely. So much so that during the course of the evening, the All Blacks confided that on the following Monday they would all be flying to South Africa to take part in a rebel tour.

Since the official tour had been blocked the year before by the injunction taken out by the two lawyers, a plan had suddenly developed for the All Blacks to tour there unofficially and apparently for handsome recompense. The All Blacks would simply rename themselves 'The Cavaliers', and the controlling body of New Zealand rugby would be powerless to stop them.

Nick listened to the plans with interest, as did the South Africans in the team. So *that* was why the All Blacks had been getting together for all those private tête-à-têtes lately. For the South Africans, the realisation suddenly grew that the same All Blacks they had been having such fun with over the last two weeks would soon be their fierce opponents.

The team seperated the following day with sadness. If Brian Lochore felt some sadness at seeing his All Blacks fly off to South Africa without him, he was also sorry to see the last of Nick on that tour. He had been impressed not only with his standard of play but also with how well he had got on with everyone else in the team. In the inimitable words of this extremely likeable New Zealand farmer, Nick was 'always keen to sort out your nuts and bolts'.

'He was inquisitive about everyone, interested to know who they were and what made them tick, and he was just the sort of guy every team needs to have at its centre. By the end of the tour I had come to regard him as a personal friend.'

For his part, Nick had also been impressed. Lochore was the only international coach whom Farr-Jones had come to know on a personal basis whose last name wasn't Jones and first name wasn't Alan.

'The thing about Brian,' says Nick, 'was that he was a real Rugby man, a man who loved the game and the people who played it. He wanted to win, sure, but it wasn't absolutely everything to him. The main thing was the beauty of the game itself. After meeting him I saw Jonesy in a different light—sure, he was a wonderful motivator, had fantastic energy to put into it as a competitive exercise, but, put simply, he wasn't a real Rugby man.'

When the Wallabies returned to Australia Jones did not mention their trip and they all suspected that he had been a little miffed at not having been invited to take part.

Nick and the other Wallabies immediately had to begin preparing for what would be a busy schedule for the Wallabies, with seven Test matches in fourteen weeks.

Early season Test matches against Italy and France were to be followed by two Tests against Argentina before they went back to New Zealand, this time for a full three-Test Bledisloe Cup series. The first four Test matches went smoothly enough, with France providing the tastiest morsel of all for the Wallabies. How delectable it was to beat the Five Nations champions by such a handsome score of 27–14. Counting their past Grand Slam victory, this generation of Wallabies now had the scalps of all of the Five Nations hanging from their belt, together with the scalps of Italy, Argentina, Canada and Fiji. In terms of world domination they could now claim North America and South America, Europe and the Pacific Islands as having fallen to their sway. That left, in the known world, only the men across the creek . . . the New Zealanders.

Always New Zealand. Twice in the last two years the Wallabies had come within a point of knocking them off, only to fail both times, and this time, Jones told them, they simply would not be denied.

At Camperdown, where they trained as always, the usual drills, the usual yelling, the usual late-night meetings, the usual amazing Jones thoroughness. Having been informed that New Zealand was experiencing a particularly wet winter that year, Jones and Alec Evans invented a series of 'wet-weather drills' with the ball, designed specifically to prepare the players for what they would be facing. They worked them endlessly and it was as usual a relief to get to the airport three days later.

So to Farr-Jones's first full tour of the Shaky Isles. Of all the international rugby tours on offer, a full Wallaby tour to New Zealand is arguably the most demanding. On most tours the Wallabies can count on at least a couple of easy games here and there, but New Zealand is not similiarly blessed. From the southern tip of Invercargill, to the Bay of Islands in the north, the New Zealand football fields are fierce in their opposition to invaders.

Yet on the plane on the way over Farr-Jones remembers feeling even more confident than usual that he would be able to play to a high standard.

'Sometimes it's just like that. You don't particularly know why, but you just *feel* like you're in form. You know you've done the work, you know the team around you is good and you just can't wait for the whole thing to get started.'

A day in the life of the tour tells a good part of the *zeitgeist* of the time. On the morning of the Second Test down in Dunedin, Jones was beyond tense. Agitated, exhilarated, intensely concentrated, darting back and forth all at once, endlessly checking to ensure that everything that could be done had been done. Did Nick understand what to do if Kirk tried a blindside move in our own 22? Did he realise that John Kirwan often cut inside his man from first-phase ball and it would be Nick's job to pick him up if he did? Have the reserves been allocated seats close enough to the ground, so they wouldn't have to waste any time getting on should the need arise? Have we got enough water bottles with us to get to the boys at halftime? Nothing was to be left to chance.

Although the Wallabies had won the First Test two weeks earlier in Wellington by the score of 13–12, in some ways it had been a hollow victory. All thirty-one of the All Blacks who'd gone on the Cavaliers tour to South Africa had been banned for the First Test and had been replaced by the so-called 'Baby Blacks', and while the Wallabies had gone to a 1–0 lead in the series many had said they would now be wiped off the field, now that the *real* All Blacks had been rushed back into the team.

But if the Wallabies won, not only could they claim the Bledisloe Cup, but also the true prize: the unofficial mantle of world champions.

With seven minutes remaining in this the Second Test, the score was tight, with the All Blacks fiercely defending a 13–9 lead and their own line. Farr-Jones prepared to put the ball into a Wallaby scrum five metres out from the line and, sensing that the All Black winger was standing a fraction wider than prudent, decided to make one of his trademark runs upfield from the base of the scrum. Just as he was tackled he passed the ball inside to number eight Steve Tuynman on the burst.

Tuynman was all but unstoppable at the best of times, but at full speed this close to the line, and this close to winning the game, the series and the unofficial title of world champions, he was completely irresistible. Although two All Blacks—second-rower Murray Pierce and winger Craig Green—actually tackled him, they were simply carried over the line with him as he fell on top of the ball.

Unfortunately the Welsh referee, Derek Bevan, refused to award the try on the grounds that there were too many hands on it, and despite the fact that the Wallabies scored a penalty soon afterwards to close the margin to 13–12, the final whistle saw the score unchanged and the New Zealanders had levelled the series 1–1.

All of which was why, when the Wallabies came off the field, Jones was so particularly upset, waiting for them just inside the dressing room door and loudly cursing. None of the players, shattered and exhausted, were in the mood for it and Farr-Jones took it upon himself to voice the collective opinion.

Jones was just in the middle of saying for the third time that it was the most *disgraceful* refereeing performance he'd ever seen when Nick interrupted, calmly but forcefully; 'Alan, there's nothing we can do about it now, let's let it lie and we'll get 'em next time.'

The Jones thunder and lightning storm had suddenly found a new target, and switched from the referee to his halfback. 'How DARE you say that to me! Don't you realise how hard I've worked for this victory? Don't you realise what we have lost by not winning today? Don't you EVER try and tell me how I should and should not react . . .'

When it was over, and Jones had momentarily spent the worst of his fury on Farr-Jones, the coach turned to the other players and said in a far more conciliatory tone, 'Anyway, don't worry, men. You played without a full-back today.'

This was a reference to David Campese, a player whom Jones had once described in a typical flourish of hyperbole as 'the Bradman of rugby'.

Admittedly Campese had played a fairly wretched game that day, constantly dropping the 'up and unders' that the All Blacks put up to him, but particularly shocking to the players was not only that Jones should say it, but also that he should say it when

Campese was out of the room—having followed his usual routine of heading straight to the showers as soon as he was off the field.

Campese heard about it two days later, and was suitably appalled. But he was already well acquainted with the coach's opinion of his game, having visited the coach in his room that evening.

Farr-Jones happened to be passing soon after Campese had gone in, and could hear snatches of Jones's words, no less forceful for having to penetrate the door. 'You've let me down,' he remembers Jones saying. 'I told the press you were the Bradman of rugby and now you've done this to me . . . I simply don't understand how you could play like that . . . you made a complete fool of yourself . . . ' Etcetera.

Taking a deep breath Farr-Jones decided to knock and go into the room so as to, in his words, 'try and defuse the situation and get the blowtorch off Campo'.

Oddly enough Jones did not immediately blow up at Farr-Jones's rude intrusion, so engrossed was he in his attack on an ashen-faced Campese sitting on the bed.

But saved by the bell . . . The phone rang. It proved to be one of Jones's friends from Australia, ringing to offer his commiserations, and the two players could do nothing but listen in.

'Yes, I've tried everything,' Nick remembers Jones as saying. 'I've shouted myself hoarse, been absolutely relentless, and I feel like giving it all away. You go through all that, cover all the angles and then something like this happens to you. Sometimes I think they're just destined to be the Greg Normans of rugby— always destined to finish a close second no matter what you do to break them out of it.'

That night there was a dinner for both Test teams in the Australians' hotel, and because the Wallabies had been delayed in their 'Happy Hour', with perhaps heavier than usual drinking to ease the pain of it all, it was the All Blacks who arrived first.

Brian Lochore remembers the Wallabies' arrival.

'They came into the room about half-an-hour late, I guess, looking really strained with the disappointment of their loss, but I remember being particularly happy to see both Simon and Nick for the first time really since the centenary tour, and they seemed glad to see me too.'

Which they were, both players making a beeline for Lochore. The Lochore ethos that 'you don't take your rugby into the evening' was theirs exactly, and the three had a good natter about everything that came to mind. Lochore, himself an ex-international, knew something of how disappointed they must have been with the result, and sympathised, as much as he could . . .

For both players it was a pleasant interlude on what had been a very unpleasant day, and although Nick happened to catch a momentary glimpse of Jones looking like thunder at them through the crowd. For now Jones's reaction was muted and the evening continued undisturbed.

After the dinner, when the All Blacks had left the Wallabies were feeling predictably flat without any particular desire to make festive and go out on the town to tour the night spots of Dunedin.

It was then that inspiration struck. In the midst of all the misery, Farr-Jones decided to fetch a deck of cards and play a game of Race the Ace, a gambling game he'd recently learned which involved dealing the cards one by one and betting which ace would win the race.

So ensued what many of the Wallabies of that time cite as their most enduring memory of Farr-Jones off-field. In the middle of the hotel bar there was the half-back, with captain Andrew Slack beside him, dealing out the cards, taking bets, yelling at people to 'have a go!', drinking, laughing and joking as he dealt, raking in the money or paying it out. The other Wallabies, as well as Australian and New Zealand supporters, stood around five deep and threw money at them. It wasn't so much making light of what had been a very unhappy Test loss, as a catharsis—leaving it all behind. So successful was the game that when Farr-Jones and Slack finally decided to 'pull up stumps' and go to bed, the suggestion was mostly greeted with groans of sorrow, with the exception of one drunken New Zealander who had lost his rent money and now tried to even the score by recalling the result of the previous afternoon's Test match.

In the words of Farr-Jones, 'If there's one thing in this world that is impossible to tolerate it is a drunken Kiwi proclaiming the greatness of his beloved All Blacks after you've lost a Test to them which you should have won.'

There was only one thing to do. They dealt a final hand and cleaned him out of his car payment money too.

It was the following evening and Jones was angry. Having just arrived at their Invercargill hotel from Dunedin minutes before, he had called an immediate team meeting and just as quickly begun to go into full *destroy* mode against the actions of 'some people'.

It was a verbal quirk of the Australian coach that even when tearing into players in front of the entire team, he would rarely name them. Everyone invariably knew who the 'some people' were, and those people got the message all right, but it made it easier to smooth things over later if the offenders hadn't actually been named.

On this occasion Jones was particularly incensed that some people who were not in the Test team had seen fit to have a room party on the Thursday night before the Saturday Test, keeping the Test players awake, and that some people had also gone out late on the Friday night and made a lot of noise when they'd come back into the hotel.

On it went. A categorical listing of the offences of some people, including offences that had occurred during the Test, missing tackles, dropping balls, and not hitting the line hard enough.

It was the last offence of 'some people', though, that hit Nick and Simon Poidevin the hardest. Jones's remarks, in Nick's memory, were along the lines of: 'And last night we even had some people spending half the night with the opposition coach. I mean, what are we about? Are we serious about beating the All Blacks? Do we really want to do it? Let us have no more examples of this, please.'

Jones now categorises any 'nonsense' about him castigating Poidevin and Farr-Jones as 'another wild distortion of what actually happened.' Yet even so close a friend of Jones as Poidevin has written that 'the reaction from Alan Jones had to be seen to be believed' and that 'the upshot was an air of bitterness and tension through the whole team.' Farr-Jones remembers 'just being totally floored that Alan could take issue with us having a drink with the opposition coach.' Lochore himself was, when he heard about it, 'absolutely shocked and appalled that rugby should have come to such a point, that it was being taken so deathly seriously that people from opposing camps couldn't talk to each other after the game'.

Australian cricket players of the 1970s say the fastest that Jeff Thomson ever bowled was after lunch on the second day of the

Second Test against England for the Ashes in 1975. Australian rugby players of the 1980s are sure that the hardest that Jones ever ran a team was on this Monday after the lost Dunedin test. Hour after hour, up and down the field, across it, around it, backwards, forwards, sideways, then do it again—all to the tune of Jones's whistle. One of the Wallabies, Damien Frawley is sure that this training session was twice as tough as the only other one that comes close—the one earlier in the tour when the cameras of 'Sixty Minutes' were recording it.

'That day with 'Sixty Minutes', it seemed like it would never end,' says Frawley. 'This day it never did end. Three weeks later back in Australia I was still waking up in the middle of the night, thinking someone was going to call me out to training. It felt like I'd got back from Vietnam.'

Fortunately this particular session was just for the 'dirty-dirties'—the reserves. The Test players, to Jones's eternal credit, were given the day off.

What Jones wanted them to do, he said, was to forget about the Dunedin Test, to go and do whatever they wanted and be ready to begin again the following day. It was time for them all to make a new beginning in order to win the Third Test, and he wanted them fresh for it. Above all, he said, do not dwell on Tuynman's try and what might have been. That's in the past and we're heading for the future.

Terrific advice for both Jones and the Wallabies to follow, but the rest of the world was not so constricted . . . In bars, clubs and pubs throughout Australasia debate raged as to whether or not Tuynman's try had been, *beyond doubt*, a fair one.

The final postscript to that question came on the Tuesday in Dunedin, when Meryl Harry, the wife of the man who would soon become NSW Rugby Union president, Phil Harry, was driving around the back streets of Wellington.

Something of an afficionado of rugby herself, she was still angry about Australia's unfair loss because of Tuynman's disallowed try, and was getting angrier by the minute when she realised she was lost.

At least there was a friendly policeman, who offered to help her find her way. As reported by New Zealand journalist, Terry McLean, the conversation from that point went like this:

'Your hotel's not far,' the policeman told her. 'If I can hop in, I'll take you to it in a minute.'

During the course of social chitchat, he asked the Australian what she was doing in New Zealand.

'I've been watching your Test rugby,' she said. 'I'm in a rage. Steve Tuynman scored. He scored right under my nose. I was sitting in that Rose Grandstand and there Steve was, just down there, just under my nose. I tell you no one could have been closer.'

A pause. Then, 'I wouldn't be too sure about that,' the policeman said presently. 'I was pretty close, too.'

'You couldn't have been closer than me,' Harry replied confidently.

'Well,' he said, 'I was actually playing. I was in fact right there.'

'And who are you?'

'Murray Pierce, the All Black lock.'

'Well,' Harry said graciously, 'I'll have to allow that you could have been closer than I.' She paused. 'But, anyway, what did you think?'

'I thought it was a try,' Pierce said.

If Jones were ever to take a bow for coaching a team to a superb performance it would be now. In the two weeks leading up to the final Test, Jones's training sessions were as well planned as they were precisely executed.

The thrust of his talks to the team were always upbeat—not only could the full All Black side be beaten, but they *would* be beaten. The last Test had exposed many weaknesses in their side, he announced, and it was simply a matter of exploiting these weaknesses. The way was simply to shut them down through overwhelming defence and then build your attack on top of that. The Test side tackled till they dropped in training then tackled some more.

Jones also took care of the environment in which the Wallabies moved. In the final days, the media were told that the Wallabies were off limits to them and anybody with a camera or a tape recorder would be turned away. If they wanted to know anything they could ask him but just leave the Wallabies alone to concentrate.

As to the people of wider New Zealand, Jones was also masterful in having them turn ever more against both him and the Wallabies, the better to create an 'us vs them' mentality in his own camp. Always good at this sort of caper, on this occasion Jones outdid himself and on the Tuesday before the Saturday's final Test he staged the infamous walk-out from the admittedly modest Thames Valley Hotel stating simply 'that this accommodation is simply not fit for international sportsmen'.

New Zealand was more than merely offended, and the good people of Thames Valley were practically apoplectic at the slight. 'THERE ISN'T A ROOM IN THE WORLD BIG ENOUGH FOR YOUR MOUTH, JONES' read the banner the following day at the Thames Valley game (which the Wallabies won handsomely, albeit after the shedding of much blood), and it accurately reflected the popular feeling. All the press in the country were in uproar.

What did Jones think of that?

Twenty-four hours before kick-off, at a luncheon in Auckland, Jones gave his inimitable answer, referring to the papers which had pushed the brouhaha as 'some of those dung-heap downtown sheets which pass as sophisticated journalism'.

It all had the desired effect. In Nick's memory, 'It felt like we had the whole country against us instead of just the All Blacks, and I guess it pushed us all together even more than before and focused our minds wonderfully. If we'd lost after all that it would have been just too humiliating to speak of. I also think that, for Alan, that sort of stuff really recharged his batteries—when it seemed like the whole country was against him he would start firing on all cylinders.'

All that remained was the Jones motivational talk, which Nick remembers as 'a beauty' and then they were out there.

The All Blacks now, running at them. Spinning the ball wide, running some more, rucking it back, ruck, ruck, ruck, ball back and spread wide again, running the ball, tackled and ruck, ruck, ruck back out for the All Blacks to run the ball some more. The only part the Wallabies recognised was the rucking part.

Everything else was strange. It was quite unlike the All Blacks to play such an expansive game plan, but the Wallabies felt they had their measure. It was just like Jonesy had said—tackle till you dropped, then tackle some more then build the attack from there.

They certainly got the tackling part right, with Brett Papworth on one occasion executing three tackles in six seconds, and 'Topo' Rodriguez soon afterwards making what was arguably the Tackle of the Eighties when with a front-on tackle he not only stopped the All Black hooker Hika Reid from scoring but also drove him backwards and put him flat on his back, lifting the Wallaby spirits a little higher. Then came the attack. Soon after the Rodriguez tackle the Australian fullback, Andrew Leeds, playing his debut Test, swept in for a try to make the score 12-6 to the Australians at halftime.

In the second half the New Zealanders, in Farr-Jones's words, had 'simply run out of legs. They had fired their last shots and come up empty.'

With seven minutes to go in the game, Farr-Jones took the ball from a quick ruck, darted away, and threw Campese a fifteen-metre pass, which set him up to run twenty metres to score, and put the Wallabies thirteen points ahead with five minutes to go. The match was sealed with the final score of Australia 22, New Zealand 9, and in the jubilation of it all Farr-Jones picked Campese up in the in-goal and put him over his shoulders. Coming back to the fifty metre line he was amazed to see that his father Max had somehow evaded security and was on the sideline, laughing and taking photos.

When the full-time siren sounded the Wallabies had become only the fourth team of the century to beat the New Zealanders in a series on New Zealand soil.

Champagne. Tears. Hugs. Photo flashes. Endless renditions of the national anthem. And the knowledge that they were unofficially the very best team in the world at that moment. Even in the midst of all the joy, Jones was thinking of the next conquest. South Africa.

'We've still got some things to achieve in Rugby,' he was quoted in the press the following day, 'and one of them is beating South Africa'.

For the moment though, that could wait.

All up, it had been a wonderful year for the Wallabies and for Farr-Jones in particular.

In the Happy Hour after the game Jones made very gracious comments about Nick's contribution to the Wallaby success, naming him as his own choice for Player of the Tour. This viewpoint was confirmed when he also got the 'Players' Player' an informal award based on a system whereby all the players voted at the end of every game as to who had been the most valuable player.

The press also handed him accolades, Greg Growden writing in the *Sun-Herald* the day after the match that 'Nick Farr-Jones had his usual magnificent Test match to boost claims that he had been the form player of the tour' and New Zealander Bob Howitt writing that he was 'undoubtedly the player of the series'.

Finally, writing an end of season wrap-up for the *Australian* in late September after the Wallabies returned, rugby writer Greg Campbell singled out Farr-Jones for particular mention.

'Nick Farr-Jones heads our rugby honour roll for '86,' Campbell claimed 'and can rightfully lay claim to being the world's best half-back. He completely outplayed the All Blacks' half and captain David Kirk, and figured prominently in each of the three Tests and is clearly the *Australian*'s Rugby Player Of The Year for 1986.'

'But not only was Farr-Jones a master on the field, but off the field and on the training paddock he featured significantly at team meetings and in nurturing team morale.'

It all boded well for a great year to come.

CHAPTER EIGHT

1987—The Decline and Fall of Alan Jones

*'In many ways I regret I ever had anything to do with
Australian rugby. In many ways, I regret that I was
foolish enough to put my name forward for the
coaching job.'*
Alan Jones, 1992

It should have been Alan Jones's finest hour, in the greatest
year of Australian rugby history. If the Wallabies won the
inaugural World Cup, being held over four weeks in May and
June in New Zealand and Australia, they would become official
World Champions, surpassing by far the feats of 1984 and 1986.

And why wouldn't they win? In the three years since Jones
had taken over, the Wallabies had played twenty tests, won sixteen
and lost only four, of which two had been by a single point.
The coach was feeling so confident that in an interview with
journalist Terry Smith, he mooted the possibility that Australia
could play Tests against both the All Blacks and Fiji on the one
day. 'I'd like to think we could do that,' he said. 'It's like Cassius
Clay wanting to pull all the heavyweight challengers into the ring
on the one night.'

If not quite so confident as that, Farr-Jones was also looking
forward to a good year. Since he'd taken over the Test half-back
role sixteen Tests earlier, he'd been a part of no fewer than fourteen
winning sides and had every confidence that this would continue.

First, there was a lot of work to be done. From early February
Jones began taking the Sydney-based Wallabies for private training
sessions at Sydney University Oval. Jones was as relentless as

ever in driving them hard, but the Wallabies were nevertheless enthusiastic—it was part of the Jones equation. Coach Jones = Hard Work = Winning = Respect for the Jones Way.

The man himself, though, seemed to have changed. The glory of the previous year's Bledisloe Cup victory had increased his public profile even more, which had brought its own pressures. While previously he had been unstintingly generous of his time for any members of his team who called him up, by early 1987 a certain impatience had started to creep into his voice over the phone and in person.

Simply, Jones was an extraordinarily busy man. Outside of his rugby coaching, he was also a highly regarded after-dinner speaker, involved in the organisation of countless charity fund-raising affairs, on the board of several companies and, most particularly, a very successful morning broadcaster on 2UE. It all demanded a great deal of his time, even if his energy for the Wallaby cause remained seemingly boundless.

The real problems with Jones's media commitments were only to show up during the actual World Cup. In the meantime the preparations continued. Part of these preparations were the hard provincial matches played by both New South Wales and Queensland (from where the Wallabies are mostly drawn).

That season the man appointed to coach New South Wales was the redoubtable Paul Dalton of the Parramatta club. An abrasive man, with nevertheless an enviable record of success in coaching club teams, Dalton set about to do with the New South Wales team what he did to every team that came under his command—bully it into brilliance.

A man after Jones's own heart, Dalton himself believed he owed his position to Jones's good graces, which is why when Jones called him up before the season began to invite him over to his place 'for a drink and a chat', Dalton went.

'It was while Jones was having a Scotch and I was having a beer that I told him of my plan,' Dalton recalls.

Dalton's plan was to replace captain Simon Poidevin with Nick Farr-Jones. In Dalton's memory, Jones was quick with his response. Not only would that not be a very good idea, Jones countered, but of the fifteen players in the NSW team, Farr-Jones would have been only his *thirteenth* choice as captain', and he was at a loss to know why Dalton would ever think up such a plan as that. Besides, there was something Dalton should know—that Nick was 'quite heavily mixed up in religion'.

Though interested in Jones's advice, Dalton was not dissuaded.

Dalton's reasons for picking Farr-Jones as captain were simple. Firstly he didn't want Poidevin. The two had never seen eye to eye, and Dalton says he regarded Poidevin as 'too emotional a footballer, too inclined to be easily rattled'.

Nick was different.

'I always saw Farr-Jones as a natural leader. He was the brain, the architect, he could read a game, decide what had to be done and have the others follow. He was already doing that from his position at half-back, but I wanted him to have full authority, to be captain.'

Easy in theory, but a problem in practice. To install Farr-Jones as captain at the expense of someone as highly regarded as Poidevin was always going to be difficult.

Poidevin was in Hong Kong at the time and heard about his demotion from a telex sent by a Sydney radio station. Infuriated not only that he had been dropped as captain but also that he had not been properly informed by his executioners—as is deemed the protocol on such occasions—he came back to Sydney angry enough for three people. With sections of the press equally upset on his behalf.

In an article in the *Mirror* Terry Smith attacked Dalton for his sacrilegious move, writing that he regarded 'Poidevin's axing as a totally unjustified insult to one of Australia's greatest ever rugby players' and that his dumping was 'rugby's biggest bombshell since Mark Ella was sacked as Australian skipper three years ago'.

Many of the players seemed equally outraged. Even so close a friend of Farr-Jones as secondrower Stephen Cutler went public in saying that 'Simon is a natural for the job and a very good skipper. He's determined and very tough. I enjoy playing under him.'

The issue came to a head on the first Tuesday night of New South Wales training after Poidevin got back, when a players' meeting was called. Dalton was present at this meeting and for half an hour found himself pilloried by the senior players—led by Poidevin himself—most particularly for the way in which he had handled the whole sacking.

In the middle of it all Farr-Jones sat, half-bemused, half-perplexed. When his turn came to speak he said, with palms upturned, 'I am quite prepared to stand down for Simon if that is what this meeting decides.'

ABOVE Nick Farr-Jones playing in his first Test at Twickenham in 1984 (vs England), with two good friends and great locks in support – Steve Cutler and Steve Williams *Colorsport*

BELOW After winning the Grand Slam in 1984. *From left to right:* Poidevin, Lawton, Lynagh, Gould, Slack, Ella and Campese *Colorsport*

ABOVE After a home Test against the All Blacks in 1984. The relationship between Alan Jones and Simon Poidevin was a close one *Action Photographics*

BELOW Former Wallaby coach, David Brockhoff, after a Test match in 1984. Farr-Jones names Brockhoff as having 'the greatest spiritual influence on my career *Action Photographics*

ABOVE The All Black team that won the Bledisloe Cup and World Cup in 1987 was one of the greatest teams of the modern era *Action Photographics*

BELOW Agin the mighty All Blacks at Concord in 1987 *Action Photographics*

'Now, before I was so rudely interrupted.' Bob Dwyer again takes the helm of the Wallabies in 1988 *Bob Thomas Sports Photography*

Sad and sorry after defeat by the British Lions at Ballymore in 1989 – 'I was targeted
and hit off the ball by six of the eight Lions forwards' *Colorsport*

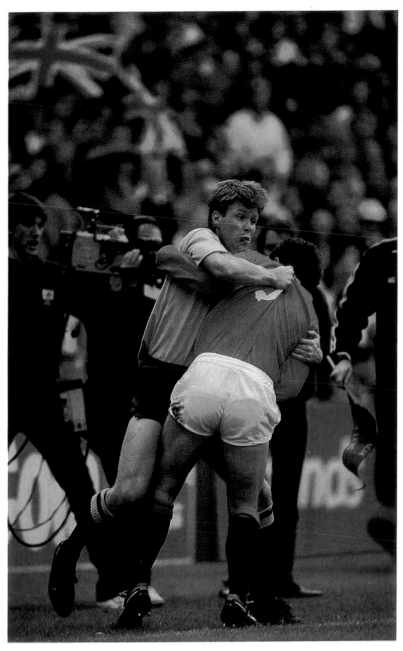

The scraps continued in the decider in Sydney – scuffling here with his opposition,
Robert Jones, 1989 *Colorsport*

ABOVE The Three Rocks: Ayers, Hard and Gibraltar. (*From left to right:* Tony Daly, Phil Kearns and Ewen McKenzie.) Three pieces of the puzzle that fitted well together, they were the platform from which much of the Wallabies' success in the early 1990's was launched *Action Photographics*

BELOW Farr-Jones launches after an Australian line-out against the French in 1990. Peter FitzSimons and Phil Kearns are in the background *Action Photographics*

ABOVE After a great win against New Zealand at the Sydney Football Stadium in 1991. The puzzle was coming together nicely *Action Photographics*

BELOW Before the Test against the All Blacks in Auckland in 1991. The relationship between Bob Dwyer and Farr-Jones was a close and productive one *Action Photographics*

When it was Glen Ella's turn to speak, a much-needed moment of levity was provided when he said that he knew that Dalton had 'lost the plot' from the moment he had picked him, Ella, for the five-eighth's position when it was obvious to everyone he was fat and unfit.

But back to business.

Poidevin's summation of the meeting in his book *For Love Not Money* is poignantly accurate: 'Much supportive talk by the players followed, although no one actually stood up and said they wanted me back as captain. The upshot at the end of the meeting was that Nick was New South Wales captain and I was last season's model.'

This season's model was gratified with the result, but hardly overjoyed.

'I was glad to have the job but it wasn't like it was any really big deal or anything. I'd always talked a lot on the field, as had Simon, and it seemed to me the biggest part of the change would be that now I would get to toss the coin before the match instead of him, but other than that things would be much the same.'

And just as Dalton was his own man despite feeling he owed Jones the position, so too did Farr-Jones operate without any sense of indebtedness to Dalton. When at halftime of one of the early New South Wales games the new captain received an abusive message from Dalton about the way he was running the backs, he sent back a curt two-word answer.

Farr-Jones's elevation to the NSW captaincy did nothing to help his relationship with Jones. As always, with the rugby season underway their relationship had cooled, but in Nick's words, 'the fact that I had been made captain against his wishes I think quite riled him, and it meant our relationship became increasingly formal from that point on'.

And so to the season's summit.

They came from all five continents—sixteen countries gathered in Australia and New Zealand to see which nation possessed the strongest rugby team on earth. The inaugural World Cup was the culmination of four years' work by the International Rugby Board to give rugby its answer to the Olympics.

As usual, the Wallabies gathered in the Camperdown Travelodge, which was to be their headquarters for the next four weeks, with only a brief foray to Brisbane. This time, though, there was something different. And it wasn't just that it was a World Cup and the Wallabies were going to try to beat fifteen nations instead of just one. Instead of training in the mornings, as they were used to, beginning the day with hard work, they would only be training in the afternoons. The reason, Alan Jones said, was because he had an 'unbreakable commitment' to keep broadcasting on Radio 2UE, which meant his working on the morning shift.

This seemed odd to the players, because Jones's commitment to the station definitely hadn't been unbreakable when the Wallabies had to go away on tour. Why was it unbreakable now?

All through the World Cup Jones continued to do his morning broadcasts from Radio 2UE and would then get back to Camperdown for training usually only in the early afternoon. Though the starting time of the afternoon training session was variable depending on Jones' commitments to speak at various lunches, it still meant that the players were now free to sleep till noon, which in turn meant that they could afford to go out till the wee hours and sleep till late in the morning.

It was of course against the rules laid down by Jones for them to do that, but things weren't what they used to be in terms of discipline. The cat was away. This lack of adherence to the rules was exacerbated by the fact that the other man who might have been expected to impose them, new manager Ken Grayling, was already weakened by cancer, which would take his life less than four months later.

The problem with Jones's media commitments didn't finish with just the timing of the training. There was also the matter of their greater intensity. When the Wallabies did train, there was enormous interest from Jones's media colleagues on how the 'Jones Wallabies' were going—which led to muttering among the team that Jones was playing up to them, driving the Wallabies longer and harder than necessary because it all looked so good on television.

These sessions were also unbelievably physical, Jones having apparently become convinced for this World Cup that the best way to prepare for the tough games ahead was to have high-impact full-contest practices now, pitting the Wallabies against each other on the training field.

Finally there was the problem, most particularly for the Sydney-based Wallabies, that their focus was inevitably fractured by the proximity of both their families and their jobs. Normally when on tour and well away from the commitments that go with being at home, it was far easier to concentrate on the job at hand. But as Sydneysiders in Sydney Town, a dissipation of attention was inevitable. Just as every morning Simon Poidevin would go to work for as long as five hours with his firm of stockbrokers and Stephen Cutler would sneak home, so too would Farr-Jones steal away in the very early morning to work and at night to see Angela or his family.

'Maybe we might have been less inclined if Alan had been dropping everything for the World Cup,' says Nick, 'but it was obvious to us he wasn't.'

Farr-Jones was in trouble with the coach on this issue early in the World Cup campaign, when he picked up the telephone in his office at 7.30 in the morning to be greeted with the angry words: 'Right, I'll see you in my room when I get back. I've *told* you I don't want you at the office.'

Farr-Jones still wonders why he didn't say, 'Hang on, Alan, where the hell are *you* calling me from?'

'It was just the way it was back then though,' he says now, 'that you didn't challenge him if you could at all avoid it.'

Right from the beginning of the World Cup the fact that things were not quite right in the Wallabies was apparent on-field, as they struggled and played sloppily against England, before finally beating them 19–6, and then appeared anything but all-powerful in beating the very weak United States team 47–12.

Then there was Japan. Under normal circumstances predicting the score of a Wallabies/Japan match would require more of a knowledge of mathematics than of rugby, but amazingly, with five minutes to go in the game the Japanese had managed to score twenty-three points and the Wallabies were only seven points ahead. That they scored two late tries to take the score to 42–23 did little to alleviate the impression that the Wallabies were in singularly ordinary form, and at one stage they were playing so badly that they were actually booed by their fellow Australians in the stands.

In the quarter-final against Ireland it looked as if Australia had at last come good, when for the first forty minutes of the game they played as well as any Australian side had in living memory. Despite losing Farr-Jones to an injured shoulder in the first sixty seconds of the game after taking a very heavy tackle by Irish flanker Phil Matthews, the Australians were well on top of their game and at halftime led the stunned Irish by the score of 24-0. Unfortunately for the Wallabies the Irish came back hard in the second half to score fifteen points to eight, to make the final score the far more modest 33-15.

At least it was a good win, though, and the Wallabies were definitely in the mood to celebrate. Unfortunately Jones decided there would be no alcohol consumed at the Happy Hour, as the team had to apply itself totally to concentrate on the upcoming semi-final against France, a week away. For the Wallabies this was an unprecedented move, as traditionally the Happy Hour is exclusively the province of the players to run as they see fit, the one hour of the week when the power balance between coach and players is redressed, and the players did not take kindly to this imposition.

Still, it was a measure of the hold Jones had over the players that, of the twenty-eight players in the squad, only one of them spoke up and said what the rest of them wanted to: 'Sorry, Alan, I'm having a beer.'

Roger Gould, the legendary Australian fullback, was a man apart within the team, particularly when it came to his relationship with Jones. Already regarded as one of the game's greats well before Jones came on the scene, he owed Jones nothing. Jones hadn't plucked him from obscurity, hadn't retrieved him from the rugby scrapheap, hadn't got him a job, made him captain—hadn't done anything at all for him other than pick him, which any coach would, such was his ability.

'Sorry, Alan, I'm having a beer,' said Gould, promptly opening one with a smile. 'I'm a problem. So drop me.'

As Gould was injured, and would be for the rest of the Cup, Jones couldn't drop him even if he'd wanted to. Besides which, Gould retained such a stature within the game, and was being such a great help to the team in the almost quasi-managerial role he'd assumed since Grayling's illness had worsened, there was nothing to be done but put up with it. Roger had his beer while the others tried to celebrate with lemonade and coke the best they could.

The only good news to come out of the evening was Jones's announcing there would be no training on the morrow and that instead he had organised a harbour cruise to refresh them. Though he wouldn't be able to join them initially as he had another commitment, he would get to them later in the day if he could.

The sun on their faces, the wind in their hair, good food in their bellies and at last with a drink in their hands as the alcohol ban was forgotten in Jones's absence, the cruise proved to be a wonderful break from the rugby. And a victory of sorts, because they had finally succeeded in getting the youngest member of the side and the reserve half-back, Brian Smith, 'on the turps'— having a drink, in Wallaby parlance. This was a particular pleasure, because to this point it had been difficult to get Smith away from Jones's side and inculcate him into more of the Wallaby ways.

Jones had selected Smith from the Queensland reserves bench the previous year and promoted him to the Wallabies ahead of both Peter Slattery, the half-back who had been the reserve to Nick in 1985, and Brad Burke, Nick's understudy at New South Wales level. The Queensland selectors did not quite share Jones's high opinion of the youngster and kept faith with Slattery by keeping him as the first-choice half-back in the Queensland firsts, but Jones believed in Smith. So much so that he was to be quoted in the *Age* that very week as saying, 'This young man is one of the most gifted players in the world. Every so often you find diamonds and you have to polish them up.' On the boat though Jones was not around, and Smith would no sooner finish his drink than one or other of the Wallabies would fill it up for him with instructions to 'get this into yer'.

Jones finally joined them in the early afternoon when the boat pulled into a ferry wharf to pick him up and he was immediately shocked to see the players drinking. The reserve centre, Anthony Herbert, was the first to receive the full force of the Jones blast as he happened to be holding a beer at the top of the gangplank when Jones arrived.

'What the hell are you doing drinking?' Herbert remembers Jones demanding. Herbert blustered the best he could, but in pique, if not outright anger, Jones announced that he'd changed his mind about giving them the day off and wanted all the reserves back at the hotel for a sprint session at four o'clock. He expected Farr-Jones too, as he had barely played the last game at all.

Not welcome news to a bunch of players who thought they had the day off and already had a lot of beer in their bellies, but most of them reluctantly tried to sober up. Only Roger Gould refused, telling them they should do no such thing. He stayed behind at the Rocks as the others went back.

If there was one thing Farr-Jones had no feeling for, with grog in his belly and clutching one arm tightly across his chest to protect his injured shoulder, it was doing sprints to Jones's command. Somehow he managed, though and finished the session at about 4.30 p.m., leaving Brian Smith behind to do what he often did—extra work after training.

When Gould got back to the hotel at around 5 p.m., he went over the road to St Johns Oval to see how it was going. Jones was still there, with a now clearly exhausted Brian Smith.

'Look at him,' Gould remembers Jones saying, 'the athlete of the year 2000.'

Alarmed at Smith's clear exhaustion and knowing how much Smith had drunk on the boat, Gould asked Jones to call off the session. It was obvious that Smith was near dropping with exhaustion. Couldn't Jones see that Smith was spent?

'Oh, he's tough, this one, don't worry. You're all right aren't you, Brian?'

'Yes, Alan. I'm all right,' said Smith, quavering only slightly.

Farr-Jones too, was just starting to feel more or less all right by the Thursday before the Saturday semi-final against France. The shoulder was beginning to come good and he felt that by Saturday he would be strong enough to play without painkillers. Which he might have been, but for some reason—and over physio Greg Craig's protestations—Jones insisted that Farr-Jones do a full-contact training session with tackles and all, and if Farr-Jones had to get a painkilling injection just to get through it, well, it was just as well to know how the shoulder would hold up now. If he couldn't get through it, then Brian Smith was always there to take over.

Farr-Jones did get through it, even though it hurt like the hammers of hell as he did so.

'I didn't understand why Jones made me do that, and I still don't,' Farr-Jones says now. 'My feeling at the time was that it probably put the recovery of my shoulder back by about three or four days, and I again had to have a lot of painkillers in my shoulder before playing against France in the semi-finals.'

It was a contest that would often afterwards be described by rugby afficionados as 'the game of the century'. (More often in France than Australia, to be sure.)

The half-back got the first inkling of what was to come in

the game when at the very first scrum he fed the ball into an Australian scrum that was just marginally giving way.

When the camera flashed briefly on Jones in the stand he looked every bit as worried as he should be. If there is one sign that a coach looks for early on in a game to foresee the end result it is how the scrum is going. If it is going backwards, as it was in this case, then the omen is very bad indeed. It means one of three things: the opposition pack has greater strength, better technique, or more hunger.

Even though Australia was ahead by 9-6 at halftime, still the omens were not good. The French somehow refused to fall away, as was their usual international form in away games, and if anything seemed to be coming at them stronger. What particularly raised their morale going into the break was a try scored by their second-rower, Alain Lorieux. From a lineout close to the Australian line the Australian second-rower Troy Coker—another Jones protégé, also plucked from obscurity by him—had actually won the ball in the lineout only to have it ripped off him by Lorieux in the ensuing maul. It was to prove a costly mistake.

After a seesawing effort that went on for the entire game, the score was deadlocked with a minute to go when, after an amazing passage of play involving no fewer than thirteen Frenchmen, the ball finally came into the hands of perhaps the greatest full-back of the modern era, Serge Blanco, on the burst.

When Blanco got to two metres from the tryline, just on the edge of the sideline, Farr-Jones was still fifteen metres away and knew he couldn't catch him. All he could do was watch in despair as hooker Tommy Lawton made a last desperate lunge for him . . . and just barely missed. Blanco scored the try and the game was gone.

The dressing room was in a predictably wretched mood at the end of the game and, for the first time Nick could remember, Alan Jones simply could not speak.

Only nine months earlier in New Zealand Jones had been able to turn the team around in the space of only two weeks; here there was no recourse. The Wallabies were out of the final and the chance to win the World Cup was gone. There was little to do that night for most of the Wallabies except return to the Travelodge and sit around in small disconsolate groups at the bar and try to cheer each other up.

'The depression was absolute,' Nick says. 'We knew we had

blown it, that there was absolutely nothing to be done.'

When highly fancied teams have very public losses, it is not unusual to see an immediate division appear between players and coach as each one tries to blame the other for the loss.

In just such a predicament it was hardly surprising that as the evening wore on and more and more alcohol was imbibed there was talk that maybe Jones had come to the end of his natural term as Wallaby coach.

From there, it all began to unravel quickly. On the Monday the team gathered in the foyer in the early afternoon as always to go to training. They might have lost the semi but they were still obliged to go to New Zealand to play the consolation final against Wales at the end of the week to see who was third and fourth.

But where was Alan?

After waiting for some twenty minutes Gould and reserve backrower David Codey ventured up to Jones's room and found him, in Gould's words, 'still only half dressed for training, an obviously shattered man'.

'We've lost it, we've lost it all,' Gould remembers Jones saying. It was as if the enormity of the consequences of losing to France were hitting him anew.

'Listen,' Codey said to the coach, 'the whole team is down there every bit as disappointed as you, and they've fronted up, they're ready to train and you've got to too.'

Eventually Jones was persuaded to get himself together and come on down. And right away, he showed that he had recovered somewhat when in his opening remarks at that training session he managed to apportion some of the blame for the loss. In Jones's eyes the three main players to blame for the Wallabies' defeat were Farr-Jones, Campese and Coker. They would simply have to take a good look at themselves if they wanted to continue to be a part of this outfit.

By this time Gould for one had heard enough, and had *had* enough for that matter. After giving it some thought he walked back to the hotel, packed his bags, made a phone call and then walked back to St Johns Oval. It had only been a light training and the others had gone, but Jones was still there, putting Smith through his paces in another private training session.

'Mate, I've got to tell you something,' Gould said to Jones as they watched Smith run back and forth. 'This has been the most unhappy experience of my life. I'm going. I'm not going to New Zealand with you. I'm leaving for Brisbane in half an hour.'

Jones turned, momentarily disoriented as Gould recalls it.

'You can't do that, Roger. We need you. We need you to help us.'

'No, you don't, Alan. You'll find all the team money is in the safe, and all the tickets for New Zealand are in there too. I'm going. This team was very very happy in 1984 and now it is very unhappy because of you, and I just can't stand to be around it. I'm going home.'

'You can't go.'

'I am. See ya.'

And turned, and walked away.

'I knew that was the only way I could do it,' Gould says now. 'Jones is an extremely hard man to argue with. He's very good at arguing and I'm not. I knew if I stayed around, he'd probably be able to turn me around, just by force of persuasion, but I didn't want that. I wanted to go and I did.'

Yet for all his antipathy towards the Jones of 1987, Gould is typical of many Wallabies in naming Jones as 'easily the best coach I ever had'.

'The best organised, the most energetic, the best at analysing weaknesses in the opposition and exploiting them. But simply not someone you could spend a lot of time with, and after four years the team had just had jack of him.'.

With Gould's departure the wheels of the Wallabies got wobblier by the minute.

Another who 'had jack' of Jones at that time was Peter Grigg, the long-time Wallaby winger who had become extremely frustrated by his continued non-selection for the important games, even though at the beginning of the World Cup Jones had said to the press that he wanted to have 'a team full of Peter Griggs'. Now the last straw: he wasn't even to be selected for the consolation final. His position had been taken by Brian Smith.

It was only a few hours after Gould had left that Grigg went to see Jones in his room. The ensuing commotion brought the Wallabies from their rooms, and they soon gathered around the door, hardly daring to believe their ears. Commotions coming from Jones's room were nothing new, but the amazing thing was that the person doing the shouting wasn't Jones. Up to now the times a Wallaby had been heard raising his voice to Jones could have been counted on the fingers of one finger—back in 1984 when Farr-Jones had 'spat the dummy' on the Grand Slam tour. But this exceeded even that.

The players around the door remember the thrust of Grigg's shouting thus: 'How DARE you put Brian Smith on the wing in my place, in a position he's never played before, EVER, when I'VE played for the WALLABIES there for years!

'You started the World Cup saying to the press that you wanted a team full of Peter Griggs, and now you haven't even got ONE Peter Grigg in the team!'

And Jones's reply? At first a great deal of shocked bluster, and then very little. The way Grigg would tell it to the Wallabies later, Jones was just standing there, dumbstruck at the extent of Grigg's fury.

When it was over and Grigg stormed out of the room, he might have been surprised to see so many of his team-mates who happened to be suddenly passing the door, but he was too angry to pause.

Just prior to this the team had been on a trip to nearby Annandale for what was meant to be a morale-boosting dinner at a local restaurant. It had initially worked, and soon after the Wallabies arrived other patrons could hear them singing. True, the songs were more 'Old Man River' than 'American Pie', but at least they were singing. Jones was there too, chatting away and occasionally laughing just a bit too loud and long to be real.

Farr-Jones too did his best to forget the loss. He ate a bit, drank a bit, sang a lot. He *felt* like drinking quite a bit, but laid off, knowing that a little later in the evening he would have to drive to the office to finish off some legal work before flying to New Zealand the following morning.

When it was all over, and the Wallabies headed back to the hotel, he retrieved one of the hire cars that had been placed at the disposal of the team and drove into town. Now after midnight, the streets were all but deserted and the trip did not take long. Which was as well, because he wanted to get to the office, knock over the work, and get back to the hotel for as much 'kippage' (sleep) as he could before the team's early start the next day.

Of course he saw the red light on the corner of Margaret and George streets but what the hell? There was no one around and he could see for himself that it was perfectly safe.

The thing about blue flashing lights suddenly going off behind you is the real horror of it is ever so slightly delayed. For the splittest of all split seconds you still have hope that the lights don't shine for you, and then the absolute certainty comes. Busted.

'Good evening, sir.'

'Good evening, officer.'

'Did you know you went through a red light then, sir?'

'Yes, I'm sorry officer, but I . . . '

'Have you been drinking, sir?'

'Well, I've just come from a function with the Wallabies and I suppose I've had four Italian beers and two glasses of red or something like that, but I don't think I'm over the limit.'

'Would you mind breathing into the bag, sir?'

Three hours later Farr-Jones was still at the police station near Central Station. Humiliated. Feeling wretched. In the time since his arrest he had been again put on the bag, again found to be over the limit, had been photographed, fingerprinted, obliged to give his name, address, occupation. His blood alcohol level was .0785, just one or two drinks over the legal limit of .05.

A nice little rotten cherry on top of the appallingness of it all was that when the police finally told him he could leave he still had to go to the office to attend to the urgent legal matters that had awaited him all this time.

Nick eventually got back to Camperdown at about 7.30 in the morning, only half an hour before the bus was due to leave for the airport to go to New Zealand.

Rotorua was just the sort of place for the Wallabies to be in their current mood. They had come to the end of the road and this felt and smelt like the end of the earth. The sulphurous geysers that the town is known for were surely the exhaust fans of Hell, and the Wallabies settled into their hotel in a humour as foul as the wind.

The unravelling of the Wallabies continued. On the last training session before playing Wales, on the Wednesday morning, Jones simply didn't turn up. No show. No explanation. Alec Evans took the session and that was that. Then, on that night, Nick received a call to go visit Jones in his room immediately. When he arrived, four other Wallabies were already there.

The reason Jones had asked them to his room he explained was because he wanted to talk to them about South Africa. Farr-

Jones remembers the thrust of Jones' talk thus: A tour was going to go ahead, hopefully with the sanction of the ARFU. He wanted them to be aware of both the desirability of them going and the need for strict confidentiality and if they had to go without the sanction of the ARFU they had to understand that they might never play for Australia again. (And without sanction he would not be able to accompany them.) Significantly, he never asked them if they wanted to go, but just assumed they were as keen as he was. It would be one way, Jones said, for them to prove they really were a far better team than they'd shown in the World Cup. He would essay to make it happen and get back to them in the near future but in the meantime, remember, absolute confidentiality.

The odd thing about all this was the way Jones went about it. Addressing the players in threes and fours, in quiet little groups. Why not simply address the whole team and have it all out on the table? Perhaps because, the players surmised, not everyone in the team had been approached. Sure enough, some muffled whispers later they found that David Campese for one hadn't been asked, and Steve Tuynman for another.

Farr-Jones pondered the venture on the way back to his room, as that infernal sulphurous smell pervaded his nostrils. On the one hand he was keen both to go to South Africa to see it and to test himself against their rugby, but on the other hand to go to South Africa was still a political decision more than a sporting one, and he was yet to work out where he stood in the complicated politics of it all. Jeez, but his shoulder hurt.

Since Monday, when the news had got out, there had been much aghast comment in the team about Jones's selection of Smith on the wing, focusing as Grigg had on the fact that the youngster had never played so much as club rugby in that position and yet he was being selected ahead of an experienced specialist winger. On the Thursday morning before the game Nick was able to alleviate the controversy somewhat when he told the coach that because his injured shoulder still had not properly recovered he would be unable to play in the Test. This meant that Smith reverted to the more familiar half-back spot, Nick gained the relative comfort of the bench, and Grigg went back on the wing.

Four minutes into the game the Wallaby back-rower David

Codey was sent off for over-vigorous rucking, and the Wallabies were down to fourteen men. On the bench Farr-Jones had the same sense of foreboding as he'd had at the last game, when he'd seen the Wallaby scrum go backward from the first scrum.

It was to be a long afternoon, and all the longer because of the nasty atmosphere at the ground among the New Zealanders. Still smarting over the hostilities of the previous season, they were all barracking hard for the Welsh to win.

Then the worst happened . . . Peter Grigg waved his hand in the air in the internationally recognised signal for 'I'm stuffed and have to come off', which meant that Brian Smith went back to the wing position and Nick took over the half-back role. Jim Webster would later note in his match report that 'when Farr-Jones came on just after halftime with his busted wing, he got the backs moving strongly'.

The Wallabies very nearly won it. But in a near-replay of the game against France, Wales scored in the last minute of the game and then slotted the conversion over to win the game 22–21.

That made two defeats in a row. It was a long bus trip back to Auckland the following morning, Jones sitting up the front of the bus, not talking at all. Behind him the players were subdued to the point of silence.

It didn't seem right. Like there was a huge party, they'd got all dressed up to go and then been refused admission at the door. On the Saturday afternoon in Auckland, at Eden Park, France played New Zealand in the inaugural World Cup final.

Only six of the Wallabies attended, while the others stayed back in the comfort and sulky security of their hotel rooms. While the All Blacks and the French were in the dressing room at Eden Park, preparing to go out for the biggest match of their lives, Nick and most of the Wallabies were playing cards, smoking and drinking in their rooms. Although winning at poker, Nick definitely felt none the better for it.

'I sort of felt like I was being a bad sport by not going to the final, but really I just couldn't face it, and most of the guys felt the same.' Whose deal?

The All Blacks won the game 29–9 in a fairly ordinary game and when, back at the Wallabies' hotel, they finally flicked off the TV, the mood was predictably black.

Despite the wretchedness of the season thus far, there was still a chance that the Wallabies could salvage a great victory out of the year. Thank providence that the new world champions, the All Blacks, were booked in to play Australia only five weeks after their World Cup victory to contest another one-off Bledisloe Cup game. If the Wallabies beat them, it still wouldn't be the equal of having the World Cup, but it would at least make Australia's failure look like an aberration in a nevertheless very successful period.

And they would at least resume the title of the *unofficial* world champions, and that would give their series in South Africa a lot more sting, though they still hadn't heard anything solid on that. Jones had gone strangely quiet on the whole thing, and no one cared to push him on the subject.

It was another sign of the times for the Wallabies that despite the published Jones opinion that there was nothing basically wrong with the Wallabies, he nevertheless dropped both his captain and vice-captain, Andrew Slack and Simon Poidevin.

Both players took it stoically enough, but Farr-Jones for one was shocked. Driving along Margaret Street, in what he suspected were the last days of his driver's licence before the court case on his drink-driving charge the following week, he heard the news of their sacking on the radio and turned it off straight afterwards so he could think.

'I just couldn't figure it out,' he says, 'how both the captain and vice-captain could be dropped and yet Jonesy insisted on telling us that there was nothing really wrong. I thought it very hard on both of them because whatever had been going wrong I was confident the replacing of Slack and Poidevin was hardly the way to turn around our fortunes.'

The new captain was even more of a surprise.

David Codey, the man who had been sent off in the last Test against Wales, was a popular figure in the team and an admittedly inspirational player when on the field, but in recent times Jones had selected Codey predominantly as a reserve. Now it was to be him leading the side.

Jones, though, had no doubts that Codey was just the man for the job.

Quoted in the *Mirror*, the coach was glowing in his praise.

'Our new captain David Codey is a forceful, aggressive, uncompromising man,' he enthused. 'He is intelligent, leads well, and has the capacity to get the best out of people. He embodies the sort of spirit and commitment we need for this game.'

Sounds like just what the doctor ordered. Even then all was not as it seemed. Codey learnt of his elevation to the captaincy through a most unusual way.

Like Roger Gould and Peter Grigg, Codey had also 'had jack' of the whole Wallaby thing and decided well before the game against the All Blacks that he wanted no further part in it. And just like Gould, he didn't want to become involved in a long discussion with Jones on the subject, preferring simply to withdraw. So . . .

'I called John Bain [the chairman of selectors] up to tell him that I was not available,' Codey says. 'There was this pause, and then Bain said to me, "Well, that actually makes things a bit difficult, David, because we were actually wanting to make you captain."'

'WHAT?'

Even then Codey, to his credit, did not immediately reverse his decision and only agreed to his inclusion on the condition that, as captain, he would be consulted on the running of the team and things wouldn't be done the Jones Way exclusively. Codey defined his conditions to Bain as 'a complete back-off from Jones on his total control of the team'. For this game there would be no more mad-dog sessions where the players would be required to beat each other around. Codey said he wanted something of a return to the old days, where the players would train hard but not foolishly and be disciplined in their approach but not to the exclusion of all enjoyment.

This was agreed to and Codey again made himself available.

On the first Wednesday of the team gathering at the Rushcutters Bay Travelodge (the team having refused to return to Camperdown) beer was served to the players after the training with their barbecue. It wasn't much but it was a beginning—not so much a need for alcohol as an acknowledgement that things were to be more relaxed.

As it was a beginning that Jones was training them again in the mornings.

And were they a happy side? Hell, *yes* they were a happy side. The day before the game, in a story in the *Mirror* headlined 'WE *ARE* A HAPPY SIDE', Jones came straight to the point: 'In spite of what some people might try to tell you, this is a very happy Australian side. Very committed and very ambitious.

'All the negative and divisive stuff comes from people who've never been to training, never spoken to a player and never spoken to me. This sort of nonsense fuels me up. It puts petrol in my tank. It puts me into overdrive.'

Overdrive?

'The whole point of why this was one of the happiest few days for the Wallabies all year,' says Farr-Jones, 'was that Alan had dropped back a gear or two. It was all a lot quieter somehow, a lot less frenetic. Jonesy seemed to have just calmed down about everything and we really did do a lot of good preparation. Going into that game I was extremely confident that we could turn it all around.'

David Codey put his own imprint on the team by insisting that the Wallabies actually stand right up close to the haka as a sign they were not intimidated, and midway through the second half the Wallabies were actually winning by a slim margin.

That the All Blacks then shifted into overdrive themselves and went on to beat them 30–16 was the cause of some regret for the team but no disgrace. The All Blacks had rebuilt from the disappointments of the previous year and had put together a side that would be looked back on as unarguably the greatest in their history.

It was a few days after the All Black game that Nick was obliged to go to court for the first time as a defendant and not as a lawyer. At the end of it he was relieved that his licence was suspended for only twenty-eight days, but aghast at what was to follow. The call came in the afternoon after the morning's hearing.

'Hello, Mr Farr-Jones, I'm from the *Daily Telegraph* and I want to write a story about your drink-driving . . . '

'Sure you do. Who's this? Is is you, Pete? Spud? Who is it?'

'Hello? No, I'm really from the *Telegraph* and I really want to do a story about your drink driving.'

'Of course you do. Now cut the crap and tell me who you really are.'

'Look, we recently did an article on Tom Carroll losing his licence, we did a little story on him advising the kids not to drink and drive, we took a photograph of him putting a blanket over his car for six months and we'd like you to do something similar.'

Farr-Jones is still not sure why he thought the whole thing was a hoax, but continued the conversation under just that impression, trying to cajole his interlocutor into giving up his real identity, but the guy kept insisting he was a reporter.

In the end, to convince Farr-Jones of his bona fides, he had Nick call him through the *Daily Telegraph* switchboard and the awful truth suddenly dawned.

'This bloke really wanted to make a big story out of it. Wanted me to give a message to the kids that they must never be as big a fool as I was and to take it from me that Nick Farr-Jones says you mustn't drink and drive.

'All of a sudden, being a lawyer, I thought, "Jeez, I can't afford this. I simply can't have my name plastered all over the paper as a drink-driver who broke the law. I've got to do something."'

Amazingly enough he got through to Jones on the third ring, without even having to go through his secretary, as was usual.

In calling Jones, he was following Wallaby standard procedure during the Jones era, that when any of them got into trouble of any sort Jones was one of the first they turned to. He was powerful in his own right, particularly well connected, and with a very good track record for helping out troubled Wallabies and even troubled friends of Wallabies. It had been a good part of his early success with the Wallabies that a lot of them were personally indebted to him for his kindness in helping them.

Could Jones get the story killed?

In the end the story ran, although Jones claimed to have succeeded in getting it moved further back in the paper.

In early August the South African issue finally came to a head. Frustrated at the continuing failure of Jones's mooted South African tour to take off, Andrew Slack and David Codey left for that country on 4 August on behalf of the players to see if they could organise it. As a courtesy they had told Jones over the telephone before leaving what they were doing and he said in an off-handed manner that he wished them well, though reiterated he could not participate himself. Slack was surprised at Jones's sudden coolness about it all, when he had initially been the one to set the ball rolling, but confident at least that the coach wouldn't do anything to stand in their way. David Codey says, 'I was still very much of the belief that Jones was right behind us.'

Two days later, on 6 August, Jones called a meeting for the Sydney-based Wallabies in his Newtown home.

He personally could not take them to South Africa, he explained, because it now looked as if the trip could now only take place as a rebel tour, and as an elected member of the Australian Rugby Football Union it would be impossible to go with them. If *they* wanted to go, then that was their decision. Before they made a decision like that, though, there were a couple of senior players whom he'd like them to listen to.

In the brief moments between Jones finishing and Simon Poidevin getting up to speak against the tour, Farr-Jones looked to his good friend Brett Papworth, who was also at the meeting and equally stupefied. There was something very badly amiss here. It seemed to them that Alan Jones, the same man who had broached the subject of South Africa with them in the first place and pushed it as the next big challenge for the Wallabies, had totally changed his ideas.

Yet not one of them then stood up and said, 'Hang on, Alan, how come things have changed so quickly? Who has got into your ear?'

Poidevin spoke, followed by Michael Hawker, and as senior and respected players their opinions carried a lot of weight. Poidevin's opinion was that it would be very risky to go over there on anything less than a fully organised and sanctioned tour. Without Alan, he for one was afraid that they risked being humiliated by the very strong opposition the Springboks would present. Hawker spoke more on moral grounds—expounding the views he had publicly held for a long time, that it would not only be wrong to go on a rebel tour, but also it would be wrong to break the international sanctions that had been put into place against South Africa.

Both players were obviously sincere, though what was not necessarily apparent to the others at the meeting was that both players had been in a previous meeting with Jones, where it was discussed what they would say.

Two days after that meeting, Jones called Wallaby winger Matt Burke (who had been unable to make the first meeting) to his house, and personally implored him to abandon any thought of him going on the tour.

'He was absolutely dead-set against me going,' recalls Burke now. 'He said I absolutely *absolutely* couldn't go, that it would be a crazy decision. I was amazed, because two months earlier he was the one that was pushing so hard that we had to go.'

And for the record, Jones denies vehemently that there was any 'turnaround' from him at all in his position from June to August. Which is as maybe . . . Yet there is no doubt that the *impression* on the players was that Jones had done a total U-turn.

'To my mind,' Nick says, 'Alan Jones was surprised to find that even without him and without official sanction most of the Wallabies still wanted to go, and went about persuading us that to go to South Africa under those circumstances would be crazy. While this is understandable, it seemed to be a total about-turn on his original sentiment in Rotorua in June. At that stage my mind was not made up as to whether or not I wanted to go but I was amazed that Jones had seemingly shifted his position so much.'

Brett Papworth is of a similar mind: 'It seemed to me that what he had been saying to us at the end of the World Cup and what he was saying then were entirely different.'

Perhaps it was all just a breakdown of communication. Yet, as Jones acknowledges, it was something that would cause a great rift in the fabric of the Wallabies.

'It is of course a matter of great regret to me,' he says, 'that all those discussions, now seemingly so long ago, built barriers between me and some people with whom I had worked to secure success in Australian Rugby.

'They are barriers which time may not be able to dismantle.'

Why Jones's apparent turnaround? The assumption of the players was that someone had persuaded him that the cost to him personally would be very high if a rebel tour went ahead— it would not work in his favour to be seen to have even the slightest involvement in a sanction-breaking tour at a time when feelings against South Africa were still running high—and that it was also not in the interests of Australian rugby to be left with a veritable Third XV to do battle with.

That assumption appears at least partly correct. In the time between Jones first approaching the players and what many saw as his about-face, his great friend and political ally in the Rugby Football Union, Ross Turnbull, had learned of the possibility of a rebel tour and, deciding it would be disastrous for Australian Rugby Football Union if it went ahead, did everything he could to crush it.

'First I had to convince Dr Danie Craven not to sanction a rebel tour,' Turnbull says, 'and secondly I had to advise Alan Jones that under no circumstances would I support a rebel tour and at the same time persuade him to my point of view.'

Soon after the meeting at Jones's house, the tour died a fairly quick death, with Codey and Slack being banned from the Wallabies for initially a year, which was then reduced to a few weeks, ironically on the intervention of Jones.

Looking back on that time now, Farr-Jones is infuriated by two things: 'At the ARU for banning Codey and Slack after they had both given such long service to Australian rugby and done so much for it; and at myself, for not publicly supporting them and saying "Well, if they're banned, then I don't want to play either."'

As the end of the Australian domestic season approached, Farr-Jones had become so badly disillusioned with the whole representative rugby scene he decided that, like all the others before him, he too had pretty much had enough.

It had been a long year, starting with the World Cup, the continued losses, the flip-flops over South Africa, the drink-driving thing, and now the upcoming tour to Argentina beckoning on the horizon. It never seemed to stop, and for the first time since he had made the Wallabies four years earlier, Farr-Jones questioned whether he really wanted to go on this tour, and told his father so. He wanted to spend a lot more time with Angie, he wanted to spend a lot more time on his work, and most importantly . . .

'I just wasn't enjoying it any more, it was as simple as that. When I started playing in '84 everything was so new and different and . . . *glorious*. It was like I just couldn't get enough of it. Now things were different and I remember telling Dad that I'd pretty much decided I didn't want to do it any more, or at least I just wanted to take a bit of time out and go back to living a normal life—not to go to Argentina.'

Max Farr-Jones thought that any such decision would be nothing short of crazy.

'The way I saw it,' he says, 'when you've got a position like Nick had, you shouldn't let it go for anything. Okay, so he'd had a year when he hadn't been enjoying it that much, so what? It was something he'd enjoyed tremendously in the past, and I had every confidence that he would come to enjoy it again.'

Nick had little interest in being persuaded over the phone, so Max decided to head to Sydney University the following Saturday, where he knew Nick's Sydney University team would be playing Eastwood.

After the game was over he went straight into the Eastwood dressing room to talk to Brett Papworth, and asked him to help persuade Nick that going to Argentina was the right thing to do. Papworth, himself a little put out to find that Nick was thinking of not going, did talk to him soon afterwards and did in fact succeed in changing Farr-Jones's mind.

'I guess I just reminded him of the terrific times we'd had on previous tours,' Papworth recalls. 'And that this might prove even more terrific because it was all new territory.'

Indeed. New territory and new beginnings. Whether Alan Jones knew it or not, this was his last throw of the dice. Win or perish. With three straight losses behind him, not only were the dogs barking, but the wolves were also circling. Once again he looked for the grand gesture, signalling that all had changed.

With neither Slack nor Codey available for this tour, he came up with Simon Poidevin as captain—the player he'd axed from the Test against the All Blacks. For the second time in succession a player who was not judged to be good enough to play in a Test found himself captain soon afterwards.

Further signalling that this was to be the beginning of a new era, Jones got the Wallabies up for 6 a.m. training runs twice in the five-day camp. Unheard of. Then, in a team meeting the night before they left, Jones read aloud a short story called *Letter to Garcia*, the gist of which was this:

In a war, in ancient times, a general gives a messenger a letter with strict instructions to take this letter to Garcia. The messenger neither questions what is in the letter nor asks why he must take it to Garcia, and the rest of the story revolves around the messenger overcoming a series of ever more hideous obstacles to in fact deliver the letter. In the end he does deliver it, albeit at great cost to himself, but it doesn't matter—he has carried out the general's instructions without question. The 'message' for the Wallabies was clear—you must give everything to the cause of seeing out your appointed task. Without question.

Such a beautiful place, such a painful injury. In the first game of the tour, against the San Isidrio Club on the outskirts of Buenos

Aires, Farr-Jones hurt his knee when he tripped while gathering the ball at the base of the scrum and then happened to get caught under the wheels of the back-pedalling Australian pack.

That night, as the team went out to sample the wonderful Argentinian hospitality at a barbecue, Farr-Jones retreated to the hotel to ice his knee, and Alan Jones arranged for Ricky Stuart, who would go on to great fame as halfback for rugby league's Canberra Raiders and the Australian Kangaroos, to come over as Farr-Jones's replacement. As a matter of fact John Bain had wanted Stuart on the tour in the first place, at the expense of Brian Smith, whom he judged 'simply not good enough', but after much wrangling the Jones view that Smith was best had eventually prevailed.

While waiting for Stuart to arrive, Brian Smith would have to play two games straight, but that was no problem. 'It won't worry him, because he is the outstanding athlete in this team,' Jones told the *Sun*, for their 12 October edition.

With Farr-Jones now injured, the way seemed open for Smith to take over the test halfback spot. The only thing that could forestall that happening would be if Smith himself got injured or if Farr-Jones recovered in time.

At first this seemed unlikely, as the day after the game Nick could barely even walk on his injured leg, let alone run, but he and the Wallaby physiotherapist Greg Craig set about the recovery program anyway.

They attacked from two angles: 'Craigy' worked on the knee, constantly moving and exercising the joint, keeping ice on it to reduce the swelling, while Nick made sure his fitness level stayed high, despite not being able to run.

While the rest of the Wallabies trained they would always look over to see how Nick was going on the sidelines. The answer was always: 'constantly'. At first he would just hop along on his good leg as far and as fast as he could until he could stand it no more, then he would hop back, then back and forth again and so on. Or else he would be doing sit-ups. Two hundred at a time. Then another 200. When all that was over he would go to the swimming pool, both to do laps and to exercise his troublesome knee. In Greg Craig's estimation, 'In a way I think he was pushing himself at least as hard as if he was training with the others.'

Jones was another interested observer of Farr-Jones's progress, as first Nick hopped and then jogged and then finally ran. Watching, but never speaking directly to Nick. By his estimation, 'In two weeks, as little as a dozen words passed between myself and Alan. I think he was just like that. If, for whatever reason, you were no longer directly contributing to the success of his team, then Alan basically didn't have a lot of time for you. All of a sudden I was no longer on his table at dinner, no longer invited to go out with him . . . not even a "good morning" as we hopped on the bus to go to training. It was quite obvious there were more important people he now had to spend his time with.'

Farr-Jones and Craig kept working on the knee regardless.

In the meantime rumblings continued to come from home that Jones's position as coach was under threat with the Wallabies' dismal showing in the World Cup and later defeat at the hands of the All Blacks.

Paul Dalton, now disillusioned with Jones, as he had heard that the national coach no longer supported him for the state coaching job that was coming up the following year, made his intentions the clearest of all: 'Give me Andrew Leeds and Nick Farr-Jones,' Dalton was quoted in the *Sydney Morning Herald* as saying, 'and he [Jones] can pick any Australian side he wants. I'll have second pick and beat him . . . flog him.'

The Wallabies of course heard about the Dalton challenge soon enough over the telephone and when they were preparing for the game against Mendoza, Jones gathered his team behind the goalposts after training and delivered a forty-minute lecture on the need for them to stay unified in the face of the '"some people"' who are trying to divide us. It is up to us, he said, to show that we are above all that, that we are not going to be affected by the dogs barking as the caravan passes.

The fact that Nick was named as part of the Dalton challenge did nothing to smooth relations between him and the coach, yet, according to Nick, 'there was no open hostility between myself and Jones, just maybe a consciousness that things had cooled further'.

Jones himself was clearly beginning to feel the pressure of it all. A few days later, when the Wallabies were losing to an Invitation XV back at Buenos Aires, the team was amazed to see that Jones had left his usual position with the reserves on the bench, and was up and shouting instructions at them from the sidelines. It would provoke a headline back in Australia the following day to the effect of 'VOCAL JONES LOSES HIS DIGNITY', but more importantly among the Wallabies it would promote the feeling, Nick says, that 'Jonesy was losing it'.

By this time Nick was back to running almost at full speed again, and though he was as yet unable to 'step' with full confidence off both feet, both he and Greg Craig had every confidence that with continued work he would be right to play in only a few days, and definitely right to play in the Test in ten days' time.

On Friday 23 October Farr-Jones was confident enough on his knee that he decided to go in for the fitness test at the end of training, which consisted of four laps of the field.

Maybe it was because he was still fairly fresh while the others were tired from the last two weeks of playing and training, or maybe it was because he just wanted to show Jones he was fit again, but Farr-Jones attacked the laps the way he did in the old days at the Sydney Cricket Ground. Top gear, full throttle, giving it everything he had. When it was over, Craig was satisfied enough to note in his diary that night that 'Nick won by a clear fifty metres'. It seemed like all their hard work had paid off and he would be right to play in the Test the following week.

Which was why Craig was so astonished when Jones took him aside the following day—onto a small balcony outside of where the post match dinner was being held—to inform him that as far as he was concerned Nick would be taking 'no further part in the tour'. Shocked that Jones should say this when surely his own eyes had told him that Nick was nearly right, Craig chose his next words carefully.

'Alan, that is your prerogative, as coach. But on medical grounds I am telling you—Nick will be okay to play in a couple of days. I'm declaring Nick medically fit.'

Craig didn't add, 'and I'll tell the press that if they ask', but it was implicit in his wording. Jones had been warned that if he wanted Nick out of the tour, then he would be getting no help from the physio.

The following day, Jones announced Farr-Jones as part of the team to play in Tuesday's game against Paraguay. A day later the Wallabies were there, accommodated in the sumptuous Paraguay Yacht and Golf Club, arguably the best accommodation any Wallaby side had ever luxuriated in.

On the Monday morning Farr-Jones and twenty more from the touring party decided to fly down to visit the famous Iguazú Falls, down on the Brazilian border, before returning for a late afternoon training run. It would prove to be a trip that none of them would ever forget . . .

In the early hours of the morning they were aroused from sleep by the phone and staggered downstairs onto a bus that would take them to the local airport where a charter plane was meant to be awaiting them. Sure enough, it was there on the edge of the potholed tarmac. If only there was a pilot to go with it they might have been able to get started straight away. A man was telephoned to find out if he would mind taking '*los gringos Australianos* down to the falls', and the group filled in the time giving their names to an aged clerk who laboriously tapped them out, one-fingered, on a typewriter that had surely been used by Orville and Wilbur Wright before they took their own first flight.

Funnily enough the plane itself, when they finally got on it, made that typewriter look positively modern. The pilot—a man with droopy eyes and moustache to match, who looked none too pleased at being woken so early—didn't actually have to start the plane by heaving on the propeller, but they wouldn't have been at all surprised if he had.

Up, up, and away. Down, down, and even further away.

A bus trip two hours north to Brazil and they were there, the Iguazú Falls. Spectacular for both the extraordinary volume of water that passes over and the depth which it falls, all the Wallabies were suitably impressed. If only they didn't have the prospect of a boring five-hour return journey to Paraguay ahead of them, their spirits would have been soaring.

As it turned out, 'boring' was not quite the word for it.

The first problem was that when the bus crossed the Brazilian/Paraguayan border, the road going suddenly from six lanes to two, the traffic slowed but their driver didn't. Confident that his big bus would come off best in any smash with all but an equally big truck, he ploughed on regardless, leaning on the horn to give all the traffic ahead fair warning that he was coming through.

Shocked, the Wallabies were all up the back of the bus, in Nick's words, 'debating what the Spanish words were for "SLOW DOWN, you mongrel dog!"', when the said mongrel dog sideswiped a car, sending it into a ditch. And continued regardless.

Eventually . . . police sirens, wild gesticulations, raised voices and handcuffs waved menacingly. After much discussion it was agreed that the bus driver would return to the scene of the accident after dropping Los Wallabies at the airport. The aghast Australians thought it might be more appropriate just to put the guy up against the wall and shoot him there and then, so as to let a policeman drive.

'When we got to the airport,' Farr-Jones recalls, 'I couldn't help but noticing the storm brewing on the southern horizon.'

The storm hit the tiny plane soon after take-off, and inside, in Nick's memory, 'it felt like riding a roller coaster in an earthquake, except we weren't sure when or if we would get off'.

In a situation like that, with all the lads around you, no one wants to be the first to show fear, and it was this bravado that initially kept the Wallabies fairly calm. Wallaby back-rower Steve Lidbury even tried to amuse them at first by selecting the Test team from the members of the touring party who were safe back at the hotel. To Lidbury's mind, Alan Jones would be sure to prop up the scrum and assistant coach Alec Evans would make dashing forays into the backline from fullback. He also reminded them of the famous story about the Chilean Rugby team that had crashed in the Andes and survived for many weeks by eating those who had already perished. He was a riot.

When the plane tried to fly above the storm, the players were truly appalled when through the open cockpit they could see the pilot staring grimly at a flashing red warning light above his head. To calm the flashing red light the pilot took the plane down to as close to the ground as he could manage, and the Australians spent the rest of the time worrying about the storm *and* the oncoming rush of treetops and branches.

At last back on the ground the shaken Wallabies didn't actually make like the Pope when he visits a new country, by kneeling on the ground and kissing the tarmac, but they felt like it.

The following night Farr-Jones felt good to be back playing with the team again. Running, passing, tackling. Showing the South Americans a couple of pointers on the game. His knee held up well. And so did he.

Peter Jenkins, reporting in the *Australian* on the comfortable Wallaby victory, wrote that, 'Farr-Jones, returning after more than a fortnight on the sideline with knee ligament damage showed no ill effects of his enforced absence.

'His service was slick and he set many backline raids into action by darting through holes up the middle of the selection team's defence.'

Still barely a word had passed between coach and player at this stage, yet Farr-Jones felt every confidence that he would be included in the Test side for the coming Saturday. He was the incumbent and had proved to all that he was back from injury and back to his best.

But fie. On the Wednesday morning before the team was announced, Jones asked to see Nick in his room to announce to him that he had a new policy, and Farr-Jones remembers the conversation thus.

'Since the World Cup,' Jones said, 'I have decided that if you haven't done the work you cannot be picked to play. We learnt our lesson then, and we will stick by our new policy. I know you think your knee has healed, but the fact is you haven't really trained with the team over the last two weeks and so I'm not selecting you as halfback. Brian Smith will play.'

The only thing Farr-Jones couldn't figure out was why, if to use Jones's words he was 'unavailable for selection', was he then listed as a reserve for the team? Ricky Stuart had arrived and been playing well, so why not put him on the bench? After all, whatever Jones said to Nick privately, the fact that he was on the bench made it look to the world as if Smithy had simply usurped him.

Within the team Farr-Jones kept his chin up and, in the memory of Brett Papworth, 'acted very much as if it hadn't upset him much at all, that he quite understood the logic of him being out and Smith being in'.

In phone calls to Angie back in Australia, though, Nick could be a lot more honest, and although to her mind, 'it is a point of honour with him not to let disappointments get to him', she does remember him sounding 'the most down he's ever been when away on tour'.

The team itself was aghast . . .

'It was just madness,' says second-rower Damien Frawley, 'and we all knew it. Nobody could figure how Jonesy had possibly come to that decision.'

For the record, Jones' written memory of it, though faulty, is thus: 'The facts as opposed to the rumours were that Nick was injured early in the piece. He simply was not fit, had not played and had not trained in the lead-up to the First Test. I was certainly keen to have Brian Smith in the side because I regarded him as an outstanding player.'

Oddly enough, despite the sudden reversal of their roles, the incumbent becoming the understudy and versa vice, there was no apparent tension between Smith and Farr-Jones. Just as there had been no tension between Farr-Jones and Phillip Cox four years earlier. But this time it was for a different reason.

'Tension' connoted 'contact', and there was simply very little contact between them on that tour. Since his arrival in the Wallabies Smith had stuck very close to Jones's side, both socially and on the training field. Invariably the bus would be held up from leaving training because Smith and Jones would always have to finish doing 'extra work', and back at the hotel Smith was very much an 'early to bed, early to rise' man.

Which was in contrast to the others. The rest of the players, including Farr-Jones, cite Argentina as possessing the greatest night life of any country they'd ever toured, and they sampled it to the full. Part of the Wallaby folklore of this particular tour is that players would often go to bed with their dancing shoes on, with the sheets pulled up to their chin, and wait till Alan Jones had done the rounds to check that everyone was settled in for the night before getting up and tiptoeing to the lifts at an agreed time. Though this is probably overstated and it is hard to find any Wallaby who'll personally admit to such a nefarious duping of Jones, it is certain that a large part of the good times of the tour happened well after midnight. With the Argentinians all working on siesta time most of the nightclubs never even got going until 1 a.m.

Often the return from the night spots would be accompanied by the sun rising, and on several occasions Jones was seen to be a little surprised at how well dressed some of the players were at breakfast.

Smith was never a part of these midnight-to-dawn forays and, as such, Farr-Jones, who often was, never really got to know him in any social context. Smith wanted Farr-Jones's spot and the latter didn't blame him for it, particularly.

It is another old tradition in the Wallabies and it is called 'death-riding'. A practice that dare not show its face publicly, it involves all those players on the tour who wish they were in the Test team but aren't, secretly hoping that the Test team will lose and the players in their own position play badly so as to maximise their own chances of getting in the next time.

As the First Test began, in front of a crowd of 50,000 at Velez Sarsfield in Buenos Aires, with Farr-Jones on the sidelines and Brian Smith selected ahead of him, Nick at least admits to 'half death-riding'.

'I wanted Smith to play badly and the Wallabies to win.'

The Wallabies could only manage a 19–19 draw, and Peter Jenkins' report in the *Australian* on the 2 November noted that in a lacklustre Australian performance, 'halfback Brian Smith had an unhappy day as well and failed to provide slick service to [the] backline', while the *Herald* said that: 'Queenslander Brian Smith played the blindside too often from the lineout when there was a space on offer out wide and his decisive passes to five-eighth Steven James were few and far between.'

The wider issue was that for the fourth game in a row the Wallabies had failed to register a victory.

There was one game left before the Second Test for Nick to impress upon Jones his worthiness to be re-included—the game against Rosario on the following Tuesday.

Again Farr-Jones went well. Smith had reverted to fullback for this game and acquitted himself as well as could be expected of one not accustomed to the position and who had played another hard game only three days before. In the dressing room later Jones did him no favours at all by saying something that would be repeated endlessly for the rest of the tour, and often in coming years, becoming something of a running joke among the players: 'Brian Smith, many players have played as well for Australia at fullback as you did today, but none have played better.'

For Farr-Jones, though, still not a word.

The report of the match in the *Herald*, 5 November 1987 tells the story the way Jones saw it:

> 'Jones said he was disappointed in the form of deposed Test half Nick Farr-Jones who seemed to do little wrong . . .
>
> 'Brian Smith, with whom Farr-Jones was vying for the Second Test halfback spot, made some nice moves at fullback, but made a couple of handling errors under little pressure.
>
> 'Smith's performance drew great praise from Jones but Argentines

will be amazed if Farr-Jones's game was not good enough to win back his test spot.'

Not as amazed as the Wallabies would have been.

'It was just unbelievable,' says one of the senior Wallabies who prefers to remain nameless. 'It was bloody obvious to us all that Nick had to come straight back into it, and equally obvious that Jonesy was still pushing for Brian, come what may.'

That night after the Happy Hour, as Farr-Jones and a few of the players lazed by the pool of their hotel and listened to a recording of the Melbourne Cup that they'd just received, he was approached by two of the Australian journalists who'd interviewed Jones after the match and was told in private some of Jones's comments, most particularly that he had been very 'disappointed' in Farr-Jones's game and that he had thought that Smith's game had been 'one of the best ever fullback performances'.

Farr-Jones: 'Basically, the journos knew that he was trying to talk me out of the team, so the guys would write in the paper "Farr-Jones not going well" and from a distance people would think Smith was justified for my job. I went to bed pretty certain I wasn't going to make it.'

Unbeknownst to Nick at the time, however, submissions had already been made to Jones on his behalf from powerful quarters. One was from Jones's great friend and supporter Ross Turnbull, who in a telephone call from Australia told Jones that 'Nick had been integral to the success of the Australian team in the past and they simply had to have him'.

'I'm not sure what influence that had on Alan,' Turnbull says, 'but I definitely made the call.'

The other was from Michael Hawker, the most senior player on the tour, who took it upon himself to tell Jones what the clear will of the players was.

The following morning Jones called Farr-Jones to his room in the Buenos Aires Hilton to tell him two things. Firstly that he was back in the team (with Smith out and Michael Lynagh replacing the injured Simon Poidevin as captain), and secondly that, while he might have told Nick last week that he wasn't going to pick *anyone* who hadn't 'done the work', the thing was . . . he was 'going to pick Troy for this one'.

'What I want from you,' Farr-Jones remembers Jones saying, 'is not to make a song and dance about it. I don't want you to go back to the other boys and say that I've gone back on my word and I suppose contradicted myself.'

'Of course I won't, Alan.'

Troy Coker was also a great friend of Jones—a player who had got his start in representative rugby simply by writing a letter to Jones, asking what he had to do to become one of Jones's players—and when it came to someone 'not having done the work', Troy was the man to talk to. He had been injured in the Paraguay game and had hardly been able to train since. But Jones had immense confidence in him, even picking him in the Test the previous week when it was obvious to all the players that he would have to drop out, so badly was he limping.

This time Jones wanted him again, despite the continuing obvious seriousness of the injury. What the footballers call 'a badly buggered knee' was in this case a torn anterior cruciate ligament, and Jones had been advised by Greg Craig that Coker was only thirty per cent fit.

'That surely means, then,' Jones said, 'that he'll be right to play full bore for twenty-seven minutes.'

'No,' Craig insisted, 'that means he's just as likely to break down completely in the first minute and will *never* be able to play at 100 per cent for this game.'

Eventually Jones gave in when Coker broke down in the first training of the Test team and had to again drop out of the side, but it was getting ever more bizarre by the minute.

As for Brian Smith, though, he was clearly disappointed with his sacking in favour of Farr-Jones, and he was later to tell fellow Wallaby Ian Williams, when they were at Oxford University the following year, that Jones had told him the reason he had been dropped was 'not because Farr-Jones is better than you in himself, but because the other players at the moment play better when he is there'.

After all this, the worries and the turmoil, the end of a long year and with home beckoning, the Wallabies ended up being thumped in the Second Test, almost predictably, by the score of 27–19. Though leading 13–3 at one stage in the first half, the great Puma five-eighth Hugo Porta chose that day of all days to play one of his greatest games, scoring twenty-one points for his team through no fewer than five penalty goals and two field goals on the run.

Jones was at least gracious in the dressing room afterwards, being quoted in the *Sun* as saying, 'It was a very important and proud day for Argentine rugby. It was very disappointing for us, but it must be good for the game here. We've had our share of wins in recent times, but this year we've had to become accustomed to defeat.'

Indeed. For the Wallabies it was now five games in a row without a win. On the morning after the Second Test there was a breakfast in the Wallabies' Buenos Aires hotel, at which Jones spoke.

In a way the meeting was to impart Jones's version of what is known in the Wallabies as the Tour Secrets Act—that 'what goes on tour stays on tour'. Usually the TSA is applied to amorous conquests while away, but in this instance Jones wanted the Wallabies to apply it to all of the tour itself.

'As I remember it,' Farr-Jones says, 'Alan's message was, "Let's not go home and break up and tell stories about each other— let's stick together. The people out there are the wolves—they're trying to get at us—they're trying to divide us—they're trying to be critical of us. Let's stay very much a tightknit sort of team, hang in there together, and I know it's been hard but if we can do that we can come back bigger and better than ever next year."'

The irony of which was not lost on Farr-Jones. In his mind a lot of what had divided them in the first place, the schisms that had caused so many of their problems, was Jones's favouring of one group over another. Asking for unity was a bit much now.

For followers of the fluctuating fortunes of Bob Dwyer and Alan Jones, the irony was exquisite. While back in 1984 Jones had been installed as the new Australian coach at the expense of Dwyer, after Dwyer had managed to guide the Wallabies to only a loss and a draw on tour in France, now, four years later, almost exactly the same scenario was being played out in reverse—except that instead of failing in France they were failing in Argentina.

Alan Jones, with the Wallabies, flew back to Australia to be greeted by the inestimable headline in the *Australian*—'JONES RETURNS TO FIND RIVALS' DAGGERS DRAWN.' The article, by Bret Harris, opened: 'The Australian rugby union team has travelled down the Argentine and the daggers have been sharpened for Wallaby el supremo Alan Jones . . .'

Ne'er a truer word written. For the last four years Jones had been incredibly successful in amassing, despite the recent string

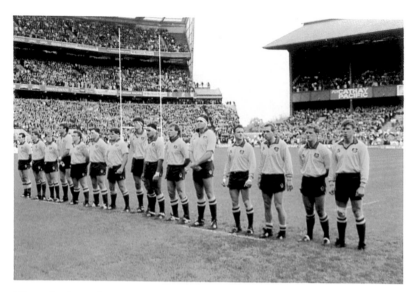

WORLD CUP FINAL, 2 NOVEMBER 1991

    ABOVE The Anthem *Colorsport*

    BELOW The Playing *Colorsport*

WORLD CUP FINAL, 2 NOVEMBER 1991
   ABOVE The Final Whistle *Colorsport*
   BELOW Receiving the Cup from the Queen *Colorsport*

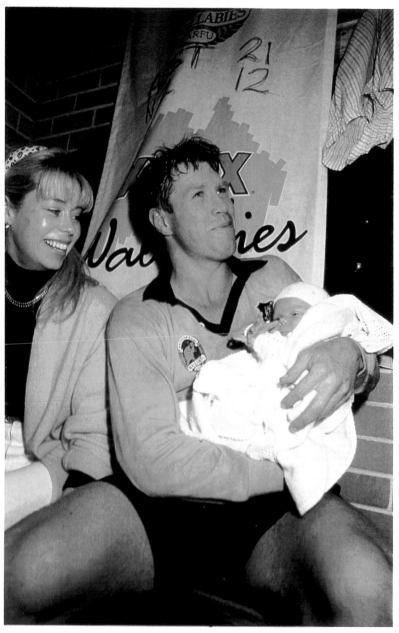

Jessica's first appearance in the dressing room, aged sixteen days (the score, indicated on the flag, was Australia 21, New Zealand 12), in 1991 *Colorsport*

ABOVE Ouch. It was this tackle in the World Cup Quarter-final against Ireland in 1991 that would force Farr-Jones to leave the field *Action Photographics*

BELOW In the baths after the World Cup in 1991 – *from left to right:* Coker, Poidevin, Kearns *Action Photographics*

ABOVE The ticker-tape welcome – Nick Farr-Jones with Bob Dwyer and team manager, John Breen, 1991 *Action Photographics*

BELOW The team celebrates after the Ballymore victory against the All Blacks to secure the Bledisloe Cup in 1992 *Action Photographics*

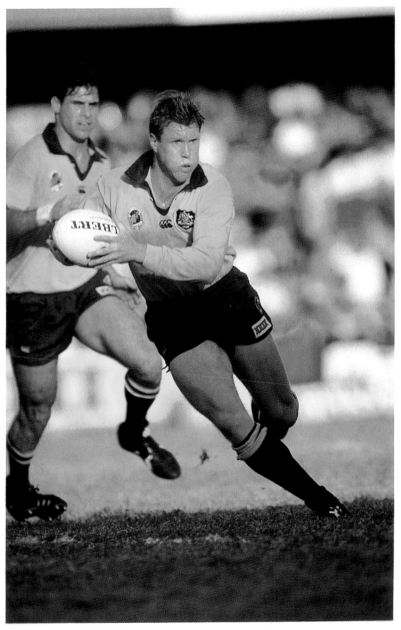

In action against New Zealand at the Sydney Football Stadium, with David Wilson
in 1992 *Action Photographics*

AGAINST THE SPRINGBOKS IN 1992 *Action Photographics*

ABOVE The calm…

BELOW …before the storm

ABOVE South Africa, August 1992 – three captains with President de Klerk. *From left to right:* Naas Botha (SA), Nick Farr-Jones, and Sean Fitzpatrick (NZ) *Action Photographics*

BELOW Playing against South Africa at Newlands in August 1992 – Nick Farr-Jones' last Test as captain of Australia *Colorsport*

of losses, an unheard of record with the Wallabies, of nineteen victories one draw and eight losses. But at cost. Being 'unapologetic in the pursuit of victory' had indeed earned Jones a lot of victories over the years, but it had also left an awful lot of people extremely angry that they hadn't been apologised to.

The result was that when he stumbled, as he had now, guiding the Wallabies through five Test matches without a single victory to show for it, there were all too many people willing to, as Harris put it, 'stick the sharpened daggers into Jones'.

Chief among these, as was to be expected, was Bob Dwyer himself. In the same article in the *Australian*, Dwyer succinctly set out the thrust of the attacks he would be making on Jones in the coming weeks . . .

There was the way the Wallabies had been playing: 'The indecision and lack of positive play in midfield is hampering the backrow's ability to maintain pressure at the breakdown.' Dwyer also raised the injustice of his own dumping from the Wallaby coaching job in the first place, with the implication that Jones had only capitalised on his own early good work: 'There was absolutely no reason to change coaches. If some genius had been on the horizon, it might have been different.

'When I was coaching Australia it was a perfect example of a team just starting to get into the swing of approaching the game the right way.'

And of course Dwyer also nagged at Jones's true point of vulnerability, the Wallabies' recent record: 'We've just gone five Tests without a win and I can't remember that happening before.

'Tempo [Bob Templeton] lost the job after losing three Tests in a row and I never even lost two in a row.'

Dwyer finished with the rather noble, but false, 'I don't care about the politics of the situation. I've got something to offer and if they don't want me, that's their decision.'

In fact, he would work just as hard lobbying as Jones had four years earlier. Phone calls, letters, the calling-in of old debts, talks with those players in the Wallabies who were most particularly in favour of his return, constant approaches to those members of the media covering the story, trying to put his 'spin' on their coverage.

He was helped in this, at least indirectly, by none other than Mark Ella, who came out against Jones on Sydney radio station 2KY just before Christmas. Ella had retired early in his career because he no longer wished to play under Jones, so this was hardly surprising, yet the tenor of his comments caused something of a stir at the time.

'I honestly feel the players will not allow him to coach them next year,' Ella said.

'I think Mr Jones is just too busy to coach the Australian side. He's got so many other interests . . . rugby has really suffered under his hands because of those commitments.'

Ella was also critical of Jones's selection policies on the recent tour to Argentina: 'Brian Smith and Troy Coker are certainly very good players but nowhere near the standard of, say, Nick Farr-Jones or Steve Cutler. Yet he pushes these guys to the forefront all the time.'

Such utterings strengthened Dwyer's challenge, but he was not the only one seeking the job. Paul Dalton also took the opportunity to throw his hat into the ring, as did former Australian coach Bob Templeton, though he withdrew just before the ballot. In the face of it all Jones essayed to play with a straight bat, falling back on his overall record rather than his record of just the last four months, being quoted in an article by Greg Growden to the effect that, 'we've lost eight Tests in thirty, and if that is the source of complaint then Australian rugby is hard to please.

'It is a fairly imposing international record we have amassed over the past four years and if I don't say that no one else will. The best judges of all this are the players—and you should ask them.'

Two of the journalists, Peter Jenkins in Sydney and Jim Tucker in Brisbane, took Jones at his word and did ask the players, every single one of them, so as to publish the results in the form of a 'Player Poll'.

Farr-Jones got his call in early February: 'Look, this is all off the record, and it will never come out what you say, but who did you support for the Australian coaching job, Alan Jones or Bob Dwyer?'

Farr-Jones: 'I think Jones has probably had a very good run and it might possibly be time for a bit of a change, but on the other hand . . . '

Jenkins: 'Who do you support. Jones or Dwyer?'

(Pause.)

Jenkins: 'Nick?'

Farr-Jones: 'Dwyer.'

It did not come easily to Farr-Jones, actually to do something that would help end the reign of Alan Jones, but all he knew was that it really was time for a change. Farr-Jones was to play no further part in the election process, refusing all further comment to the press and refusing to be drawn into any of the player factions as they jostled for position behind one coach or the other.

Not that the faction behind Jones was particularly large. In the aforementioned poll only nine of the thirty-one players contacted who had been a part of the World Cup campaign or the Argentina tour said they would like Jones to return. One of the few players on Jones's side actually to stand up and be counted was Simon Poidevin, being quoted in an article by David Lord in the *Sun* just before Christmas as saying, 'I'm in an invidious position, because Bob [Dwyer] is my club coach and does a great job and Alan [Jones] is my Wallaby coach and he too does a great job.

'[But] my loyalty is to Alan Jones.'

Too little, too late.

The day after the poll was published, on 24 February, Jones said on Radio 2UE that, 'The big issue here' which no one is speaking about is South Africa. Last year I opposed people going to South Africa and now some of those forces are arrayed against me.'

Indeed they were. In the end the result was a foregone conclusion even before the vote was taken . . .

CHAPTER NINE

Dwyer and the Captaincy

*'Rugby is a nonsense, but a serious nonsense and the thing
to do is to win, but with style.'*
Cliff Morgan, former Lions five-eighth and later
BBC commentator

Jones was gone. The news went round Australian rugby in
a trice. After four years in the wilderness Bob Dwyer was
returned to the helm of the Wallabies. The news came
through around midday on a Friday afternoon of late February
1988. Nick found out from a secretary at the ARFU offices, when
he called to check the result. Though feeling a twinge of something
akin to sympathy for Jones in spite of everything, he did not
make an immediate consolatory phone call.

'I probably should have. Jones and I had our differences, but
at the end of the day his record speaks for itself. We all learnt
a lot from him about how to win a rugby game, and if there
were tough times in the last part of his reign there were at least
a lot of good times before that.'

Having not made that phone call in the first few days, it became
all but impossible in the ensuing weeks, as Jones made it known
that the people he blamed most for his dismissal were the disloyal
senior players who had not supported him, of which Nick was
one. It would be some time before their relationship would be
back on a more even keel, and even then . . .

The man of the moment was Robert Stewart Francis Dwyer.

Soon after his ascension Dwyer invited Nick, Simon Poidevin and Stephen Cutler to break bread with him at his beachside Coogee home. On his way there, Farr-Jones reflected on what he knew of Dwyer.

He had first laid eyes on him in early 1984, when Sydney University had played an early season trial match against Randwick down at Latham Park. As Randwick's club coach, Dwyer seemed to get progressively more unhappy as the match went on. Actually, he was probably unhappy before the game even started. He had recently been deposed as Australian coach, had presided over a lower-grade Randwick defeat, had suffered the sun beating brightly down on his lily-white skin. Now this, Uni—of all teams—flogging his beloved Randwick. As one who had played 347 grade games for the myrtle greens Dwyer loved the team, beyond just coaching them.

Thus Nick's first memories of him in the flesh—a tallish man with a big moustache, parading up and down the northern touchline, screaming abuse at the Uni players in general and the referee in particular. When the latter sent Randwick backrower John Maxell off for fighting, it seemed as if Dwyer might start gnawing on the fence, so furious did he seem.

Actually Dwyer was far more relaxed in person when there wasn't a losing rugby game paraded before him, and Nick had again come across Dwyer the previous year when the latter had coached the Sydney side for a couple of games. They had got on well but had since had little contact.

And now he was going to the man's place for dinner.

This then was going to be an entirely different sort of Australian coach to the only one Farr-Jones had known to date.

Not only did Dwyer pass the salt when you asked him but it was obvious that he was genuinely interested in his guests' ideas as to how the Wallabies should proceed. To Nick's mind, although one of Jones's strengths had been that he had a very clear idea of what he wanted done, his major weakness had been a lack of flexibility when that plan no longer worked and a reluctance to confer with the people actually taking the field.

Dwyer made it clear he wanted to keep what had been the best of the Jones Way of doing things and dispense with the worst. He wanted their opinion as to which was which.

At one point Farr-Jones remembers taking a moment's pause,

sitting back and reflecting that here they all were with the Australian coach and they were all enthusiastically talking at once. With Alan they had been hard put to get a word in and you never, but never, attempted to talk over him. Poidevin's presence at the table also spoke something of the sort of man that Dwyer was. Poidevin had been the chief spokesman for the pro-Jones forces in the recent tussle and yet Dwyer obviously harboured no rancour.

Farr-Jones took his leave that night, impressed. As was Dwyer. He even told his wife Ruth, as they did the washing up together, that he was particularly keen on some of Nick's ideas.

Two months on, in April, Farr-Jones went on an all-expenses paid trip with Angela to Monte Carlo to play in the annual Monaco Sevens tournament. It was one of those 'junkets' that come the way of international rugby players every now and then where, in exchange for their celebrated services, they get a trip to an exotic destination, often with their partner, and the organisers can count on more people coming through the gate to see them play.

Actually this was more than a mere 'junket'.

The pleasant April sun, the nicely chilled champagne, the Mediterranean stretching before them from the balcony of their magnificent hotel room and . . . and . . . Hello? Room Service? Send up another two dozen oysters if you would, *toot de sweet*.'

On the night before the tournament began Angie and Nick went to a dinner at Monaco's famous Hotel de Paris, where the dripping chandeliers reflected acres of red carpets, royalty, celebrities, fellow rugby players, pomp and circumstance.

Even the rugby was fun. Farr-Jones wanted his team, the Bahrain Warblers, to win, sure. Just as Simon Poidevin, who had also made the trip, was keen to see his Monaco side do well. But for once winning wasn't everything. As their two teams played throughout the day, both progressing to the final, it was a timely reminder of just why they loved rugby so much in the first place. Running with the ball, passing, risking, trying to create something out of nothing. All without the amazing pressure that attaches itself to Test rugby and can in some cases kill the pleasure of it all.

The true indication of how absorbed they had both been by the rugby for the rugby's sake was Simon not even looking that upset when Nick's side eventually got up to win the whole thing. It was just that sort of day. Another wonderful dinner, a visit to the Casino, and thence to bed.

The next morning, even with the curtains firmly closed, the persistent sun still found its way into the room enough to illuminate the warbling bedside telephone.

Nick picked it up as Angela continued to sleep beside him. It was Angela's mother. And the news was good. Amazing, but good. Mrs Benness had just heard on ABC radio that Nick had been made captain of the Wallabies.

A little more chat, a final whispered, 'thank you, Mrs Benness', and then Nick put the phone down. Angie was only just beginning to stir and he had a little time to think before telling her.

Somehow Bob had decided on him as the captain. Previous to this, the thought had never occurred to him. If he'd bothered to think about it at all, he'd just assumed it would be either Poidevin or Michael Lynagh, the two who had captained Australia in the last two Tests. Poidevin would be upset, for sure, and Nick genuinely felt sympathy at what would be his great disappointment. For the fourth time in twelve months their positions in a rugby team vis à vis the captaincy would be reversed.

'What was that all about?'

'Bob's made me captain of the Wallabies.'

Said just like that.

Not *'Bob's made me captain of the Wallabies!'*, as one might expect. No double air punches, no whoopees, no nothing.

'It was a little like he was telling me that he was going to go down to the shops to get some milk or something,' Angie recalls. Not that she was particularly surprised at his sober demeanour, because 'Nick's just like that—he never likes to go overboard when something amazing happens to him because he thinks it's bad form. If it's for others, or for the team, or me, then that's different.'

It took the famous All Black number eight, Murray Mexted, who was also over in Monaco for the Sevens, to pump his hand in warm congratulations that afternoon before Nick even broke into a public smile about it. Even then he was very reserved.

'I really couldn't figure it,' Mexted says, 'how he was telling me this fabulous news so matter-of-factly, but I guess that was just his way.'

It really was a big deal, for all that. Australia-wide there might be more prestigious positions a sportsman can hold—captain of the Test cricket side, for example, or a rugby league side, or skipper of an America's Cup-winning boat. But in the patrician world from which Nick had sprung—Newington, Sydney University, the law school, big city law firm—to be captain of the Wallabies was pretty much the summit as far as sporting appointments went.

Back in Australia, Max and Ro heard the news only moments after Mrs Benness, when they started receiving telephone calls from people who'd heard the same radio report. And if they'd been proud when their son had made the Wallabies for the first time, and doubly proud when he had played his first Test, they could now barely contain themselves.

It had always been their custom to go to the airport whenever any of the boys returned from anywhere, but this time, when they went to meet Nick, they had to fight their way through a forest of journalists and photographers who also wanted to get to him.

The TV lights hit him just as he came out of Customs, and Nick looked behind him to see which pop star or politician he had unintentionally preceded. Amazed at the media attention, Farr-Jones answered all their questions as best he could, though he was still possessed of that slightly ethereal, other-worldly feeling one gets when looking at a situation from without.

There was even some controversy to deal with in this, his first press conference — a minor kerfuffle having broken out about Poidevin's initial omission from the team and then later inclusion. Nick's reply was that, 'If he [Poidevin] didn't want this in the press then he made a bit of a blue mentioning this to a friend of his.'

Poidevin had indeed 'made a bit of a blue' by mentioning the selector's flip-flop to Alan Jones, who had been pounding the podium about it over Sydney radio for the last two days, despite Simon's protestations. But enough already. It had been a long trip. When all the questions had been answered, and all the photographs taken, the new Australian captain and his girlfriend finally got into Nick's parents' car and were driven off.

With the wisdom of five years' hindsight, and Nick now installed as the most successful Australian captain ever, it is tempting to look back and say, 'Ah yes, of course. Farr-Jones was the obvious choice for captain all along.'

After all, with four different captains in the previous four Test matches, what the Wallabies most needed was a captain who would endure and stabilise the ship. Farr-Jones would go on from that point to record thirty-six all-but-successive Tests as captain, encompassing one historic World Cup win, one Bledisloe Cup, and the ascension of the Wallabies in the process to world domination.

At the time, however, his selection as captain wasn't obvious at all. Alan Jones, for one, according to the muddy grapevine, apparently thought it was a most unwise decision, and Jones's doubts were mirrored by others—a fact illustrated by the *Sydney Morning Herald*'s headline the next day: 'HAVE THE SELECTORS TAKEN A GAMBLE ON OUR NEW RUGBY CAPTAIN?'

In coming up with an answer of 'no' Greg Growden quoted Dwyer's reasoning for the appointment: 'Nick is a great student of the game and he is respected by all his peers.' (To which Dwyer would add now that 'of all the candidates, Nick was the only one I was absolutely sure would hold his spot in the Test team'.)

There was, too, the fact that when Farr-Jones took over the captaincy he was almost uniquely qualified among the team-members to know how to rub along with people, and if necessary lead them. The same things that made him assimilate so quickly with the Wallabies back in 1984 also worked in his favour now. As one who had grown up with two brothers, who had gone to an all-male school at Newington, then an all-male residential college at St Andrews, not to mention the numerous rugby tours he had been on, Farr-Jones was nothing if not an expert on what the collective male psyche was all about.

It was his time at St Andrews college, however, that probably influenced Farr-Jones' captaincy the most.

'I loved my time there,' he says, 'but one of the things that bugged me was the whole idea of institutionalised seniority, like the longer you've been there the more important you are.

'When I took over as captain I was dead keen to reinforce something that Andrew Slack, in particular, had already begun— which was that the Wallabies would be a team, pure and simple, not with a faction of old guys and a faction of young guys. A team where there was no particular seniority other than one of natural respect for each other.'

Of course at that stage it was all academic anyway. What mattered at the moment was that he was captain and they had a game against a combined World XV, which it was now more than ever Farr-Jones's responsibility to ensure that Australia won.

Legend has it that at the beginning of his first Wallaby training session, Dwyer started with the immortal words: 'Now, as I was saying before I was so rudely interrupted . . .'

Farr-Jones remembers it a little differently.

'Right from the beginning Bob had an entirely different style from the one we were used to with Alan. Everything was a lot less intense—not whistles blowing and a bunch of shouted commands—a lot less life-or-death, while still being done seriously and with purpose.'

There was at least something about Dwyer that was exactly the same as Jones. Just like Jones, Dwyer loved to wear the green and gold colours of Australia to training. While it might have been the dearest wish of all the Wallabies before they made it to the national team to wear those colours, they soon became blase about it after they got there. Both Jones and Dwyer, they noticed, loved to sport the green and gold above all else, and at any moment when the team was together could be counted on wearing it.

While Dwyer might have made the mistake the last time he was Wallaby coach of trying to change things too quickly, this time he proceeded with more caution. One of the 'good things' of the Jones Way, it had been decided, was the emphasis on having a secure 'platform' from which to launch, meaning a good scrum and lineout, and this would be retained. Jones's preoccupation with height in the lineout was also retained, with the two-metre men, Stephen Cutler and Bill Campbell, both selected in the second-row. In the trainings, most of the skill-drills used were ones initiated by Jones.

They beat the World XV 42–38, with Brian Smith, who had switched to the five-eighth position, ironically playing far and away his best game for Australia, scoring twenty-six of the forty-two points.

Dwyer's approval of some parts of the Jones Way also resulted in the appointment of an Assistant Coach, as Jones had had, with former Queensland and Wallaby coach Bob Templeton being appointed to the post. Dwyer also continued with Jones's notion of having a specialised team of professionals as part of the Wallaby infrastructure—with a physiotherapist and doctor always on hand. Dwyer would in later years expand this, adding a physiologist, a strength trainer, a dietitian, a sports psychologist, a masseur, an 'assistant Assistant Coach' in Jake Howard, and even a full-time public relations man to keep press access to the team organised.

The most noticeable difference in approach between Jones and Dwyer was off the field. Dwyer was far more laid back than Jones had ever been. The usual problem with coaches treating their charges as equals is that it generally doesn't take long before the players start to believe them, and the consequent loss of authority is quick. Dwyer, in Farr-Jones's eyes, got around this 'by having a fairly clear division between what was rugby and what was life.'

'If it was rugby, then there was no question that he was the boss and his opinion was ultimately the one that counted, but outside of that he didn't pull rank.'

Which is perhaps another reason Dwyer and Farr-Jones got on particularly well. While the relationship between Jones and his succession of captains had often been likened to a headmaster and his favoured head prefect, Dwyer was more of a benevolent big brother. For the first time in his career Nick was consulted on everything, and the two would spend long hours discussing such things as selection policy, training, and all matters pertaining to the team.

Neither can recall a situation where they particularly argued in that first year. There was even understanding from Bob when Nick might make a very bad mistake on the field, as he did in the following test against England, at Ballymore.

Seventeen minutes into the game, the new captain ran from the scrum base and, trying to link up with his inside centre Michael Cook, delivered an intercept pass to England centre Bryan Barley on the burst, who then set up a seventy-five metre try for England under the posts. It was obvious that Farr-Jones had made a blue, equally obvious that he knew exactly what that blue was, and Dwyer, in Nick's memory, barely even mentioned it after the game.

The main thing for Dwyer was that even after Lynagh made a similar mistake four minutes later and Australia suddenly found themselves down 13–3, the Australians 'kept their composure' (always a buzz phrase with him) and came straight back into it, helped by a precise Farr-Jones chip-kick just before halftime.

It bounced perfectly for Ian Williams to regather, and the Wallabies scored a much needed try.

The Wallabies won the First Test against England 22–16 and consolidated this a week later in Sydney, winning the Second Test 28–8.

The only real divergence between captain and coach was when it came to talk vs action on the training field. Dwyer was always a great man for talking, for getting the players to understand *exactly* what he wanted from them . . . and what he wanted was complex, to say the least. In contrast to Jones, who appeared to have loved coaching primarily for the thrill of the win itself, Dwyer's pleasure seemed to come in the intellectual thrill of working out a system of play superior to that of the opposition.

Dwyer's proposed structure required not only that the backline stand a lot closer to the opposition and run straighter, but also that they engage the opposition tacklers and not run around them, and see if we can't, in this situation, see, have our blind winger come across here . . . *suddenly you are getting sleepy* . . . and their fullback will have to move left to cover him . . . *very sleepy* . . . their inside centre will have to move left and . . . , and 'BOB, CAN WE GET ON WITH IT?'

Farr-Jones again, trying to keep the training moving, in a sense to get back to the Jones Way of doing things. He preferred to have urgency at all times on the training paddock and to do most of the talking off it.

'I wasn't against the technical stuff—I just would rather have done it on the blackboard the previous night.'

History has proved that Dwyer was talking sense through all his verbosity—his ideas are now regarded as state-of-the art in backline play—though it took some time before the Wallaby backs could really wrap their minds around what he was on about.

At least though they were never in any doubt as to the depth of his technical knowledge. Indicative of this were his halftime messages.

During Wallaby matches, Jones's communication to the players had always been in general that, 'we've got to make our tackles count! Tackle hard!' Dwyer's in contrast would be almost unbelievably specific. In that First Test against England, for example, Farr-Jones opened the piece of paper handed to him by the runner, to find that Dwyer was of the opinion that the Australian scrum was a fraction too low on the right-hand side, that the Australian lineout needed to close up the gaps between positions five and six, and that the Wallaby centres had to look out for the gap being created when the English inside centre was drifting wide on open-side moves near the line.

'We all had the impression that Bob was *seeing* a lot more than Alan,' says Farr-Jones now. 'Jonesy was a marvellous motivator, but to my mind his technical knowledge of the game was not nearly as great as Dwyer's. As a halfback there was nothing Alan could actually teach me about the game, but there were things Bob knew that I didn't. Jones's coaching would have been almost as likely to have achieved similar success in any sport, while Dwyer's knowledge was specific to rugby.'

In the early stage of his second tenure, Dwyer would probably have settled for just a little more of simple Jones-like success. Particularly during that year's three-Test Bledisloe Cup series.

A newspaper picture snapped behind the goal posts of the First Test against the All Blacks on 2 July 1988 tells something of the flavour of the times. Appearing in the *Herald* it shows seven Wallabies standing behind the goal posts after an All Black try, six of them with their heads down and one with his head up—though still looking as if he has just seen someone run over his dog. That last player is Farr-Jones.

The All Blacks had just scored their last try in what was then a record-breaking demolition of the Wallabies by the score of 32–7, and the only difference between Bob Dwyer and General Custer was that Dwyer had to watch a tape of the slaughter the following day. It was not pretty and was to get even uglier as the series went on.

Though they would be able to salvage a 19–19 draw in the Second Test in Brisbane a week later, the All Blacks again routed the Wallabies in the Third Test to win by 30–9.

Even if the consensus was that this was the best All Blacks side that had ever been put together—and it wasn't just that the Wallaby side was a bad one—it was still a difficult and humiliating time for the entire team. In the midst of his personal disappointment, however, Farr-Jones had still very much enjoyed the role of the Australian captaincy. 'Like quick tap kicks, for example,' he says. 'I liked not having to ask, "Can I do this?" I'm captain! I gave myself permission.'

The Wallaby captaincy was also a pleasure off the field, and brought its own duties, invitations and responsibilities; for the most part Nick found these very much to his liking. Making speeches at rugby clubs all over Australia, addressing schools, being asked to donate Wallaby gear for charities, representing the Wallabies at sports awards dinners, as well as giving addresses at charity nights himself . . .

The only problem in all this was the one quickly pinpointed by Angie: 'His inability to say "no" to people.

'Right from the beginning,' she says, 'he was always conscious of what he saw as his "duty" as Australian rugby captain, and if any rugby club from anywhere wanted him to speak, he'd always go.' And usually still be going well into the wee hours . . . Nick's former Sydney coach, Peter Fenton, tells a story of going to speak at Temora Rugby Club and finding all the locals extremely disappointed at the end of the evening that he wouldn't stand on his head and drink a beer . . . the way Farr-Jones had the previous year.

If, as a result of fulfilling his 'duty' Farr-Jones had a little less time to devote to the law firm, that was still generally acceptable. As Australian captain, the finder in the firm of Minders, Binders, Finders & Grinders was becoming a finder par excellence, as senior partner Michael Holden might have phrased it.

The fact that he had less time to be with Angie was more problematic. When she did see him, he looked more or less like the old Nick, only more tired.

At least he carved out some time one wet Saturday in late September to take her down to Shelley Beach's famous Le Kiosk restaurant. They had just left the car and were walking down the esplanade when the rain really started to come down hard, forcing them to huddle even more tightly under the umbrella as they walked. Still, Nick could see she was going to get all her left side soaked.

'Here, put this on your finger,' Nick said, giving her the engagement ring he'd been keeping in his pocket.

And wasn't that about typical? Only three weeks after this she again had to drive him to the airport, as the Wallabies were going away—this time to England and Scotland. It wasn't easy having a relationship like this, with Nick so often away, so often tired, so often upset at the way things were going with the Wallabies (that year particularly), but they managed.

Securely in his luggage this time, as always, were ten letters from her, each with a date on the front, which he would open every morning on tour for the first ten days. By which time the other daily letters she would have been sending from home would be reaching him at whichever hotel he was at. He, in return, would, time permitting, pen her as many letters as he could before leaving, similarly dated.

Angie would be kept particularly busy this time in his absence. Not only with her job in personnel management, but also in planning for next March's wedding and in buying them a house. Nick simply didn't have time to 'muck around looking at real estate', he had explained to her, so whatever she found would be fine with him. (She did find it, a townhouse at Sylvania on the water. On his return from the tour Farr-Jones would go straight from the airport to see the place he had purchased, sight unseen.)

Only hours after arriving in London, Farr-Jones was taken aside and warned that, as Australian captain, he should be 'extremely careful' of any young ladies he met on tour who might be of amorous intent. He never knew but that they might be in the employ of one of the British tabloids, and he could find himself like British cricket captain, Mike Gatting, with allegations of 'Sex romp with British barmaid' plastered all over.

'It was an unecessary warning,' says Farr-Jones, 'but interesting all the same.'

In hindsight, this tour to England and Scotland was one of the less important ones of the decade, though they weren't to know that. While the loss that the Wallabies suffered against England at Twickenham on the first leg of their tour is all but forgotten now, at the time it seemed a disaster.

Bob Dwyer simply could not speak, sitting slumped on a bench as the Wallabies trudged into the Twickenham dressing room. Alan Jones had been sacked the year before primarily because the Wallabies had gone without victory for five Tests in a row and he had now coached them to four such winless Tests. Farr-Jones felt as wretched as if he personally were responsible for Australia's 28–19 loss—the first time in six years that Australia had gone down to England.

At least Farr-Jones was at his best at the Test dinner that night at London's famous Guild Hall, when he rose beneath the flying buttresses to make his speech on behalf of the Wallabies. For the next half-hour Nick regaled the room with funny stories of the tour so far, congratulated the English on their win and promised that the Wallabies would work a lot harder and do a lot better for the remainder of their time in Britain. Beyond the day's result, though, he thought it fitting to reflect on their incredible good fortune to be involved in such a game as rugby, which had brought them together in a place like this on such a night as this. And what a good thing it was, he said, to see that for the first time in its history the English Rugby Union had invited ladies to grace their Test dinner; may this, too, be the beginning of a long and glorious tradition, one of the traditions that the wonderful game of rugby is so steeped in.

His speech was met by a standing ovation, led by the English players themselves and followed by Australian players amazed that he could speak that well. As he sat down, Dr John Moulton, the Wallaby medico, congratulated him for making what he says was 'quite the best speech I've ever heard'.

Still, a faxed copy of a *Sydney Morning Herald* article the following day put things in a harsher perspective.

> No matter what happens in the final three weeks of the Wallabies' tour of Britain, the team have already failed in their major test and prime reason for coming halfway around the world.
>
> Yesterday's (28–19) loss to England is certain to cast a deep shadow over the rest of the tour which moves to Scotland.

Farr-Jones took the lead. Although after many of the games leading up to the English Test he had assured Dwyer, 'Don't worry, it'll be all right in the Test,' it was now obvious to all that things were not going to be all right unless things changed. For the rest of the tour he could be seen leading the senior players of the side on runs back to the hotel from practice, pushing himself even harder than usual on the field of training.

Dwyer too did everything he could, working the players hard and at night reading up endlessly on the books full of state-of-the art theories on sports motivation. Always a man of great technical bent, Dwyer had started to become interested in such books as yet another resource to be tapped into for the greater good of the team, and his vocabulary had started to become littered with the psychobabble that was found therein.

Part of the team's problem, he confided to Nick, was that the players weren't getting their 'arousal levels' up high enough before the game. And he knew just the man to put that right. Bob Dwyer.

From the first game in Scotland, Dwyer attempted to work the team into a frenzy prior to every game. At his most intense, Dwyer was like a madman in control of a verbal machine-gun, spraying the room wildly with words and phrases—'hit!' 'smash 'em!' 'yell out "give me the fruit!"' 'ruck!'—and then, finding a particularly inviting target, such as a forward who appeared to be listening, he would fire volley after volley right into his ear: 'drive it, drive it, drive it, hit, hit, hit, if you want the fruit say "gimme gimme gimme" then up and away and bash 'em, bash 'em, bash 'em, and in the scrum keep it on, keep it on, keep it on!' Another wild spray around the room, another concentrated volley.

Many of the players were, frankly, more amused than motivated, and would have preferred a little more quiet to concentrate, but it was a difficult subject to broach, so suddenly convinced was the coach of its effectiveness. Bob's own 'level of arousal' was so high that on occasion Farr-Jones remembers being tempted 'to take Bob outside, hose him down a bit to cool him off, put some boots on him and then get him out on to the field'.

The problem was that as the Wallabies began to play well and win again, Dwyer became ever more certain that it was because of the 'higher arousal levels', and continued to double the dosage. With suddenly four wins in four games he was definitely doing something right, but in hindsight it was probably more the extra effort the Wallabies were putting in on the training field, and their more disciplined approach off it, that helped them turn the corner.

At least their efforts were rewarded, for the Wallabies won the game against Scotland with the handsome score of 32–13.

A person standing outside Edinburgh's Carlton Highland Hotel that night, as the snow wafted down, might well have caught sight of them through the window, standing with their arms linked, bellowing out 'Auld Lang Syne' in a rough approximation of the tune.

With the Wallabies' win the tour had been saved, as had quite possibly Dwyer's position as Wallaby coach.

On 4 March 1989 Nick played a game of golf with his two brothers at the renowned Australian Golf Club in Kensington, of which they had all been members for many years. A fraction more mature now, Nick didn't wrap his golf club around any trees, as in the days of yore, didn't swear loudly when he missed a putt, and was in fact on his very best behaviour the whole time. They played eighteen holes and would have played on but for another commitment that took them all away from the course. Nick had to get married and Peter and Simon were to be his groomsmen.

Six years to the day since they'd first gone out on a date back at Sydney University, Angela Louise Benness and Nicholas Campbell Farr-Jones were married in the grand old sandstone church St Thomas's in North Sydney. White dresses and black ties for the wedding party, everyone else in equally formal wear. Commensurate with the groom's increasingly high profile, their marriage was something of a minor media event, with photographers and social scribes of the Sunday papers turning up at the church, and the whole event making the evening news on TV.

They might well have watched but for the fact that they were already back at the golf club for the reception.

One might have thought that on their Hawaii honeymoon Nick, particularly, would have been content for once just to relax and take it easy, to revel in being well away from the pressures of rugby and the law practice.

On their second day at the resort the honeymooners played what they agreed would be a one-set only tennis match. Just sort of fun at first, as Nick kidded around and Angie went to a 3–2 lead. Having played competition tennis back in Adelaide Angela knew how to make the ball do what she wanted, but Nick equally knew he had her measure. Still, at 4–2 to her it was a bit of a worry, and he started to hit the ball with more force so he could begin to haul her in. Angie in turn started to hit her returns on even stronger angles as the sun beat down. No talk now. Just hit, hit, hit. The bridegroom belting it with everything he had, Angie running across the court and spooning it to where he wasn't. A point to make, a point to prove. Going,

5-2 . . . going, 5-3 . . . *gone*, 6-3. Game, set and match to the player in the crisp white dress.

'Let's play another one.'

'No, I don't want to play another one, Nick. I'm tired and I'm happy with just one set, thanks.'

'Let's play ANOTHER ONE.'

'No.'

The British Lions were coming. Comprising rugby players from Ireland, Wales, Scotland and England, the Lions are as prestigious an outfit as exists in rugby and their three-Test series against the Wallabies would be the principal challenge of 1989.

Early news coming from the first Lions games back to Wallaby HQ (Dwyer's office) was good. The Lions seemed poorly organised, badly unfit, lacking in any real venom. Their results on tour in the first stages had been anything but impressive and the series boded well.

The last real chance to look the invaders over would come a week before the First Test, when the Lions were due to play New South Wales at the magnificent North Sydney Oval. But would Dick Laffan, the affable New South Wales coach, be able to get the Blues fired up enough to give the Lions a good work-over? Damn right he would. Dick was in no mood to let the brutes escape without giving them a very good physical pasting indeed. And he had just the way to get the boys in the right frame of mind.

At the beginning of the last training session before the Saturday game, Dick asked all non-playing personnel to leave the changing room. This was it. When the last one had gone he locked the door and turned back to the team purposefully. After dwelling for a few minutes on the Lions' style of play, the tactics they were likely to use, and what reprehensible mongrels they really were, deserving nothing better than a good flogging on the weekend, he paused. Looked around the room. Waited for the right moment. Now, surely now.

'One in,' he said with a steely, though somehow expectant glare. The players looked at Dick, then at each other to see if anyone knew what he was getting at, then back at Dick.

'*One in*,' Dick said again, this time with a little more emphasis, and an even more expectant look.

A tentative voice in one of the corners belonging to the centre from New South Wales Country, Michael Hayes, responded: 'Er . . . all in?'

Bingo.

'ONE IN!' Dick shouted once again in triumph.

'All in,' was the reply of the now rather embarrassed players. The exception was good ol' Michael Hayes, who really gave it a very good and gusto-filled 'ALL IN!!'

A wonderful rugby man, Dick. Still, perhaps he really was doing something right because, during the game, at the very first sign of a brawl, it really was one in, all in, and New South Wales came within an ace of winning the game, eventually losing 23–21.

It was the week after that that the Wallabies played the First Test against the Lions, the first time a rugby Test match would be played at the Sydney Football Stadium.

The really *nice* thing before the game began was that the big electronic scoreboard at the southern end of the ground flashed up the words of the Australian national anthem as the band played the tune, and for what seemed like the first time ever the entire crowd really joined in and sang 'Advance Australia Fair' with zest. Just the thing to get the Wallabies in the right frame of mind before kick-off.

Too easy really. The Wallabies won the game by 30–12 and it seemed as if a 3–0 win over the men from the mother countries beckoned.

In the meantime the response of the sizeable British press contingent covering the tour was scathing. Typical were the opening two paragraphs of the report by John Mason of the London *Daily Telegraph*.

'So we can't play rugby union either. The British Lions joined our cricketers in scathing defeat at the eager hands of Australia in the First Test in Sydney.

'The Lions, representing the cream of British and Irish rugby, were sorely outclassed and conceded four tries to nothing.'

To the proud men in charge of the Lions, coach Ian McGeechan of Scotland and his back-rower captain Finlay Calder, such words were of course anathema, and the Wallabies felt sure that in the next Test at Ballymore a fortnight later the Lions would be an altogether more difficult opponent, playing in the classic manner of 'wounded champions'. Farr-Jones even said as much in his address to the team before they went out to face them: 'Fellas,

I promise you this will be twice as hard as last time. If we give these blokes a sniff, we're going to be in trouble.'

As Farr-Jones was about to feed the ball, in the very first scrum, his opposing half, the Welshman Robert Jones, stood on his foot and Farr-Jones pushed him away. They began to wrestle and . . .

'Next thing I knew, Finlay Calder came off the scrum and belted me.'

It resulted in the first of what would be many brawls that day. By Farr-Jones's count he was 'cleaned out' with hits 'off the ball' by six of the eight opposing forwards in the course of the game. Bit by bit his face became bloodied, his back was raked, his eye swollen and blackened, his lip torn. The Lions won the game 19–12 to even the series going into the Third Test; Angie burst into tears at the first sight of Nick's face after the game, and the criticism began. Little of it in the press, most of it in the Australian rugby underground. The Wallabies were too soft, unable to counter roughhouse tactics if they didn't receive the protection of the referee. Farr-Jones was too easily put off his own game once hit, and unable as a captain to marshal his troops and send them storming back into the fray.

The words of one former Australian captain to a journalist, though they were unattributed to him in the ensuing articles, were that in that game 'the Wallabies unravelled around their captain'. Two years later, in one of the first camps to prepare for the World Cup, the Australian National coaching director Dick Marks would say that one of the few weaknesses of the Wallabies was that 'Nick can get flustered when put under enough pressure'.

When Nick collared him later and wanted to know what the hell he based that assumption on, Marks cited 'Lions, Second Test, 1989'.

Farr-Jones rejects out of hand that he became flustered on the field, but admits a lack of composure, that night when the team went out to dinner and started talking over what they had been through.

In his book *The Winning Way*, Bob Dwyer has said that 'the Lions who toured Australia in 1989 were at times the dirtiest team I have ever seen in international rugby', and that 'with them, dirty play was a persistent, deliberate, all-embracing tactic'.

Rightly or wrongly, that accurately sums up the feeling around the table that night. Not only had the Lions been dirty, not only had they been engaged in something that wasn't at all cricket, but the prevailing thought was it had been a pre-planned tactic from the opening whistle. There was talk that perhaps the Lions had reactivated the famous '99' call of their 1974 tour to South Africa when, so rugby lore has it, a call of '99' was the signal for every man in the lineout to start belting his opposing number on the reckoning that the referee could hardly send them all off and the Springboks would be suitably intimidated. Both McGeechan and Roger Uttley, the forwards' coach, had after all been part of that Lions tour.

Well, if that was the way they were going to play, Farr-Jones had an idea of his own. The only way to counter that sort of stuff was to fight fire with fire and be ready with a similar call of their own come the opening of the Third Test.

His lip throbbing now, his head hurting and his body aching from the pummelling it had received, he told a few of the forwards that that was what they were going to do. Take the Lions' heads off.

'"We've gotta go the biff", was how he put it,' the Wallaby prop Dan Crowley remembers. 'He was just very upset, very angry, and I think he was probably . . . just a bit knocked around by the whole thing.'

Of course, in the week leading up to the Third Test, when things had fractionally calmed, Farr-Jones thought the better of it, and the plan was abandoned. But it is a measure of the passion of the times that one who abhorred foul play as much as Farr-Jones even considered it an option.

That plan aborted, there remained the far more admirable option of the Australian forwards at least standing up man to man against the Lions' aggression, ad hoc, as it happened. This is surely what the legendary hard man of Australian rugby of the late 1970s, Steve Finnane, had in mind when he was quoted in a newspaper article saying, 'There is one simple answer. They have to hook in.' Asked for his own philosophy of what one should do if the fists began to fly, Finnane came right to the point.

'If someone hit me, I'd hit the closest bloke to me. If he asked: "Why did you hit me?" I'd reply, "Pass the message on to the bloke who did."'

Finnane's comments were reflective of the public opinion that the Australian pack didn't have what it took to mix it with the Lions in 'the tough stuff'.

The Third Test turned out to be almost a duplicate of the Second, with one exception. Again the Lions were more than passing aggressive, again the Wallaby forwards seemed to wilt under the fire, but even with all that, the Australians still could have won the match.

The game, and the series with it, came down to a single mistake.

If Australian rugby has greatly profited over the years from the erratic genius of David Campese in attack, it has also been made to pay the piper every now and then for his laxity in defensive play, and this was one of those times.

Six minutes into the second half, Australia was ahead 12–9 when the Lions' five-eighth Rob Andrews attempted a field goal to even the score. He missed, but the Lions struck gold anyway. The ball drifted out to the right and into the hands of Campese standing in-goal. Standard procedure on such an occasion is to simply ground the ball in the in-goal, which would have allowed Australia to restart play twenty-two metres downfield.

Never a man for the boring and predictable, Campese took the exhilarating option, which was to run it and, when the Lions's defence mounted, suddenly threw a pass to Wallaby fullback Greg Martin. Taken by surprise Martin fumbled, and Lions winger Ieuan Evans, on the fly, gleefully fell on the ball for the easiest of tries.

When, thirty minutes later, the Lions won the game 19–18, and thus the series 2–1, many was the rueful head that was shook all over Australia saying, 'If only Campese hadn't . . . '

But he had, and a brief media storm erupted over the next few days to decide, in the words of the Australian rugby writer Greg Campbell, whether Campese was a 'legend or a liability'.

Farr-Jones, as captain, was always notable for taking a protective stance when one of the Wallabies was attacked, and on this occasion his support was much needed by Campese.

On 19 July 1989 a letter to the sports editor appeared in the *Sydney Morning Herald* from the Australian captain. It began . . .

> SIR:
> Not only as captain of the national team, but as an Australian, it disturbs me to hear and read the constant and at times villifying attacks by rugby followers and the press on one of our greatest sportsmen, David Campese.
>
> . . .
>
> Campo's blunder last Saturday was careless and costly. But few of the Australian players would be satisfied with their performances,

including myself. Campo will hopefully learn by the mistake and the whole team, I am sure, will not only show the tremendous spirit in Australian rugby but will improve on individual performances when matched against the might of New Zealand in August.

To Campo I say: Yes, one bad mistake on Saturday which I know you will learn from, but, mate, if I was a selector you would always be one of the first picked, with no handcuffs or chains to inhibit you.

Nick Farr-Jones.

And so back to sober reality . . . In their married life together there had been the best of times and the worst of times. This for Angie was the worst of times. And it wasn't just that she would sometimes wake in the night to hear Nick yelling in his sleep— 'GO LEFT!' 'HANG OFF!' 'OVER FORWARDS!' 'YOUR MAN GAV!'—for that was common enough around tense Test periods. It was that when he was awake, she could never remember seeing her husband so down. Moping around the house, doing nothing much at all, uninterested in just about everything. If a lifetime of extreme competitiveness made you all the more likely to be a winner come contest time, it made losing hurt all the more.

'The thing about lost tests and series,' Farr-Jones said once, 'is that they never come again. It doesn't matter what you do, you'll never be able to get them back.'

For many internationals, this is one of the things about Test rugby that sets it apart. A tennis player who doesn't win Wimbledon one year can always come back and win it the next or the year after that. But in Test rugby it was different. It was a here and now thing, take it or lose it. For that month of their lives, fifteen guys from Australia did battle with fifteen guys drawn from the British Isles, and the guys from Australia lost. They were led by Nick Farr-Jones into their defeat and it didn't matter a damn that when they wrote the history of the twentieth century the Lions series in Australia in 1989 wouldn't get a footnote on page 385, for the guys who took part it was important, and for the rest of the century and halfway through the next every time the subject came up fifteen guys in Britain would get a twinge of joy and fifteen guys in Australia would get a twinge of sadness.

Particularly Farr-Jones.

CHAPTER TEN

Surviving and Growing

*'There is the greatest practical benefit to making a
few failures early in life.'*
T.H. Huxley, 1870

Nick, I've decided to make a few changes for this coming Test.' Bob Dwyer told his captain just before the announcement of the side.

Dwyer wasn't kidding. In the wake of the Lions' wins he had decided that some of the Wallaby personnel just weren't up to the task, and determined to bring back one old player and introduce three entirely new players into the side at once.

Nick knew the old player all right, Simon Poidevin, and he had a glancing acquaintance with Phil Kearns, but who the hell were Tony Daly and Tim Horan? He met them at Sydney's Kingsford-Smith airport for the first time before their plane left for New Zealand.

'Gidday, Nick Farr-Jones. Pleased to meet you . . . '

And pleased to meet you, Nick.

Daly could tell Nick was looking him over, even as they shook hands. 'It was like he had one eye on my face and one eye on my shoulders, seeing how big they were.'

As the new Wallaby loose-head prop, Daly's shoulders were to be called on to help tame the beast that was the All Black scrum, and at least they looked encouragingly big. Prior to his selection for this Test match Daly had never played a single senior representative match in his life . . . but at least he was a regular first grader. The hooker Phil Kearns on the other hand was only a Randwick reserve grader, while inside-centre Tim Horan to that point had only managed to play for the Queensland 'B' side.

Farr-Jones remembers thinking on the plane trip, 'How odd it was to be going to Auckland to front the All Blacks on their own turf, playing with some guys who I'd never even met before. But I presumed Bob knew what he was doing.'

Bob did. What seemed like wild selections to much of the rugby public were based on Dwyer's reckoning that 'while in some cases the new players might not have been quite as good as the players they replaced, they were picked on the basis that they would *become* better players, if only they got the experience.

'These were the guys who, in my estimation, could get us to where we were wanting to go.'

While Nick might have had a few initial reservations about such quick radical change he was at least pleased to learn that although Kearns was only a reserve grader, he *had* been a player for the Newington Second XV in his final year—a sure sign of a great player waiting to happen.

Dwyer's new charges acquitted themselves more than admirably in their First Test. For the first time in the last three years the Australian scrum showed signs of unsettling their All Black counterparts. The two newcomers in the forwards also did well in general play, while in the backline Tim Horan was outstanding from the start—tackling everything that moved in black and making many breaks of his own.

That the All Blacks eventually won the game 24–12 was testament to the fact that the Wallabies still had a long way to go before they could overcome the New Zealanders, but it was at least judged to be a promising beginning. In hindsight, it was the real beginning of what was to be Dwyer's successful piecing together over the next two years of a player jigsaw puzzle, the formation of a team capable of beating the best the world could throw at them in the World Cup.

At the centre of the puzzle there were only three pieces that were secure in their spot—the 'holy trinity' of Farr-Jones, Campese and Lynagh. The All Black test showed that the newcomers were possible additions, though there remained some testing and reshaping to be done before they would definitely fit. That still left a lot of gaps in the fifteen-piece puzzle.

In the meantime the puzzle master had to ensure his own survival. Dwyer had now clocked up three losses in a row and it was rumoured even then that Alec Evans would be challenging him for the post. The remainder of the Wallaby season entailed two Tests against the Frenchmen in France—a notoriously difficult combination to beat as Dwyer well knew from 1983 when he had taken the Wallabies there. On that occasion he had lost the coaching job in part because the Wallabies had failed to win a Test. What chance deja vu all over again?

The Test against the All Blacks might have given Dwyer a lot of heart, but for Farr-Jones it was yet another loss in what had been a disappointing year, and he again began to wonder if it wouldn't be a good idea to have a break from it all. Not to retire exactly, but at least to forgo the upcoming tour. It wasn't something he announced to the press particularly, but he did mention it to Dwyer and a few others. Maybe, with all the other changes that had been made, it would be a good chance to give his more than capable deputy Peter Slattery a go. Nick had also heard what a long unhappy haul the last French tour had been in 1983 and, finally, there was the law firm to think about too.

Taking time off over the years had been fine in moderation, but it was starting to get ridiculous. If he went on the tour to France his net billable hours for the firm would be . . . let's see . . . multiplying by French francs and dividing by dollars, exactly nil.

Dwyer talked him into it.

It was in a hotel in Toulouse. The day had been spent flying across Canada and the Atlantic to begin the French tour. Most of the Wallabies are 'shot ducks', and retire to bed early. Three of the Wallabies though, Farr-Jones and the two Canberra boys Brad Girvan and Mark McInnes, are having a quiet drink and a game of cards in the hotel bar when they decide to investigate music coming from a nearby ballroom. *Voila!* A full-blown wedding. Almost instantly the groom recognises the Wallaby skipper and immmediately finds a place at his table for the three Australians. On into the wild night they go, battling jet lag, quaffing Bollinger and roaring along on sheer rollicking adrenalin, in roughly equal measure, until 5 a.m. Between the Wallabies and the wedding party there is an almost total lack of linguistic comprehension, but no one really notices.

If Farr-Jones feels any guilt about being the captain, drinking and being up at the wee hours, it doesn't show—either at the time or the following morning when the other Wallabies hear about it.

It is what he and Dwyer would later talk about as the 'off/ on' button that every Wallaby had to have. When it is 'off', as in when there is no important rugby imminent, it is quite okay to enjoy yourself in whichever way pleases you. When it is 'on', everything but everything must be focused on the task at hand. The first button to keep them from becoming humourless automatons, the second to stop them from becoming a bunch of good-time losers.

Farr-Jones again had the button switched to 'off', three nights later after the Wallabies had just beaten Toulouse . . . .

It is two o'clock in the morning and for the last two hours Farr-Jones, Tom Lawton and Peter FitzSimons had been loudly solving all the world's problems in a nearby bar. They now find themselves walking along the cobblestones in a miserably dark and gloomy back alley, looking for a nightclub rumoured to be in those parts. It is all slightly spooky as they stagger, only slightly drunkenly, along.

Suddenly up ahead in the gloom they see three figures approaching. Enemies? Friends? Muggers? In this dark alley, in a foreign country, they close ranks marginally and keep moving forward, muscles slightly tensed, to meet their fate.

'Tom, *mon ami*!' a voice rings out.

It proves to be Pierre Berbizier, the French rugby captain, with two of his friends. They, too, are looking for the same nightclub. Berbizier knows Tom well from their recent World XV tour of South Africa and shakes his hand effusively. FitzSimons' too.

Berbizier's reaction to Farr-Jones is telling. Not only is Nick his opposing captain in the Test match due in a few weeks, but he will also be his most direct adversary of the match, as the Frenchman too plays half-back. After the most perfunctory of all possible handshakes, Berbizier somehow manages to place his body in such a position that Nick is excluded from the emerging circle while he talks nineteen to the dozen to the other two Australians. It is a direct snub and doesn't he know it. In the dim light the expression on Farr-Jones's face is just visible—grim, and deathly calm like: 'Pierre, for this slight, you will be buried.'

True enough. Three weeks later the Wallabies won the First Test with the historic score of 32–15, the biggest defeat on French soil for a French XV since 1908, and the brother band of Wallabies had put paid to all predictions that they weren't up to it. On a personal level Farr-Jones had played so much over Berbizier that the Frenchman was to be dropped for the next Test.

More importantly for the jigsaw puzzle, not only did the Auckland newcomers to the team again perform well, but another piece had been found that fitted so well between two of the existing pieces it was as if the spot were made just for him. Outside-centre Jason Little, at nineteen the youngest member of the team, had in his debut Test match fitted in so well playing outside Horan (his friend since schooldays back in Toowoomba) and inside Campese that the team later that night at Happy Hour extracted a holy oath from the two youngsters to resist the lure of the Rugby League scouts until at least after the '91 World Cup.

On the way to the Second Test in Lille, in the deathly quiet that is always deemed appropriate prior to Test matches, Farr-Jones turned to FitzSimons beside him on the seat and whispered: 'This is it. We win this, we'll become the first team to whitewash the French in a series on French soil. It'll stand with the Grand Slam and the '86 Bledisloe Cup win.'

Despite the Wallabies' leading at halftime by the score of 13–6, they end up losing the game 25–19.

Even then there was something more to fit in the puzzle. Not another piece so much as a pattern. Just as the loss against the Lions would institute a new selection policy with Dwyer, this loss would beget in Farr-Jones a new consciousness of the difference between the right way and the wrong way to go about playing winning Test rugby. It was a theme that would recur often in his coming pre-match speeches . . .

'Fellas, remember Lille! Remember what happened there, how the feeling between us was so good before we went out, how we were so keen to do well and maybe too keen. Too keen on the winning and not keen enough on the *how* to win. Remember how every time we got the ball we tried to score a try, we tried to get the scoreboard turning.

'We pushed passes, we knocked on, we turned over possession, we made mistakes and gave the ball back to France—they didn't play wonderfully that day, we gave it to them. We played badly.

'But all we've gotta do today, fellas, is each of us concentrate on just beating our man, doing our job, to build the try, and the scoreboard will take care of itself. Let's just concentrate on that today—all of us doing our part as perfectly as we can. We've got to *make* it happen, instead of just wanting it to happen.'

If the Lille loss was disappointing though, there was yet another disappointment to come from that tour—one that hit Nick particularly hard.

The first he heard of it was in London on the way home a week later—where he'd stopped off to play with the British Barbarians against the All Blacks—when he and Angie (who had flown over for the Second Test) had gone out to lunch with Angie's brother and girlfriend and were joined by Professor Benness, just arrrived from Sydney.

At the first available opportunity Nick's father-in-law took him aside and said, 'Look, it breaks my heart to do this, but there's something I have to show you. It's better that you know it, and hear it from me first.'

He then produced from inside his coat pocket a newspaper cutting from Sydney's *Sunday Telegraph* which he'd picked up at Singapore airport on the way over.

It was the headline that hit Nick first.

'NICK OFF!
'Australian rugby union players have been critical of the leadership of captain Nick Farr-Jones following the tour of France.
'One test player has said Farr-Jones does not set a good example to his players on or off the field.
'While former coach Alan Jones has called for the sacking of coach Bob Dwyer, past and present players have pointed the finger at the team's on-field leadership.'

The article went on to quote a 'former player' as saying,

'Nick is an inspirational player but not an inspirational captain. There is a subtle difference.'

Even more damaging were some quotes from 'a member of the touring team who played in both tests against France', who said this:

'Nick is still a great player but I don't think captaincy helps his game. He is playing nowhere near his best.

'His on-field leadership is not up to scratch but I think it goes further. He tends to be too informal at functions. It's not a great example for the younger players and not what I'd expect from the Australian captain.'

'Thank you,' Nick said to his father-in-law as he carefully folded and put the cutting in his top pocket, the better to endlessly peruse later. Though he mumbled his way through the rest of the meal, not telling the others the news, still his mind tried to work through who it could possibly be making those allegations. Time and again he went through the list in his head and still came up dry.

Of course, the question he was also obliged to ask himself was, 'Could it be that the criticism is justified?'

The answer he always came up with was the same one that had generally been reached by the Australian rugby community at home—no, it was not justified. Farr-Jones was certainly one of the more relaxed captains on tour that Australia had ever had, but as for setting a bad example to the younger players, this was a palpable nonsense.

On the field during that series he was just as he had always been, a yapping sheepdog behind the forwards, continually rounding them up and sending them in the right direction— 'HANG OFF! GO LEFT! HIT! HIT! THERE'S THE BALL! THERE!! GET HIS HANDS OFF IT! NOW OVER FORWARDS! GET OVER IT!'—and when the ball came back to him sending it special express delivery to the backs, and then he and the forwards would go again, Farr-Jones barking all the way. His own form was good enough that at the end of the tour the French sports daily, *L'Equipe*, was gracious enough to note that the Australian captain was '*sans doute*, the best halfback in the world', a rare enough bouquet to be handed out by them.

Off the field Farr-Jones certainly had the button turned to 'off' a good deal, but in context that was simply part of an environment forming within the Wallabies where high spirits and good times were quite compatible with rousing on-field performances. Dwyer himself was notable on this tour for making a point of enjoying himself and encouraging his players to do the same.

'Whereas Jones on tour had been inevitably totally absorbed with the next tour game or upcoming Test,' Farr-Jones remembers 'analysing videos, working out detailed training skills, determining "who had done the work and who hadn't", Dwyer, though similarly applied before Tests, always made time for sightseeing, eating out at fine restaurants, going to musicals and shows—believing that rugby touring offered unique experiences not to be missed.'

The captain's sentiments exactly. It wasn't every night you could go to a French wedding till 5 a.m. without even knowing the happy couple, or visit French nightclubs after victorious games, and he'd be damned if he'd miss out on any such nights, as long as they weren't directly before a match or three or four nights before a Test match.

As to the allegation that Farr-Jones was 'informal at functions', the answer must be guilty as charged. Therein, however, lay a lot of his charm. His was not the usual glib repetition of well-hewn phrases after a match, with the captain of the visiting side saying, 'thanks, enjoyed it, rugby was the winner on the day, see ya later', but rather he would actually try to *say something*. On that particular tour he would insist on saying it in particularly bad French, but even that charmed his hosts, being the first touring captain in their memory to make the effort.

It *was* very informal and unorthodox to organise the Wallabies, at a given signal, to stand at the final Test dinner in Lille and sing 'La Marseillaise' from prepared song sheets, with the words spelt phonetically for them. Just as it was extremely informal before that dinner began to organise a quick whip-round among the players, raising some 2000 francs for a fund Nick had just heard had been set up for the Down's Syndrome baby daughter of French winger Patrice Lagisquet.

Nor was this generosity of spirit contrived for public occasions. On another occasion on that tour, finding himself in a lost village in the wilds of *la France profonde*, Farr-Jones happened upon a four-year-old *garçon* who, for no reason that he could tell, started to follow him around. The kid was only just old enough to be speaking French, let alone English, so there was no communication between them, but Nick was enchanted anyway. Getting a pair of Wallaby socks from his kit, he tied them securely around the boy's wrist and sent him home. The whole village knew that the great *Fa-jon* was in town and his mother or father no doubt soon worked out where the socks had come from.

Somehow, perhaps partly due to his Christianity, which was still bubbling away, and perhaps partly just maturity, the same guy who'd had such a filthy temper as a child—throwing tomahawks and stumps at his brothers, and tantrums at his team when they lost—had transformed into quite the opposite as a man.

Not that it was all sweetness and light. The unreasonable anger on a short fuse was still there, as the young winger on that tour, Darren Junee, found to his cost once in Toulon, when he made the hideous mistake of leading clubs instead of hearts in a game of five hundred with money riding on it, only to be told that any low-down *stupid* mongrel *dog* knows you always lead *hearts* first off on a no-trumps call. Mostly, though, the beast was under control and if the younger players garnered a bad impression of the captain it wasn't obvious to other senior players on the tour, nor apparently to the youngsters themselves, all of whom immediately leapt to his defence when asked for comment in the press.

Phil Kearns was particularly forthright. 'I can't speak highly enough of his captaincy, either off the field or on the field,' he was quoted in the *Herald* as saying. 'At training, if any complacency or lack of discipline crept into our preparation, Nick would pull us into line and get our mind back on to the job. He, in particular, impressed on us young guys that it wasn't enough just to get into the test team, but we had to win it. I think he is a great captain.'

So where did the barbed criticism come from?

It turned out to be a player who had been extremely upset when he'd heard that Nick, as one of the selectors on the tour, had been in favour of dropping him for another player. Which was true enough—Nick had been in favour—and one of the reasons he soon afterwards stood down from being a selector was so as not to risk engendering any further bad feeling. That and the fact that at the time he stood down, late 1990, there had been whispers that Peter Slattery deserved the halfback spot ahead of him, and Nick wanted no possible conflict of interest.

On his return to Australia after the French tour Nick found that he wasn't the only one who had been under attack. Bob Dwyer had arrived at Sydney airport to discover that Alan Jones had been extremely critical of the Wallabies' performance in

France. 'DWYER'S RECORD ABYSMAL' had been the headline on the back page of the *Daily Telegraph*. The article was riddled with Alan Jones's alleged comments on Radio 2UE. Further quotes were included.

'. . . a tragedy to see the talent of so many squandered by a few.'

'. . . a tragedy to see kids losing when they could so easily be winning.'

'. . . will Mr Dwyer now admit that his second stint as Australian coach has been even worse than his first?'

It was the beginning of what would be yet another bitter campaign for the job of Australian coach, this time with Jones's former assistant coach, Alec Evans, standing for the position.

In reply Nick went into bat for Dwyer, being quoted in the *Herald* thus: 'I don't want to get involved in political grand-standing of who should be coach; it is not the players' responsibility to comment on those sorts of things. But in Dwyer's defence, after some of the criticism slung at him, I thought he did a great job in France.'

So did enough of the ARU delegates voting for the coaching position that Dwyer narrowly survived the challenge and was able to continue putting the jigsaw together.

It was July 1990, and it was the bus driver up at Brisbane airport who told them. One of the French forwards—who'd just played in the three-Test series against Australia at home—had died in Noumea on the way home. In Brisbane to play a one-off Test against the United States before heading over for a full three-Test Bledisloe Cup series against New Zealand, the Wallabies were hit hard. Only two nights before, they'd been with the French for a wildly warm end-of-series soiree at Sydney's Regent Hotel— drinking, singing, cavorting, exchanging blazers—and they all wondered which of the French forwards it could have been and what had happened.

It turned out to be Dominique Bouet, the French prop who'd played in the Third Test, and he had apparently partied so hard in celebration of France's only victory of the series that he ended up asphyxiating on his own vomit. The Wallabies were collectively shocked, and were moved to hear that the French team had refused to leave Noumea until the body of their team-mate was on board in its coffin and the paperwork be damned. They simply would not leave without him.

In response to the tragedy Farr-Jones was at his best, quickly instituting three things. Firstly, despite the ARFU's initial resistance, he insisted that they send a Wallaby representative to the funeral, and suggested Simon Poidevin, who was not involved in the upcoming Test. Secondly, he immediately wrote a letter to the captain of the French team, Serge Blanco, expressing the Wallabies' sadness that they, too, had lost a *'frere en rugby'*. Thirdly, he arranged something for Bouet's widow. Another piece added to the Wallaby puzzle that series was the gargantuan tight-head prop Ewen McKenzie who, following tradition, had swapped jerseys with the Frenchman at the conclusion of the Test. The jersey of the dead man was still at home and unwashed, and Farr-Jones made arrangements for it to be couriered to Bouet's wife immediately.

Barely three minutes into the second game of the Wallabies' New Zealand tour, against Auckland at Eden Park, the All Black centre Bernie McCahill got the ball and prepared to run a crash-ball into the Wallaby backline. In reply Tim Horan crouched and steeled himself to make the tackle, when just to his right a flying black flash launched and exploded just in front of him. Over the next two years Horan would through force of habit get used to that happening, although this first time it gave him quite a turn. It was Willie Ofahengaue doing what Willie did best— tackling an opposition player so hard that other players swore they could hear the teeth rattle.

McCahill has been sent flying backwards, losing the ball in the process. The World Cup campaign had found itself a backrower and another piece fitted into the puzzle.

One piece in, one piece out. The same game also marked the disappearance of FitzSimons from serious contention. Having given away three penalties just in the second half alone, which the All Black five-eighth Grant Fox promptly slotted for nine points, the Wallabies went on to lose by only six points and there was suddenly a big opening in the jigsaw puzzle for a second-rower who didn't give away stupid penalties. After some experimentation that spot would be filled by the young Queenslander John Eales, in the First Test of the following year.

Player in, player out, player in, player out, and so on. Sifting through the pieces looking for the right shape, reshaping others that almost fitted. All of which was fine in theory. But if Dwyer had not been able to get the Wallabies up for a win in the Third Test in Wellington, after the Australians had lost the previous two and been labelled 'The Woeful Wallabies' in headlines back in Australia, it all would have been academic. Dwyer's chances of surviving a challenge by Queensland coach John Connolly really would have been something less than 'abysmal'.

In the same timespan that Dwyer had been with the Wallabies for his second tenure, Connolly had built an even more impressive record with his provincial side, and was ready to launch if Dwyer faltered.

The day before the Test, Farr-Jones, together with Michael Lynagh and FitzSimons, went to a Chinese restaurant in downtown Wellington with two knights—New Zealand businessman Sir Robert Jones, and New Zealand's greatest ever fast-bowler Sir Richard Hadlee.

In the course of the lunch Hadlee recounted how ten years earlier, in a test cricket match against the mighty West Indies in 1980, when their only chance of victory was to bowl the Windies out for a pathetically low score, they had stumbled upon the key to success for that day. They had started to say the word '*win*' to each other between every ball, '*win*' when passing each other at the end of the over, '*win*' when throwing the ball back to the bowler as he walked back to his mark—slowly and shyly at first, then louder and more often as the wickets began to tumble and '*win! win! win!*' as the Windies' tail came to the crease and were picked off one by one for a famous New Zealand victory.

Lynagh and FitzSimons wanted to know what you ordered for dessert in a Chinese restaurant, but Farr-Jones was fascinated by the story and got Hadlee to recount with ever more detail the mechanics of it—who had suggested doing it, who had decided what the word was, how it had got started, and so forth.

Klak-a-klaka-klak-a-klaka-klak-a-klaka-klak-a-klaka.

Ask not for whom the boots toll, they toll for thee. In the dingy and dark Wellington dressing rooms the sounds of the All Blacks' boots clunking past on the bare concrete outside was the final reminder to all that the match would soon begin. Time for Farr-Jones to speak.

'Okay, guys, if I could just have you all over in this corner please . . .'

It worked. Led by a particularly ferocious Sam Scott-Young the Wallabies, for the first time in the series, were *really* knocking the All Blacks over, mouthing '*win!*' to each other, then knocking them over some more and '*win! win! win!*', pounding them in the scrum and '*win!*'. No matter that the All Blacks were then on a four-year winning streak, encompassing twenty-three straight Test victories, and that as usual when they lined up for the *haka* the veins on their neck seemed to throb in unison. It was the day that that generation of Wallabies came of age, playing in a fashion to make the All Blacks doubt for the first time, that they would win the World Cup in a year's time. A 21–9 win to the Wallabies, on New Zealand soil yet, was after all comprehensive.

The accolades for Farr-Jones's own game were many and warm, perhaps the most touching being of all places in the *Otago Times*, which reported that while the Wallabies had many heroes in their triumph, 'the greatest of all was Nick Farr-Jones, their captain'.

'The great captains,' it went on to say, 'the great halfbacks, have vision, and that is what Farr-Jones displayed in the Wellington wind and rain.

'He saw the ground as a chessboard. He made all the right moves and pulled the right strings as he urged (or rather demanded) even more from his men.'

Overall Farr-Jones could also take some of the credit for the greatly improved relations between Australian and New Zealand rugby people as a result of the tour. In contrast to the 1986 tour when relations had become very strained under the 'win-at-all-costs' attitude of Alan Jones, this tour was notable for a far more open and friendly attitude—the team treasurer Anthony Herbert on two occasions having to mildly reprimand the captain for having promised some of the money in the team fund (money raised by the team through the sale of game tickets and T-shirts, etc, to be divvied at the end) to charities in towns that the team passed through. In Taranaki the Wallabies contributed $800 to a fund for a boy with a broken neck, while in New Plymouth they kicked in another $500 for a children's charity. Both times the man making the promise was the captain.

'Nick was just like that,' says Herbert. 'He assumed we were all as generous with our money as he was and I guess, over time, we were . . . though it took a while for his attitude to filter through completely.'

The New Zealanders themselves were not slow to pick up on

the difference and applaud the Wallabies for it, the program for the Bay of Plenty game going so far as to editorialise that, 'The social attitude of the Wallabies has helped erase the sour memories of the 1986 tour by the Australians under Alan Jones, a spitfire who seemed to use a post-match conference as a soap-box and who usually reacted as if he was trying to domesticate Cleopatra's asp.'

A fraction hard on Jones, perhaps, whose manoeuvrings were more designed to keep the Wallabies winning than anything else, but at least indicative of the prevailing attitude.

There was nothing like a win in the last test of the season to send you sailing happily through summer. Whatever else had occurred before, the last Test win always boded well for the coming Test of the following year and made the interim pass all the more happily.

Between Nick's usual end-of-season activities of addressing tens of rugby clubs throughout the land and any number of charity organisations at home, he made time to go down to Adelaide with Angie in early November to take part in a BMW Celebrity Race just prior to the Grand Prix.

The phone again.

'Nick, it's Bob.'

'Hi Bob.'

(Chat, chat, chat, blah, blah, blah.)

'Bob, it's not even eight o'clock in the morning down here. What's on your mind?'

'It's 2 November, Nick. Exactly one year from today we'll be winning the World Cup. I want you to have a drink of champagne today to toast our coming victory.' (All the pieces of the puzzle were in fact getting a call that day.)

'Yes, Bob. Beauty. Bye.'

If Angie and he were glad to be down in Adelaide that day for such an event as the Australian Grand Prix, they were doubly excited on this morning because it was the day they were going to meet the great Sir Donald Bradman and his wife Lady Jessica.

Two months earlier Max Farr-Jones had attended a dinner for Stepping Stone, a Sydney charity for homeless children, and when at the end of the night an auction was held for a bat signed by Sir Donald, Max had highest bid. Thrilled at the acquisition, Max wrote a courtesy letter to Sir Donald to thank him for donating it and received a swift reply where among other things Sir Donald said, 'I've long been an admirer of Nick. He has set excellent standards both for rugby and for sportsmanship— qualities too often lacking in modern society.'

From there, one thing led to another and now they were to have lunch with Sir Donald and his wife Lady Jessica on this very day. And although Angela would have to go to pick them up alone, as Nick unfortunately had to go to driver training in the late morning, he had at least organised the table at Adelaide's finest restaurant, Ayers House. In the process he had informed the management of who was coming, and wondered would it be possible to get a private room so Sir Donald wouldn't be hassled by autograph hunters? The restaurant demurred, insisting that the public would have to make do with the brasserie and that for Sir Donald and his wife the whole dining room would be far more appropriate. Which is what they got, with two waiters exclusively for them.

They came into the restaurant, led by Angela: Sir Donald and Lady Jessica Bradman. She, 'petite and sparkling'; he, Nick says, 'somehow a lot smaller than I had imagined, perhaps because you always imagine that people of his stature are also going to be big in person'.

Oddly enough there was no stilted formality between the couples at all. The fact that Sir Donald and Nick briefly competed to pull Lady Jessica's chair out for her had set the two menfolk off on the right foot with few words spoken, the more so when the younger deferred to the elder.

Surprisingly, for a man living far from the rugby mainstream, Sir Donald knew a great deal about rugby and chatted quite knowledgeably about the ins and outs of recent Wallaby campaigns. A little he picked up from the newspapers, he said, and most of it from ABC television coverage.

Though Nick was conscious that he could not even begin to mention his own career in the same breath as Sir Donald's, there was nevertheless a lot of common ground between them, albeit a half century apart and in different sports.

How it had felt to play their first Tests for Australia, their favourite victories, the hardships of touring, the occasional difficulties of being captain and so forth.

One of the most interesting things Nick gleaned was that at the height of Sir Donald's career he had had to employ a private secretary to handle the three hundred letters *a day* he would often receive while away on tour—and he still often received twenty to thirty letters a day now.

In the meantime the older and the younger woman had been comparing notes on how it was to be mostly left home while their husbands were away on sporting tours. On one occasion, Lady Jessica recounted, Sir Donald had become so ill while away in England that in some momentary confusion with the telegraph a newsagent's billboard had appeared in Adelaide declaring 'BRADMAN ON DEATH BED'.

Though this was certainly overstating it, Bradman was very sick, and it was while very worried about this that Lady Jessica was contacted by Charles Kingsford-Smith, Australia's most famous aviator, who informed her that he was flying to the UK in three days' time in a two-seater, and he'd love to take her with him.' Lady Jessica told Angela that she would have loved to have gone, but after consultation with her husband they decided it might be safer after all if she went over by ship.

Finally lunch was over. In all, the two couples had been together for well over two hours before Nick had to go to practise again for his race and Angie had to take the Bradmans back to their house—the same one they had been living in since 1935.

The beginning of Nick's rugby career, at Newington, had started in the month of May. As he'd grown older and the rugby more serious, by the end of school that date had moved to April; university pre-season had generally begun to get serious in March and for the World Cup in 1987, Alan Jones had got them started in February.

It had to come . . . For the 1991 World Cup Bob Dwyer drew the Wallabies together in a camp in mid-January in Brisbane.

Indicative of how things had changed over the last four years was the schedule of the weekend. While Jones had simply worked them hard, this weekend saw the members of the squad hung down, strung down, poked, prodded, pulled, put through their paces, tested, all by *experts*. Physiological, dietetical, bio-mechanical, psychological. While the employment of 'science' had always been a part of Dwyer's scheme for building a better rugby team, for the occasion of the World Cup he had really let himself go. This first camp was in fact just part of a wider individual work-out program that the players were supposed to have been pursuing on their own since early December.

Over those two days the Wallabies were on the one hand tested to determine just where their physical and psychological strengths and weaknesses lay, and on the other plied with information as to how they could maximise their strengths and minimise their weaknesses.

Some of the Wallabies, such as the young Phillip Kearns, couldn't get enough of such technical information, and eagerly jotted down that the best way to maximise carbohydrate intake in a game was to have five small meals in the day as opposed to three medium ones, and that in weight training it was best to go in six-week cycles as opposed to the previously thought ten.

Others, such as Farr-Jones, who wouldn't have known the difference between a carbohydrate and a block of flats in the first place, listened with only half an ear if that. But, as he says, 'This was something that Bob wanted to do and he was the coach, so I went along with it, no problem. I would say, too, that while I realised that I wasn't going to get a lot out of it, a lot of the younger players did, and I was happy for that.'

Having come this far in his rugby career without the help of science, his reluctance to absorb the meaning of a lot of the new-fangled terms being bandied around, like 'plyometrics', 'carby-loading', 'corrugated iron' and 'marmalade jam', is perhaps understandable. Dwyer, though, was all but beside himself with enthusiasm, the ends of his moustache twitching as he spoke.

'To win the World Cup,' he told them in one of the many meetings of the weekend, 'I don't want twenty-six players who want to win. I want twenty-six players who want to *prepare* to win.'

In a way it was Dwyer's version of Nick's 'Lille scoreboard'. Instead of focusing on the World Cup itself, the players must focus on doing the work meantime that would get them to be the best in the world and then the World Cup would take care of itself.

The players left that weekend with yet more screeds of paper on which their updated individual programs were mapped out, and with strict instructions to follow them to the letter. Nick's program is possibly still under the bed or in the woodshed, he's not sure.

With the break-up of that camp, the World Cup campaign

was officially off and running, but even then there was room for late additions to the jigsaw puzzle.

Marty Roebuck, for example—the man who would turn out to be the crucial last line of defence for the Wallabies during the World Cup—was discovered by the high representative selectors a full four months after that first camp, all but out of the blue. One of those players who had been around for years without ever quite making it—either through injury or a rare bad game at the wrong moment—Roebuck finally served notice that he wanted the World Cup fullback spot at almost the last possible moment.

On the way back from the NSW tour to Argentina in May of that year the team stopped off in Auckland to play against the North Harbour side. The ground was buzzing that day because the 'Bring Back Buck Shelford' campaign was gaining momentum and seemingly the whole nation was tuned in to see how Shelford— the former All Black captain, who had been dropped under controversial circumstances the year before—would perform in his first game back for North Harbour after getting back from overseas.

Sure enough, twenty minutes into the second half Shelford, arguably the most damaging man with the ball in his hands in world rugby gouged the ball from a maul and set off up-field. Three shoulder charges and one palm-off later, he was through. Almost. The only thing that remained between Shelford and the try line was the slender Roebuck.

Wha . . . wha . . . WHAM! In three precise movements Roebuck drove his shoulder deep into Shelford's midriff, straightened his legs to lift him high above the field and then drove him straight down into the turf.

The mud spattered at the point of impact. Around the ground the momentary stunned silence gave way to an excited buzzing.

On the field Marty gazed down upon his still prone and dazed quarry with the truly appalled expression of one who didn't even know the gun was *loaded* let alone pointing in such a dangerous direction, but by then it was too late. The damage was done. The 'Bring Back Buck Shelford' campaign was derailed and Marty—toot! toot!—was slowly shunting his engine onto the track the other way with a 'Roebuck for test Fullback' banner on it.

When Dwyer soon afterwards asked Farr-Jones his opinion of Roebuck, the halfback had no hesitation. He'd been personally spattered by the mud where Shelford had hit the ground and it was obvious for all to see that that had just been the beginning of Roebuck's great form. So, damn right, slot that piece in at the back of the puzzle.

It was all coming together nicely at the right time. The holy trinity was there, along with the seasoned warrior Poidevin, and the young yet now experienced players such as Kearns, Daly, McKenzie, Ofahengaue, Horan and Little, together with players like Roebuck and Bob Egerton, who had also been around for a while and risen to the occasion at the right time. What they all had in common, apart from talent, was that they had all worked this year as never before, in '*preparing to win*', as Dwyer kept endlessly repeating.

The Welsh at Ballymore were the first unfortunates to feel the brunt of the Wallabies' new preparedness. The Wallabies ripped 'em by the unbelievable score of 63–6, which was satisfying, although the score was so stunning that the public suspicion grew that it was less a case of the Wallabies being great than of Wales being truly awful.

The woes of the Welsh were highlighted in the function held after the Test when a scuffle broke out between members of the side over who was to blame for the debacle.

Farr-Jones was not there. Even as the first niggle turned into a shove turned into a punch, he was on a plane back to Sydney to be with his now heavily pregnant wife. The little one was not meant to arrive for at least a few days yet, but as a precaution an extra halfback was flown to the camp in Brisbane with them in case the baby should take it into its head to push ahead early.

The baby was due to be born some time before the English Test the following week, and Farr-Jones made it known that if he had to make a choice between playing the Test match against England and attending the birth of his child, then there would be no choice at all—he would be with Angie.

The days of the Camperdown Travelodge had been left behind and preparations for Sydney Tests were now held an hour away in the peace and quiet of Wollongong. By Wednesday when the Wallabies were due to leave, the baby still had shown no sign of arriving so Farr-Jones left for the south in good faith that he would be called at the first sign of any movement at the station.

On Wednesday evening, at around seven o'clock, when Farr-

Jones was showering for dinner after training, the call came through. Angie was in labour and on her way to hospital. A quick word to the lads in the dining room—'it's happening and I'm outta here'—and he was gone.

By the time he got there at 8.30 p.m., Angela's contractions were about five minutes apart. If only Nick hadn't been too busy to attend the pre-natal classes he might just have known what that meant.

Some seven hours later, at 3.15 a.m., the 4.52 kilogram Jessica Kate (named after Lady Jessica Bradman) was born and the elated Australian captain eventually got to bed at dawn.

Two hours later he was up again, back to the hospital for a day with wife and child, and then eventually back to Wollongong at 7.00 p.m., where his fellow Wallabies awaited him with champagne glasses raised, and the hotel had laid on a cake in Jessica's honour. And so into exhausted sleep.

It had not been the best of preparations for a Test match, but not to worry. Angela and Jessica sat up straight in bed on Saturday and saw the Wallabies flog the English to within an inch of their life, and then two inches. The Australians won the game by the score of 40–15, in what Bob Dwyer has since called 'the best eighty minutes of rugby I have ever seen an Australian team play'.

Thence straight back to the hospital again to see Angie and Jessica. He took with him Willie Ofahengaue, whom Farr-Jones had developed a particular affinity with of late—partly through a natural warmth that Ofahengaue seems to bring out in most people, and partly because Willie O. had an even deeper commitment to Christianity than Farr-Jones himself did, something which Nick admired and wished he could 'more effectively emulate'.

Whatever. The main thing was that mother and baby were doing fine and, for Nick, 'the sight of little three-day-old Jessica being nursed by Willie in his Australian blazer is something I shall always cherish, as corny as that might sound'.

From there it was back to the Test dinner at the Manly Pacific Hotel, and although he arrived late he at least brought a box of cigars for each team, each cigar tied with a pink ribbon.

All up, the win over the English had been an impressive victory, but not half so impressive as the Test against the All Blacks that followed two weeks later, when at the Sydney Football

Stadium the Wallabies smoked the All Blacks by the all but unbelievable score of 21–10. If ever Messrs Dwyer, Templeton and Farr-Jones wanted confirmation that the work and preparation the Wallabies had put in was starting to bear fruit, they had it now.

For the captain, the high point of that particular match came when his Sydney University team-mate Bob Egerton followed through on a Lynagh kick, plucked it out of the All Black winger John Kirwan's hands, and raced some fifty metres to put it down under the sticks.

'It was just so fantastic to see Bobby do that in front of his home crowd against such a player, for such an important try. Then I remember we trotted around the ground after the Test to the cheers of our supporters and when we went into the changing room my little sixteen-day-old Jessica was brought in to meet all her uncles for the first time. It was a big day.'

The biggest of the year for the Wallabies, by far. Beating England and Wales was one thing. But to defeat the All Blacks by such a handsome score was eye-watering.

The true measure of how things had changed, though, came a fortnight later in Auckland. The All Blacks won the game 6–3 and the level of rejoicing among the All Blacks and their supporters at the defeat of the Australians had previously never been witnessed. Cheers, tears, lots of whoop-de-do from the supporters streaming on to the field and from the normally dour All Blacks themselves. In only the recent past they had almost taken it as their God-given right to beat the Wallabies, yet let the record show that in August of 1991 it was regarded as a very, very big deal indeed.

And although it mostly went unsaid at the time, there was almost a feeling of relief among the Wallabies at the loss. Scheduled to play them three times in 1992, there was a strong, unspoken feeling among them that it was always going to be a difficult proposition to beat them three times out of three in a single year. If they had to lose to them one time in a year, then better it be that match than the World Cup.

Farr-Jones's private thoughts were that 'if we do meet the All Blacks in the World Cup, there will be plenty of sting left from this loss to give us a lot of added *ooomph* when we face them'.

However, at the Happy Hour that night at the Auckland Racecourse Dwyer had very stern words with the Wallabies to the effect that it just wasn't good enough. That they lost to the All Blacks was a problem, sure, but it was *the way* they lost that really got Dwyer's goat.

'It is simply not good enough if we are going to win the World Cup and, make no mistake, that's *exactly* what we are going to do,' he said.

CHAPTER ELEVEN

The World Cup

For when the one great scorer comes to mark against
your name,
He marks not whether you won or lost, but how you
play the game.
Grantland Rice, US Sportswriter

In her four months of life Jessica Farr-Jones had never heard a noise quite like it. Sitting on her mother's knee, with her injured father beside her, 50,000 Irishmen were going berserk, cheering, hollering their joy because the Wallabies looked to be right on the point of going down the gurgle-hole of history.

When, with six minutes to go in the quarter-final of the World Cup between Australia and Ireland, the Irish flanker Gordon Hamilton broke through on the left flank to run half the length of the field and score in the corner, it looked as if against all the odds Australia would lose to the valiant Irish team. Ralph Keyes' conversion to Hamilton's try put Ireland ahead 18–15. On home turf. In front of a delirious crowd. For what would be an historic upset if they held on.

The Irish would not be easy to throw from this point on, and most frustrating of all to Nick was that he was entirely powerless to alter the fate of the game. In an earlier pool game against Western Samoa he had injured his knee and recovered only enough to get on the field to injure it again early in this game. Just as it had been in the World Cup four years earlier, he had been knocked out of the quarter-final against Ireland too early in the game to be able to affect its outcome.

So the man most in power to affect the fate of this game now was Nick's replacement as on-field captain—Michael Lynagh—and how very fortunate it was that the Queenslander's own finest hour should coincide so exactly with the time when Australian rugby needed him most.

Leading his players away from the scene of the catastrophe (the spot where Hamilton had put the ball down), Lynagh took the players into a little huddle under the goal posts and gave his instructions in just the sort of concise, clear terms one might expect from the sports psychologist's son that he was.

1 Do not panic.

2 From the kick-off we will kick the ball long and to the left.

3 The forwards must do everything possible to secure clean ball and as a team we must *keep it* and not lose control of it.

4 We'll score and win the game.

It happened just as Lynagh had said it would, only better. After a long back-line movement, David Campese was tackled just short of the line on the right-hand side of the field, and bounced a 'Hail Mary' pass behind him to the left. It was Lynagh himself who regathered the ball and, despite being hit by two Irish tacklers, managed to hold on to the ball long enough to get the ball down over the line just inside the corner flag.

They say you could hear the silence from three kilometres away, in the all but deserted streets of downtown Dublin. So sudden and eery that for moments some of the Wallabies thought they couldn't have scored at all. Usually after a Test try there are screams of either exultation or distress, but this was something else again. All of the Landsdowne Road crowd, which had been so noisily ecstatic only minutes before at the prospect of such an amazing upset victory, was now aghast, refusing to believe that they had somehow lost it, that the World Cup was finished for them.

Only the screaming of the Australian commentators up in the stands as the referee put his arm in the air to signal 'fair try' leavened the momentary silence, together with the excited bubbling of the Australian bench and the genuine sobs of relief of the injured captain, Nick Farr-Jones.

'I was just overcome,' he says. 'We had come so close to losing the whole thing, to blowing all those months and months of preparation . . . and now we had survived in such a fashion as that.'

With only a quick kiss for wife and child, he hobbled quickly down to the dressing room and stood at the door to greet the team as they arrived. Without a word, he embraced every one of them before they entered.

When it came Phillip Kearns's turn to be embraced he remembers being a little surprised at how emotional Nick was.

'And not just him,' he says. 'Everyone in the squad that hadn't been out on the field looked just totally drained and emotional, crying and hugging us, while those of us who'd just come off the field were wondering a little what all the fuss was about. Sure, it had been a tight game, but we always felt we had their measure.'

Sure they did.

'We *did*.'

Nick's recovery program on his troublesome knee began right then, as physiotherapist Greg Craig put ice on his knee and he hobbled onto the bus with the ice pack around it to keep the swelling down and the moisture dripping into his socks. It had been a familiar feeling since he'd injured it ten days before and was to become all the more familiar in the coming week till they played the All Blacks, again in Dublin. On the occasion of his knee first giving way, in the middle of a maul during a previous pool match against the extremely tough Western Samoan side (for what was Nick's fiftieth Test), he had told the press, quasi tongue-in-cheek: 'My first reaction was that I'd broken my leg. But, fortunately, I'm a tough bastard.'

Injured or not, Dublin was still a wonderful place to be at such a time as this, just as it had been back in 1984 when the Irish leg had been the Wallabies' favourite part of the Grand Slam tour. They were all particularly impressed by their knock-about spirit and at how well the Irish coped with their loss.

'It was just *unbelievable*,' says Nick now, 'that despite being so incredibly disappointed with their loss, all the Irish remained so good hearted towards us.'

In his book, *The Winning Way*, Bob Dwyer records with wonder what happened to him in the stands immediately after the final whistle: 'An Irish official came up to me and said, "Congratulations, Bob. You were far the better team." I turned to Bob Templeton a moment later and said, "Did you hear what he said? I couldn't have said that. Even if I thought it,

I wouldn't have been able to get the words out."'

That sort of comment was to prove typical of the Irish good humour, and with the upcoming All Black match there was a distinct feeling among the Wallabies that they would have the Irish behind them.

Absolutely correct. Rightly or wrongly, the perception of the Irish was that while the All Blacks were extremely closed and unforthcoming, keeping the media at arm's length and refusing to sign autographs for the public, the Wallabies were quite the reverse.

Vincent Hogan, who helped cover the World Cup for the *Irish Independent*, recalls how 'amazing it was to us all just how friendly and inviting the Wallabies were during their whole time in Dublin. Some of the people still say they were the best behaved sporting team ever to come through here.'

A similiar opinion was enshrined in an editorial published in the *Irish Times* on the occasion of the Wallabies returning to Dublin on their tour to Ireland a year later.

'The Wallabies are the most welcome of visitors to the Ireland rugby scene,' it said. 'They are a credit to themselves, to the game and to sport, and they have an attitude worthy of emulation that is in sharp contrast to the arrogance of those of lesser achievement in this part of the world and the charmless attitude of their immediate predecessors as world champions.'

A bit hard on the All Blacks, perhaps, but apparently indicative of the warm feelings engendered in the Irish by the Wallabies.

The Wallabies had begun to stand out as a team apart right from the beginning of the tournament. On the night before the first game the World Cup Organising Committee had held a black-tie dinner for all sixteen teams at the grand Royal Lancaster Hotel, together with assorted rugby heavyweights and sponsors, totalling some 1300 people in all.

Paris-based rugby journalist Ian Borthwick who was there that night remembers it well. 'It was a very hot, very closed atmosphere and a lot of the teams had taken their coats off and loosened their ties. Yet the Wallabies to a man kept their navy blazers on and ties done up. They looked disciplined and immaculate.'

The unwritten law of the Wallabies on such formal occasions is that no one is to remove their coat until the captain gives the nod by removing his, deferring to his judgment as to when it is appropriate. Nick decided to keep his on and that was that. Nary a word from anyone in complaint.

Yet mixed with this small act of discipline of keeping their blazers on despite the heat the side also retained a strong sense of fun. The men seated at the official table that night were not to know the full reasons for why the Wallabies seemed to be beaming at them so rapturously when they took their seats. They weren't to know that before the Wallabies had arrived at the dinner each of them had tossed five pounds into a winner-take-all pool and tried to estimate how many 'Alicadoos' (Wallaby short-hand for 'rugby officials') would be on the top table that night. No one had won it—for none of the Wallabies could have guessed that the numbers would go as high as . . . forty-four! A new post-war record.

On the field in those first few pool games, the Wallabies had been victorious but not triumphant. A 32–19 win over Argentina hid the fact that at one point the Wallabies had been leading only 20–16 with twenty minutes to go with the Argentinians pressing them hard. Then there were the Western Samoans . . .

Back in the early 1970s, the World Heavyweight Boxing Champion George Foreman had what other boxers called an 'Anything Punch', in that anything it hit it broke. The Western Samoans, for their part, had Anything Tackles—quite legal, but so hard that in their first three games six opposing players had to leave the field injured because something or other broke.

The Wallabies played them on the muddy amphitheatre of Pontypool, in howling wind, sheets of rain and a cold so bitter it was said the wolves in those parts had been eating the sheep for the wool alone. Nick recalls it as 'the worst conditions I've ever played in'—and the Wallabies only just managed to win. Leading 6–3 with five minutes to go, Michael Lynagh had slotted another penalty goal to give the Wallabies the slightly more respectable margin of 9–3, but it had been a close-run thing. Even allowing for the unexpected quality of the opposition and the hideousness of the playing conditions it was not the form expected from a team with pretensions of being the best in the world and Dwyer let them know that in no uncertain terms.

In the following game Wales had fallen far more easily to the Wallabies by 38–3 at Cardiff Arms Park, but then again, that was only Wales—a once proud rugby nation at a particularly low ebb. In contrast to the wild scenes Nick had known in the dressing room back in 1984 when the Wallabies had beaten Wales at the Park, he remembers this as being 'very calm, very controlled, just another step on the way forward'.

Despite their patchy form in the pool games, though, the bottom line was that the Wallabies had survived them. Now having so narrowly survived disaster against the Irish, many of the players started to feel that destiny must surely be on their side.

'It wasn't like we felt that all we had to do was turn up at the coming matches and we'd win,' says Marty Roebuck. 'But on the other hand it felt like things must really be starting to go our way after a difficult beginning to the Cup. There was still a lot of work to do, but maybe we were getting there.'

Added to their increased confidence was the fact that the coming challenge was one they were very familiar and comfortable with— beating the All Blacks.

For all of the Wallabies, the game against the All Blacks was not only to be a very important semi-final of the World Cup, but also revenge for the 6–3 defeat they'd suffered against them in Auckland two months earlier.

'Personally,' Nick says, 'I couldn't get out of my head how terrible I'd felt when after that game was over Gary Whetton had lifted the Bledisloe Cup above his head and showed it to the roaring crowd. I really felt humiliated, and remember thinking at the time "yer going to pay for this". If one thing gave me focus leading up to that game it was the memory of that.'

Though for the first part of the week Nick was unable to train with the side as he had to continue getting treatment for his knee, he was pleased to hear that 'the boys were really whacking each other'. Particularly pleasing was a report coming back after an additional forwards' training held on Tuesday afternoon at Trinity College (where no less than Oscar Wilde had once studied) that Simon Poidevin had practically clobbered Phil Kearns when they had been practising a lineout drill. Kearns had been acting as an opposition forward, trying to break through the line where Poidevin was standing, and the red-headed breakaway had stopped him a little too effectively for Kearns' liking. Fisticuffs were narrowly avoided . . . and upon hearing about it Nick was delighted.

'It might sound funny to some people,' Nick says now, 'but generally if the forwards are starting to fight among themselves during training then it means that things are going well.'

The forwards' tension at the coming battle was understandable—it was they who had received most of the criticism for the Wallabies' poor form against the Irish. The morning after the game in their team room at Dublin's Westbury Hotel, Bob Dwyer (who could occasionally live up to his semi-affectionate nickname of Barbed Wire) had opened the batting with a long rant against the abominable form of the forwards, and he was joined in his harangue by the two forward coaches, Bob Templeton and Jake Howard.

The basic accusation was that the forwards had lacked urgency, lacked structure, lacked venom—had played like lackeys instead of the best forward pack in captivity. In response the forwards decided they would meet at the beginning of each day to set strategies and goals to achieve at training—with their principal goal being to ensure that they would play the coming game at a furious pace, yet without losing any of their structure. *Urgency* was to be the watchword.

Nick was able to rejoin the team for full training on the Wednesday and was happy to get through it unscathed, his knee appearing to hold up well. When Angie saw him that afternoon—when he went on a brief visit to see her and Jessica at the nearby Burlington Hotel—she remembers 'how relieved he looked, I guess because he knew he really would be able to play the All Blacks'.

Perhaps, too, it was partly relief at simply seeing wife and child, Nick recalling it as 'A wonderful respite from the constant rugby and pressures of it all. To be be able to go and take Angie and Jessica for a walk down by the river helped get my head right.'

It wasn't exactly usual for a player to have his wife so near by on a Wallaby campaign—the old-time dictum being that having wives and girlfriends around diluted team feeling and spirit—but this was no ordinary campaign and Nick had never liked that dictum much anyway. And, besides, with Bob Dwyer's wife Ruth also having come over for the Cup, the coach was in no position to complain even if he wanted to.

For her part, Angie says, 'We wouldn't have missed it for anything. This was obviously going to be one of the biggest things of Nick's rugby career and we [she was accompanied by her mother, Pam] wanted to be there, as much as Nick wanted us there.'

The morning of the game, a Sunday, Nick went with Willie Ofahengaue to meet Angie and Jessica at a church near their hotel. Farr-Jones often prayed on the morning of matches, but this time it was different. Usually he prayed for wisdom in his decisions as captain, for the physical wellbeing of his team as well as the opposition, and for it to be a good game generally. Not this time.

'I prayed for victory as well. It might seem kind of blasphemous to some for me to be praying for something so ultimately trivial as a sporting victory, and I'd only ever once done it before, but I simply felt at the time it was *that* important that we win.'

Willie prayed too, the two Wallabies sitting side by side on the wooden bench as the huge Gothic buttresses towered over them and Irish worshippers all around looked at them, many recognising them as two who would be taking the field against the All Blacks that afternoon. Presently they were joined in the church by Bob Templeton. Ever a restless man on the morning of a Test match, Tempo had spied them walking away together up the street and, suspecting where they were heading, had followed them.

Walking back quietly to the hotel through the streets of Dublin after the service was over, Farr-Jones recalls, 'There was just a kind of feeling among us that we were going to win and an impatience for the match to begin.'

Finally, with the bus driver outside getting anxious that the Wallabies would make it to the ground on time for the semi-final, the Wallaby captain got up to speak.

'. . . and just before we finish, fellas, I'd like to read you part of a letter I got just a couple of days ago from a friend of mine by the name of Matt Laffan . . .'

In fact the twenty-year-old Laffan was already well known to the the NSW-based Wallabies, as the severely physically disabled son of the former New South Wales coach Dick Laffan. Matt had long been a devout follower and supporter of the Wallabies fortunes, without ever having been able to play the game himself, and was a close enough friend of Nick and Angela that they had made him godfather to Jessica. Nick continued reading . . .

'. . . but inspiration also comes to me from what might be regarded as an unlikely source for a wheelchair-bound individual—the Wallabies . . .'

'. . . it is a subtle inspiration which simply instils the spirit with a full sense of purpose so that in the moment of need the strength required to succeed is inexplicably called to the fore.'

The message Farr-Jones was trying to get across—the one he felt most strongly himself—was that whatever difficulties they would face against the All Blacks that day, they were as nothing to the ones that Laffan had already overcome and that what they also had to realise was what a victory against the All Blacks would mean to their supporters at home. In the closed atmosphere of a Wallaby team about to take on the All Blacks, such a message resonated well and they soon afterwards filed onto the bus with a particularly gritty sense of purpose.

This was to be the fortieth Test that Farr-Jones at half-back would be feeding to Lynagh at five-eighth, a world record far surpassing the previous mark of thirty-two held by the Scottish duo of John Rutherford and Roy Laidlaw.

'Our relationship on the paddock has always been excellent,' Nick says. 'I always knew where 'Noddy' would be and it always gave me a feeling of relief when he was there. I know that all I've got to do is get the ball out to him at the right time and he'll run the backline from there. In the past on those rare occasions when he hasn't been there I've felt a much greater burden in the captaincy.'

But this day he was there, praise the Lord and pass the ammunition.

Then there was Campese. Once, after Campese had scored a particularly wondrous try in the Lions series of 1989, Farr-Jones had said in a highly complimentary manner that 'his brain doesn't know what his feet are doing'. Farr-Jones himself generally didn't have much of an idea what Campese's feet were doing, but he at least had developed a finely honed instinct over the years of what they *could* do, and at appropriate moments had always got the ball to him. So much so that of the forty-five Test tries that Campese had scored to that point, Farr-Jones had delivered the final pass or kick to him on no fewer than sixteen occasions— an extraordinary number for two so far apart on the field as the half-back and winger.

Whatever the innate talent of Campese though, Farr-Jones knew it was a talent endlessly expanded by Campese's own assiduous preparation.

Few of the Wallabies had been blessed with his talent, none had worked so hard to develop it. Gymwork, sprints, flexibility exercises, diet, the lot. The result was that in attack at least he was without peer, as his performance in this game would illustrate once again. Oddly enough, for some reason Farr-Jones had a strong presentiment in the dressing room just before walking out to face the All Blacks that today really would be Campese's day. Campo, as usual, was reading the poem about 'Winners' that his mother had given him many years before. Ever since, he had carried it around in his wallet and read it before every Test.

Campese first struck early in the game when, finding that Michael Lynagh was buried under a ruck from which the ball was emerging on the Australian side, he took the totally unorthodox option of coming in from his right wing to Lynagh's five-eighth position on the burst. When the ball emerged, Farr-Jones could hear the familiar 'Yes, Nick!' on his left, and realising what was happening nailed the gold flash with a pass that went straight to him.

The irony of what happened next is best seen in the context of Dwyer's coaching philosophy. The First Commandment since he had taken over the Wallabies had been Thou shalt run straight! The whole pattern of Dwyer's attacking play is thrown out of kilter if ever a player succumbs to the temptation of running at all laterally (in the process allowing inside defensive players to cover outside attacking players) and many is the Wallaby back who has found himself angrily and publicly berated by Dwyer if ever he has done so.

Yet on this occasion Campese did just that, running at almost a forty-five degree angle across the field, right under the guns of the momentarily mesmerised All Black defence. It seemed as if none of them could make out what on earth Campese was up to, perhaps each expecting the other to tackle him, and at the death Campese was able to slice neatly inside the All Black winger John Kirwan for a try that would take Australia to a 4–0 lead. In a way it was only fair that Kirwan should be the one so humiliated because in the past he had many times similarly embarrassed Campese, though never in such a spectacular fashion or on such an important occasion.

Soon afterwards Lynagh slotted a penalty to give Australia a 7–0 lead and thence to The Try . . .

Six minutes before halftime, from the base of a ruck, Farr-Jones passed the ball out to Michael Lynagh, who angled a narrow chip kick just over the head of the mounting All Black defence, and Campese (who else?) burst behind the All Black lines in an effort to retrieve it.

It was a day when he seemed to have the ball entirely at his command. The leather could have gone anywhere, but instead came swinging back right to the winger as a baby monkey might to its mother's arms—*phwoooomp!*. In Farr-Jones's mind, the ball 'had come back into the hands of maybe the only player in the world who could set up a try out of that situation'.

Indeed the try was far from scored at that stage, as the All Blacks moved quickly to block off the threat. Roaring down the right touchline with the centre Tim Horan inside him, Campese first darted left, then right, then left again, and just at the last possible moment when the New Zealand defence had turned themselves so far inside out that they were ready to tackle him again and were about to do so, he hurled an absolutely *impossible* pass over his right shoulder, completely blind, to where he assumed Horan was.

Another *phwwoomp!* Another baby monkey. Horan crossed the line without an All Black hand being laid upon him and scored a try that Lynagh would convert to give the Wallabies an unbelievable 13–0 lead at halftime. Talking about it now Farr-Jones says, 'I've seen that try literally hundreds of times since and it still has the power to raise the hairs on the back of my neck.'

With such a lead all that remained was for the Australians to totally shut down the All Blacks in the second half through vigorous defence, and this they did with alacrity.

One of the many cards Farr-Jones could lay on the table when it came to advancing the Wallaby cause was an ability to see where the next breach in the Australian defensive line might come before it actually happened, and then guide his forwards to get there. In the final forty minutes of the game he kept playing this card until the All Blacks' noses started bleeding.

'GO LEFT! GO RIGHT! HIT! HIT! HIT! HANG OFF LEFT, WILLIE! NOW GET HIM! YOUR MAN, TONY, YOUR MAN! I'VE GOT HIM!'

And so on. Barking at his forwards until they assumed the pattern he wanted, tackling himself when he had to. When the final bell tolled the Wallabies were the victors by 16–6, only the third time the All Blacks had lost a Test match since 1987, and each time it had been at the hands of those dastardly Wallabies. The 6-3 loss in Auckland of two months earlier had been avenged.

The accolades for Campese would be many, although Farr-Jones too was widely feted for his own game—Clem Thomas of the *Observer*, for example, noting that while 'it will always be remembered as Campese's match, one should not disregard the impact on the game of another magnificent player, Nick Farr-Jones. The Australian captain was at his authoritative best, and if the try-scoring was by courtesy of Campese it was Farr-Jones who looked after the nitty-gritty'.

For his part, Farr-Jones handed out his own accolades, and one in particular was indicative of what sort of an outfit the Wallabies were in the northern autumn of 1991.

'This has been Bob's best year as coach by far,' the Australian captain told assembled journalists of the international media. 'There have been a couple of players over the years who have had some negative sentiments about Bob, but everyone in this team has been very positive and been raving about what a great job Bob has been doing.'

'Coaches, like players, go in and out of form, and I think Bob has been in his best form since he took over for his second stint.'

It was yet another measure of the curious relationship between coach and captain that Nick should feel free to speak about Dwyer like that—not in the usual manner of a player congratulating a coach, whereby he has to reach up to do so, but instead straight across, man to man, as it were. During the Jones era the thought that Slack would ever have been so presumptuous as to give his coach a public report card was unthinkable.

That night in Dublin the Wallabies had a big team dinner, to which all family and friends there for the occasion were invited as well as Michael Hawker and Steve Williams, the two distinguished Wallabies of the recent past.

Williams remembers the mood of the Wallabies that night:

'A lot of people had been saying that the game between the Wallabies and the All Blacks was the *real* final of the World Cup and the game against England was just a formality, but none of them had that attitude at all. Nick, particularly, seemed very pensive . . . '

Guilty as charged.

Farr-Jones: 'I remember thinking that night not just how great it was that we'd beaten the All Blacks, but how awful it would be if after all we'd been through we then went on to lose to England. I knew England were going to be bloody difficult to beat, simply because they're always extremely good at Twickenham. Remember, the last time we'd played them there [in 1988] we'd got thumped.'

The following morning there they were again—at the airport. The All Blacks. It was almost as if they were waiting for them. Did these guys never give up? The Wallabies were catching the plane to London and glory while the All Blacks were off to Cardiff for the consolation final against Scotland.

Tough duty, but someone had to do it and, as Nick says, 'I think all of us Wallabies who were survivors from the first World Cup thought of how terrible it had been for us when we had to go and play against Wales in Rotorua at a time when we were still feeling crushed from having lost to France. This time we felt it couldn't have happened to a nicer bunch of guys.'

Farr-Jones's irony notwithstanding, all the aggression of the previous day had disappeared by this stage and the New Zealanders impressed upon them that if they had one wish at this stage it was to see the Wallabies beat England in the final.

'It was heartening in a way to hear the All Blacks say that,' Farr-Jones recalls, 'sort of like if we had the New Zealanders themselves on our side, then we fair dinkum must have a lot of support behind us going into this final.'

They did.

The Wallaby victory over New Zealand had set up a World Cup final that was going to be an intriguing contest, and one which it appeared most of the rugby world wanted the Wallabies to win. For in contrast to the enthralling Wallaby game against the All Blacks on the Sunday, where both sides had pulled out all the stops, England's performance against Scotland had been one so lacking in enterprise, so devoid of boldness that even an Englishman, Martin Johnson, writing in the *Independent*, wrote that the game was 'so awful that it emptied virtually every bar in Dublin'. (From where he happened to be writing.)

For many of the international rugby community the Australians on the other hand were playing rugby as it was *meant* to be played, and while popular support would build behind the Australians with the support even of the Scottish team (who would all wear green and gold scarves to the final), the Welsh, and of course the blessed Irish, the English side were reduced to taking up the cry of the famed English soccer side, Millwall: 'No one likes us, we don't care.'

There was an added dimension to this game too for the Wallabies, in that they would be playing, not just to prove themselves the best in the world, but also to beat England—always a special occasion for any Australian side, and it would be all the sweeter they knew if they could beat England on home turf.

In typical fashion—undiplomatic but basically harmless—David Campese was quoted in the press thus: 'England would never beat us in the World Cup because they are a bunch of Toffs, and we are convicts.'

The country that was watching with the most interest of course was Australia. The reaction in the great south land was phenomenal, rivalling only the reaction back in 1983 when a boat bearing the name of *Australia II* was about to take on a boat called *Liberty* in the America's Cup.

And now, as the Wallabies prepared themselves for the most important game in Australian rugby history, much of Australia settled down to wait for the big moment, many of them passing the time in sending faxes through one of the six machines especially installed in the hotel.

Farr-Jones was to get some idea of how crazily enthusiastic things were getting back in Australia when on the Tuesday morning one of the fax machines spat out a copy of an article appearing on the front page of a newspaper in Melbourne, of all places (not traditional rugby territory), announcing that a baby girl born on the day the Wallabies had beaten the All Blacks had just been named, Harriet Elizabeth Nicola Farr-Jones Davina Campese Wallaby Geddes. Truly.

Farr-Jones (the senior) shook his head in very wonder at such a thing, put the fax in his pocket for later perusal, and got ready to go to the Wallabies' first serious training for the final.

The atmosphere on the bus on the way to that session, on Tuesday morning, was very loose, very relaxed. But who the hell were all those people there waiting for them? Surely that crowd of 100 or so weren't all journalists, were they? Just about every damn one of them. Journalists with photographers, cameramen, soundmen, the lot. A bristling media forest, sprouted right there, just for their training. Attention that had been divided up among sixteen teams and then eight and then four, was now only having to be shared between two teams. And with such a big event as the World Cup final, media interest had moved well beyond just the sporting section of the news.

Farr-Jones: 'It was when we saw all those media people on the sidelines that I suppose we realised that what we'd been involved in, in the five weeks of the World Cup to this point, had just been the *preliminaries*. Now, we had finally arrived at the big one.'

As the Wallabies were warming up and the cameramen began to swarm, it became obvious that the man whom the media cross hairs were really trained upon was Campese, and the only way any of them were going to make the evening television news or the following morning's newspapers was if they warmed up beside Campese. It began as a trickle, turned into a rivulet and then became a gusher, all of the Wallabies eventually swamping Campese, falling all over him and pushing each other out of the way as they all tried to get in the photo.

All harmless fun, and typical of the Wallabies to date, yet in a certain way the levity of it all was a little worrying to Bob Dwyer. The previous evening he had confided in Nick his fear that with the actual World Cup final looming some of the Wallabies might be so overwhelmed by the pressures of it all that they would succumb to the temptation of not concentrating, of kidding around instead of focusing on the task at hand. Apparently some of Dwyer's sporting psychology books had warned of just such a phenomenon as this.

And so after the photographers had finally had their fill and the Wallabies had finally stopped laughing, Dwyer assembled the team away from the media microphones and gave them a brief speech, along the lines of: 'I don't mind you having fun and relaxing, but, remember, you must know how to switch the button from "off" to "on". And now is definitely the time to turn it to "on". Let us have total application, total concentration, let us have a commitment to getting it *absolutely right*.'

To Farr-Jones's mind, 'The message worked and the lads trained the house down. Not a long hard session but a precise and efficient one that got the week's training off on the right foot.'

Not that their commitments to the team ended with the training. For Farr-Jones particularly, as captain, it seemed every waking hour of the day came with its own commitment that he must meet. The pattern had been much the same since the beginning of the Cup.

After training there would be a team lunch, then in the afternoon he would have to juggle international media interviews with continued treatment on his knee (which although it had stood up well through the semi-final was still not quite right). The early evening would usually bring a team meeting to watch a video either of one their own recent past performances or of the upcoming opposition, or if it was the evening before a Test then they would often have a one-hour meeting covering every aspect of the game—how the opposition would likely play it, how the Wallabies wanted to play it, things to particularly concentrate on, moves they would execute, etc.

After that there would be dinner, and then often Farr-Jones would go to have an informal chat in manager John Breen's room, frequently with Dwyer and Templeton there too, to have a quiet glass of red wine and make sure everything was running smoothly. Should we accept this invitation to send a delegation of Wallabies to visit the local blind school? (Yes.) Do we want to accept an invitation to go to this charity's cocktail party? (Yes, but just the reserves and none of the Test players.)

Finally, depending on the current state of his knee, Farr-Jones would often retire to Greg Craig's room to get ever more treatment and on several occasions he had actually fallen asleep in the physio's room with the ice still strapped to his knee and Craig patiently working away in the wee hours, getting more movement into it.

On top of all this there had been the daily visits to see Angie and Jessica and various functions to attend throughout the Cup— some official rugby functions, which he attended in his capacity as captain; others, commercial gatherings, where for the sake of a twenty-minute speech Nick could often return to the Wallabies with as much as 1000 pounds to kick into the team fund, which would later be divvied up by all twenty-six of them. Perhaps word of these talks had got out, because he had begun to get calls from one Harry M. Miller back in Australia, a famous impresario who wanted to sign Farr-Jones up for his speakers' agency as soon as he returned. The phone calls from everywhere seemed constant. There was also his other duty as captain, which was to ensure that everyone within the team was happy and that none of the players had any problems of note that would distract them from the task at hand.

The inevitable result of all these commitments was that Farr-Jones became very run down, and at the conclusion of Wednesday morning's training he suddenly began to feel shaky and weak, and soon afterwards began to throw up.

'I guess it was just because I was so exhausted and though I wasn't really that worried I still had no doubt that what I had to do was cancel everything and go straight to bed for the rest of the afternoon.'

Which he did, sleeping the sleep of the dead. The following morning, to anxious enquiries, he was able to report that he felt fine.

That day at lunch the famous British decathlete Daley Thompson, who had become a good friend of Nick's a couple of years earlier when on a visit to Australia, came to the hotel. He remembers the atmosphere well:

'Basically relaxed but with a kind of hard edge to it. The Australians seemed to have a totally professional approach to this game, basically, "Whatever it takes, we're going to win."'

And Farr-Jones in all that?

'He was the one they all seemed to be looking to, the one that all the other players were conscious of—where he was and what he was saying. And he was very, very focused. Nick's always been a bit surprising to me because he can look so much like an accountant, with his glasses and his haircut . . . like butter wouldn't melt in his mouth on the field and he wouldn't be hard, but I think really he was the most intense of the lot of them.

'I saw in him exactly the way I am before a decathlon—he was talking normally, and maybe having a bit of a joke here and there, but he also had this total *alertness* about him. It's hard to explain but it's like the rest of the world is in slow motion and you're the only one who's got time to analyse every little thing that happens, looking around to make sure that everything is as it should be in order for you to win.'

The call came through to Angie's apartment in downtown London at about 6.30 p.m. on Friday. It was Nick. He had decided he didn't care that it was the night before the final, that it was raining cats and dogs and cows, that the wind was howling, that he was well over an hour away by cab, he wanted to come to see them. So see you in a few hours, he would call the cab as soon as the Wallaby's last meeting was over that night. *(Click.)*

He walked through the door about three hours later, kissed his wife and mother-in-law hello and went straight to the room where Jessica was sleeping, to gaze on her for thirty seconds or so before returning to the lounge room. In the memory of Mrs Benness, he was looking 'as relaxed as ever I'd seen him. Usually before a Test match Nicky was very, very tense, but this evening he seemed almost unnaturally calm.'

The three chatted briefly, then all sat down on the lounge together to pray for a good game, for no injuries, and for victory. Then Nick got up to get his coat and call for the cab.

One more thing, Nick said just before he left. He knew it might be difficult, but he absolutely had to see Angie and Jessica before the game. Just had to. Please make it happen.

Then he was gone. Ten minutes from 'hi' to 'bye'.

The rain still pelting down, the London cabbie silently weaving his way back to the hotel, Nick sat in the back of the cab feeling indeed very relaxed. Tomorrow the Cup.

It was the now familiar sight of Twickenham that beckoned them in the distance as the Australian bus approached England's temple of rugby on that Saturday afternoon of 2 November 1991. Always it was the same thing—you'd see the hulk of it in the distance, catch a glimpse of its actual architectural details as you approached, and then you'd see the people. Hundreds of them, *thousands* of them in the west car park, lunching off the boots of their Jaguars, Daimlers and Rolls Royces, nibbling their chicken drumsticks, sipping their wine and chatting merrily away. It was always so genteel, sometimes the thought would occur to you that as a Test rugby player you were not unlike a Roman gladiator—fired up to fight to the death while all around you the well-bred had paid good money to see you do so.

It was standard form before most Test matches for the coach to work in somehow that this was 'probably one of the most important Tests that Australia had ever played, blah blah blah'. But this time it was different—it clearly *was* most important. Determined now to get off the bus and into the dressing room with as little fuss as possible, so as to keep totally focused, the Wallabies grabbed their bags and set out through the pressing crowd, for once refusing both autographs and eye contact, just wanting to get to the dressing room sanctuary without delay and . . . and . . . and *what the bloody hell is the hold-up?*

Oh. That's all right then. (It was the Queen of England and her entourage, wanting to go through the same gate.) Still, it was difficult standing there mute, in the middle of the crowd, for a full three minutes, still trying to maintain the mood of the bus, despite all the people wanting to talk to them, touch them, and just generally be *close* to the men who were going to be the main entertainment of the afternoon. Finally, though, the passage was cleared and they were able to reach the dressing rooms and thence almost immediately straight out on to the field to have a look at the pitch. It's always like that before a Test— both teams getting out on to the ground as soon as they can after arrival to see what it's like, check the wind, get the feel of the place.

This day the pitch looked good to the Wallabies, very good indeed. What was now known as 'Twickers' in international rugby circles had begun the century as a market garden with the name of Billy Williams Cabbage Patch, and since being purchased in 1907 by the English Rugby Football Union it had traditionally ever after grown a particularly lush carpet of grass. But on this day, of all days, that growth had been shaved to a height of only one-inch—apparently its closest crop ever for a Test match.

Perfect. Perfect, for the expansive fast sort of game that the Wallabies wanted to play, against what they expected would be the usual stodgy English play. God knows what possessed the Twickenham groundsman to cut the grass to suit them so well, but then again God bless him too.

Back inside the dressing room the build up to this game was to be different from most. For starters, because of all the formalities that had to be got through before the game could begin, the presentation of the teams to the Queen and so forth, they would be required to leave the dressing room a full eighteen minutes before kick-off. There was simply no point in getting themselves too pumped up in the dressing room then, because it would simply not be possible to maintain the rage for that long without somebody to knock over in the interim.

And, besides, there was simply little left to say. It had all been said, over and over, and for such an occasion as this it was essential for each man to get himself in the best possible frame of mind in his own way and—

'Nick, Angie's here,' John Breen whispered to him about ten minutes before they were to go out. Somehow she had made it with Jessica through the crowds, the crowds, the crowds and the myriad security. It would later be claimed by the British press, who got wind of it, that this was the first time in Twickers' history that two females had made it into the inner sanctum of the players' enclosure before a Test match. Whatever. A quick kiss for both, the comforting knowledge that they were both there and safe, and then back inside.

—and it was for each man to do that the best way he knew how. Tony Daly liked to walk about, thumping his fist as he looked around him, Willie would silently pray, Jason Little and Tim Horan would generally stick very close together, quietly talking.

As a team, though, there was one brief address by Nick, where he once again implored them to stick to their task no matter what and not be distracted by any of the coming pomp and pageantry.

However, there was one other collective motivational flourish that looms large in the Wallabies' memories. A few hours before the final Bob Templeton had taken Nick aside and asked him whether he thought it would be a good idea to read out a famous poem about the Wallabies penned by Peter Fenton, the same man who had picked Nick to go on that first Sydney tour in 1984.

The captain thought it was an *excellent* idea to read out 'The Running Game', and now with five minutes to go before lift-off he signalled Tempo to do his thing.

Templeton called for their attention, cleared his throat, then began.

There's a spirit in the Wallabies,
Mere words cannot describe.
It's as if they had descended
From some legendary tribe.
There's a kinship, a tradition,
As in days so long since past,
Of crusades, of knights in armour,
And of men before the mast.

There's a thrill you can't appreciate,
A pride you cannot tell,
Lest you wear your nation's jumper

And you wear it really well.
When you mark before the forward rush
So doing turn the tide,
When you make that vital tackle
And your line is open wide.

When you go down on the rolling ball
And dare the tramping feet,
When you lift your aching body
And the opposition meet,
When you burst away from tacklers
And you make the winning run
And you come back heart a'thumping.
And your team-mates say, 'Well done.'

But it isn't just the winning
Nor the scoring nor the cheers,
It's the friendships and the memories,
That last you through the years
It's the camaraderie
That's born of valour, not of fame,
It's the sheer exhilaration
When you play the running game.

The players listened quietly, one or two with tears in their eyes, then filed out. The crowd, the Queen, the anthems—'Gee, that must be funny,' Nick remembers thinking, 'to have everyone singing "God Save the Queen" when you *are* the Queen'—and thence to the game. With the kick-off, they were into it before an audience of 60,000 at the ground and other hundreds of millions around the globe.

After great Test matches it is usually possible to look back upon the landscape of the game and see clearly distinguished the mountains that are the tries; the high foothills made up of near-tries, great tackles, breathtaking passages of play, and before them again the forests of lineouts and scrums that can also be pleasing to the eye. This was not such a match.

In this particular game there was only one modest-sized mountain, very few foothills and fairly stunted-looking forests. In the end the single most outstanding feature of the game's landscape was simply its final result.

Midway through the first half Lynagh scored a penalty goal to take Australia to a 3–0 lead. The Wallabies soon afterwards found themselves in a lineout so close to the English line that they could almost spit on it. For the only time in the tournament Willie Ofahengaue, standing at No. 5 in the lineout, heard the shouted code numbers that meant the ball would be coming to him.

Willie's leap was as perfect as hooker Phil Kearns's throw, and he returned to earth with the ball securely in his possession. The maul immediately formed and moved inexorably forward towards the English line with the Australian captain barking incessantly behind them. In the middle of it all, the two props Ewen McKenzie and Tony Daly had control of the ball more or less jointly, feeling the powerful surge of the other Australian forwards hitting the maul behind them, then breaking away from it as an ambulant beast with two backs and as soon as they were over the line dropping down together for the try.

Though it was not clear to the commentators which of the two had actually grounded the ball first, one of the touching things after the game was that in response to the many media inquiries, neither appeared to particularly care who appeared in the record books. The Wallabies had scored it and that was all that counted. As mealy-mouthed as it might sound, on such team spirit was much of the Australian campaign built. (For posterity though, *T. Daly* is marked in the book as the try scorer.)

Lynagh's conversion took the Wallabies to a 9–0 lead, which they held on to going into halftime.

Soon after the break it almost seemed as if someone had thrown the switch to send the English forwards into high gear, so quickly did they begin to dominate proceedings, and the Wallabies suddenly found they had to move into continuous tackle mode to counter the surfeit of English possession.

A penalty apiece for Michael Lynagh and English goal-kicker Jonathan Webb brought the scores to 12–3 and then with another English penalty goal making it 12–6 it seemed to many as if the match must surely go in to overtime, for the English forwards were now winning so much ball an English try seemed a probability. All the Wallabies could do was tackle themselves red raw and wait for the storm to pass.

Now the tension around the ground was palpable, and perhaps the man who felt it most was Bob Dwyer, up in the stands and dying a thousand deaths every time the Wallabies got the ball and exposed themselves even to the slightest risk.

On one occasion when an isolated David Campese and Michael Lynagh tried to put on a 'move' right in front of the mounting English defence, Dwyer could contain himself no longer and leapt to his feet.

'KICK IT TO THE SHITHOUSE!' he bellowed, with both hands cocked around his mouth so as to send the sound further. A woman dressed in red a few rows away didn't turn to look at Dwyer, but she was the only one. Then again she was the Queen of England, so might very well have judged it politic to pretend she hadn't heard.

Out on the field the battle continued, while back in Australia Alan Jones listened to it all blow by blow on his car radio, as he drove back to Sydney from a speaking engagement in the country, and in the stands the anxious Angie sat with Jessica. Behind her somewhere in the stand her mother was pacing back and forth, praying, refusing to watch, and only coming back every now and then when the roar of the crowd indicated that something had happened. In another part of the stand Nick's parents focused on every move, hardly daring to speak.

With just minutes remaining, with the World Cup beckoning the Wallabies from the sideline, the English centre Jeremy Guscott suddenly brushed off a midfield tackle, broke free and charged away downfield.

Farr-Jones set off in pursuit and in the balance was quite possibly the World Cup. If Guscott had scored on that occasion then the most likely result would have been the match going into overtime. But the way Nick's father would later tell it, which was accurate, 'Nick lined him up, accelerated on to him, and cut him down.'

The whistle blew soon afterwards and it was all over. As Farr-Jones walked up the stairs to get the World Cup from the Queen, the thought running through his mind was that, 'This is just like winning the FA Cup final, going up the stairs to get the Cup from the Queen, except that people weren't throwing scarves all over me like I'd seen them do when I used to watch it back at Peter Baker's house in Lilli Pilli.'

When he actually received the William Webb Ellis Trophy, there was much comment afterwards that almost his first action was to hold it above his head and look underneath it, almost as if to see whether it was 'Made in Taiwan'.

But no.

'That's the way they used to always do it in the FA Cup Finals.'

'The melancholy of all things completed,' Nietzsche called it. It wasn't that there was no tremendous exuberance in the dressing room afterwards, with loud and joyful whoops. There was. Together with all the cheers, back-slapping, bellowing and proud renditions of 'Advance Australia Fair' which filled the room as the World Cup was passed from hand to hand and filled with champagne, with at least as much again going down their jerseys. There was too a cry taken up of 'Phil Kearns, world champion! Tony Daly, world champion! John Eales, world champion!' as they all pointed to the various players one after the other.

But not too far below the surface, in the breast of some players, there was also a sense of *so this is it*?

Few are the players who will admit publicly to feeling a little sadness when they should be experiencing their greatest joy, though at least Bob Dwyer and David Campese have gone on the record as saying that they, for two, felt a surprising flatness after their World Cup victory. Dwyer characterised it as 'a feeling almost of let-down and anti-climax', while Campese admits that he felt 'none of the elation you are supposed to feel on these occasions'.

And Nick was another one.

'You're happy, of course you are, basically. But really mixed up in the middle of it all is maybe the sense that in conventional terms a lot of people would regard this as probably the pinnacle of your life—and now it's fifteen minutes behind you and getting further away all the time.'

The joy would come, of course, but only later. When there had been time to reflect and get among the people who had been so uplifted by the victory

And maybe, too, hindering their delight was the simple fatigue factor. Whether great joy and overwhelming fatigue can co-exist in the same spirit is a moot point but certain is that Farr-Jones had never felt fatigue like this, ever. Physically, emotionally, mentally. It felt a lot like a dream he once had where he was asleep on the train tracks and the train was coming and he semi-woke, but decided he didn't care, he just had to sleep.

After a few quick comments to the press and a few hugs here

and there, it was all he could do to drag his body to the bath, there to quietly soak for half an hour. And it was also perhaps the measure of an extraordinary day that when through the mist of the shower and baths he saw the British prime minister looking over at him, obviously wishing to speak, it didn't strike him as at all odd.

He wishes now he'd thought to drape himself in a towel. Undoubtedly there have been other times in history when someone has spent 15 minutes chatting to a British prime minister while stark naked, but Farr-Jones is surely one of the few, if not the only, to have been standing up at the time.

Funny thing is, it just didn't occur to him once he roused himself out of the bath to drape himself appropriately and the photos look odd to this day. John Major, wiping the glasses that kept getting fogged up with the steam, Farr-Jones, starkers, and happily chatting away regardless.

After all the players had finally showered and changed and sated the voraciousness of the media's appetite to get the definitive answer for the perennial quesion of 'How does it feel?', the Wallabies finally got back onto the bus that would take them back to their hotel. With them on the packed bus were not only all the friends and family that would fit, but also 'Bill', as they had christened the William Webb Ellis trophy. Nick and Angie sat up the front, with Jessica on their knees, discussing the best way to stop Jessica crying as the bus full of Australians moved south through the dark streets of London.

That night, at the World Cup Victory Dinner back at the Royal Lancaster in the centre of London, Michael Lynagh got a rather unpleasant surprise presaged by a tap on his shoulder. It was Nick.

'Mate, I'm crook,' he said. 'I'm going to go back to the hotel, so you'll have to make the speech for me.'

'Hang on, Nick, you can't . . .'

But he was gone.

'I don't know quite what it was,' Farr-Jones says now, 'if it was exhaustion, or a bug, or whatever, but I was feeling faint and nauseous, and I just knew I wanted to get out of there and back to Angie and Jessica at the hotel.'

In the aftermath of the Australian victory there seemed no limit to the accolades that came Farr-Jones's way, even from the unlikely source of New Zealand where, writing in the New Zealand *Herald*, respected rugby writer Don Cameron sounded not only the familiar theme that Farr-Jones is 'the best halfback in world rugby' but also that 'the Wallabies are the best organised, most talented and enterprising international side in rugby at the moment.

'They brought charm, class and natural humour to the 1991 World Cup. They were not unsmiling giants, nor noisome braggarts.'

For his part, the famed former All Black captain Wayne Shelford who, writing in London's the *Independent on Sunday*, stated that not only was Farr-Jones's tackling 'out of this world', but that 'it was Farr-Jones who kept things together when the Wallabies were under the greatest pressure from England in the second half'.

The English magazine *Rugby News*: 'The Wallabies' triumph proves conclusively that nice guys can win. The courtesy and manners shown by men like Bob Dwyer and his captain Nick Farr-Jones were exemplary.

'These two and their colleagues were the finest ambassadors for their country. Their rugby matched them, the game and its much cherished reputation was in excellent hands.'

The respected French rugby newspaper *Midi Olimpique* named six Australians in its World Rugby Top Ten. David Campese was voted number one and Nick Farr-Jones number two. And so on.

So big did the World Cup loom in the lives of those who had participated in the Australian victory that their conversation for a long time afterwards would be peppered with three basic timeframes: 'before the World Cup', 'after the World Cup' and, most particularly, '*during* the World Cup'.

It was only after the World Cup, though, that the Wallabies truly realised how cherished their victory had been at home. Their arrival at Sydney airport was met by an enormous crowd, and played on all the television news services that night. Everyone seemed to be talking about it, complete strangers stopped them in the street to shake their hand; many of the schools from which they'd sprung invited them back to address full-school assemblies.

From just being famous in rugby circles, the success of the World Cup had moved all of them closer to mainstream fame, some more than others.

If there were two players who reaped individually the better part of the collective Wallaby glory, it was Campese and Farr-

Jones. While Campese had been the star player of the Cup, Farr-Jones had been the captain of the winning side, a superlative player in his own right, and the man who had first lifted the cup to show Australia and the world.

And here was the rub—in Campese's absence because of commitments to his rugby club overseas, it invariably meant that whenever the media and the public's attention was focused on an individual player, that player tended to be the man who had informally become known in the tabloids as 'Captain Courageous', Farr-Jones.

Two days after returning from the Cup, the faxes and letters he had received containing offers, commercial and otherwise, stood a couple of centimetres thick on his lounge room coffee table. Would he like to speak to this Rotary Club? Could he find the time to attend this charity function? That speech day? Had he ever thought he might like to do a spot, advertising this particular product?

Exactly one week after the final, Farr-Jones was elected, as the youngest member ever and with the most votes of any of the thirty-two competing candidates, to the board of the National Roads and Motorists' Association, a prestigious and extremely wealthy motorists' organisation.

Soon afterwards he was working in his office in a brief break between media interviews, when the phone rang. It was a state Liberal Party official, wanting to know if the Australian rugby captain was interested in standing for preselection in the blue ribbon Liberal Party seat that had previously been held by New South Wales Environment Minister Tim Moore . . .

Farr-Jones listened for two minutes in mute amazement that he should be approached to enter the political field because of his success on the football field, and then interrupted.

'I basically thanked them very much for their kind offer but told them I could think of about thirteen reasons why I couldn't possibly accept, and after that I terminated the conversation very quickly.'

In fact, the '13 reasons' Farr-Jones claims, boil down to 'just one really . . . I had no real interest in going into politics at that time.'

Things were crazy there for a while, and in many ways haven't really calmed down since. In short order Farr-Jones signed a contract with a TV station to do occasional commentary work, had agreed to do a column for the *Sydney Morning Herald*, had accepted some thirty invitations to speak at functions over the following two months and was invited to dine with both the Queen and Prince Philip on their forthcoming Australian tour. For the team there was a tickertape parade, right through the heart of the city, and though the Wallabies initially wondered whether anybody but a few of their friends and family would turn out, in fact the city had never seen anything like it.

In the first car of the parade Nick was seated beside Michael Lynagh as they held aloft 'Bill' for everyone to see and both were practically buried under all the papers falling from the skies. At the conclusion of the procession Nick was personally presented with the Key to the City by the Lord Mayor of Sydney as the first of many honours that would be bestowed upon both he and the Wallabies.

CHAPTER TWELVE

South Africa: 'One Million . . . If You Count the Blacks'

*'Now is the time to show what mettle is in you—and
there shall be a warm seat near the hall fire, and honour
and lots of bottled beer tonight for him who does his duty
in the next half hour. This is worth living for—a half
hour worth a year of common life.'*
Thomas Hughes, *Tom Brown's Schooldays*

There is an old saying in the Wallabies that a Wallaby tour is a lot like sex. When it's good it's FANTASTIC, and when it's bad . . . yeah, well, it's *still* pretty good.

The 1992 tour to South Africa was of the latter variety.

As a high pressure two-week sojourn into a troubled land forcibly isolated from the rugby world for much of the previous two decades, there was to be little free time for simply gambolling about to get to know the place informally, little time for anything much but for playing, training, travelling, attending functions and feeding the ravenous South African media. All the while mentally preparing for what they knew to be the most important game of the year.

Out of a clear blue sky on a Sunday morning of mid-August then, the African continent suddenly stretched below them, the first such sighting by a Wallaby team for two generations. On the long flight from Sydney the mood on the plane had been as openly Boys' Own Revelry as usual, though tinged with an unspoken tension. Not only were they flying into a tense political situation, but also the lair of notoriously hard opponents. Some of the props were so 'built', it was said, that on those rare occasions when they smiled they did so using the muscles at the back of their necks.

At least, for the holders of the William Webb Ellis Trophy, as they came out of the Customs Hall at Jan Smuts Airport it was an initially familiar sight—the usual solid wall of people, television lights, and thrust microphones before them. But they soon realised the differences. For starters, there were so many people—including all twenty-three members of the South African Rugby Board, in their blazers, come especially to welcome them, and another thousand or so South African rugby supporters— so many lights and microphones, with every media organisation in the country represented, and such a different atmosphere. In the air was a mixture of welcome . . . and warning. Along the lines of 'fantastic to have you Wallabies here to end our isolation for the last two decades . . . *but you don't think you're really world champions till you beat us do you?'*

It was a refrain they would become forcibly used to over the following two weeks.

Somehow, from the opening hours of the tour, things were not quite what the Wallabies expected. It was cold, shivering cold. You didn't expect that of Africa, just as you didn't expect everything to be so dry, brown and lifeless—countryside in the middle of a great drought.

From the bus on the way from Jan Smuts into Pretoria they also saw the huge headquarters of the South African Army built into a hill five kilometres south of the capital—and if they'd expected to note some military presence while in such a country as South Africa, the enormous dimensions of the base sobered them all the same.

Then there was Pretoria proper. That part of the Afrikaaner character which is serious, conservative, button downed and rigid backed all comes together in the capital on a Sunday morning. To the Wallabies, as they first ventured out from their base at the downtown Burgespark Hotel, the city seemed all but shut down. Traffic on the streets a bare minimum, pedestrians on the main thoroughfare only very sparse.

After all the hoopla of their departure from Australia and arrival at the airport, it was all a bit of a let-down—the feeling of the morning after an enormous New Year's Eve party . . .

'How many people live in Pretoria?' Farr-Jones asked one of

the South African officials accompanying them to training that first afternoon.

'Oh, about 300,000.'

'Only 300,000? Gee, it looks a lot bigger city than that somehow.'

'Well, it's a million . . . if you count the blacks.'

'Well, why *wouldn't* you count the blacks?'

Was the grunt in reply a 'slightly embarrassed' one or the grunt of someone who knew the political reality exactly but couldn't be bothered explaining it to a no doubt liberal out-of-towner?

Farr-Jones wasn't sure and let it pass, but it was a small part of what would be his continuing education in the ways of South Africa over the next two weeks. And in fact, to this point, no one acquainted with his public utterances in Australia would have said he *was* particularly 'liberal' on the subject of South Africa.

His general view on sporting sanctions had been that they were unfair to sportspeople and he always put that case forcefully when asked by journalists and sometimes when he wasn't. He had also visited the Republic on two occasions in recent years as a guest of the South African Rugby Union and enjoyed himself immensely, becoming even more of a pro-sporting-contact believer as he was feted with overwhelming hospitality. But now that he was there as captain of a team that the South Africans desperately wanted to beat, he was starting to see things in a different light.

Like the time when, coming back from one of the Wallabies' early training sessions in Pretoria, he happened to be idly looking out the bus window when he spied a newsagent's billboard, blaring 'ALL OF SOUTH AFRICA ARROGANT—AUSSIE CAPTAIN!'

The story was on the front page:

'That's what Wallaby captain Nick Farr-Jones along with his team-mate David Campese has accused South Africans of. But whereas the outspoken Campese's statement is limited to the rugby field, Farr-Jones reckons all South Africans are arrogant—that is what he told the *Sydney Morning Herald* . . . '

Well, he never.

Farr-Jones had merely mentioned in passing in a speech to the National Press Club in Canberra the month before that in his opinion, when it came to rugby and cricket, the South Africans were in fact arrogant, automatically believing themselves to be the best even though they hadn't had a chance to test themselves yet—a not unreasonable viewpoint.

It was after all a leading South African rugby administrator who, profoundly unimpressed by the quality of play he saw in the World Cup, was quoted in the *International Rugby Review* soon afterwards as saying, 'I can now reveal the Springboks' schedule for 1992. We'll take England at 12.30 p.m., the All Blacks at 2 p.m. and Australia at 3.30 p.m. Just to make it interesting we'll give them all twenty points.'

If that wasn't arrogance what was?

Still, it stood as one of the few, if not the only time, in Farr-Jones's career that he stood accused of anything other than total diplomacy in the countries he visited, and while Campese might have been used to making such impolitic waves wherever he went (seeming to thrive on it, in fact), Nick was not and was both hurt and angered at the *Pretoria News* for making a big story out of what in his eyes had been no more than a passing reference to a known truth.

Part of this slightly more wary attitude can be seen in the speech he made to the team just before the Wallabies played their first game at Pochefstroom, two hours south of Pretoria on the Tuesday after arriving. On the way there the bus had charged down the highway at 150km per hour under police escort—partly because of security and partly because they were late—and from the bus the players could see for the first time the famous black township of Soweto flash past on their right. It was only the briefest vision, but again it was a reminder of the sort of place they were in and contributed to the feeling they all shared of being in a really *different* sort of country. The joke circulating among the team at the time was that 'the South Africans like to watch 'Roots' backwards so they can always have a happy ending'.

It is traditional in the Wallabies that just before the team alights from the bus at the stadium, one of the 'dirties', or non-playing members of the side, gets up to make a brief speech. At Pochefstroom that person was Phil Kearns, and he spoke briefly . . . He knew they would do their best, and he wanted them to know that they went out on to the field with the best wishes of the entire touring party, etc . . . A smattering of applause (the atmosphere at such times is always restrained and loud applause would be inappropriate), and the players made the first moves to get off the bus.

But the captain had something he wanted to say and waved them back to their seats, as the enthusiastic supporters outside kept tapping on the bus, waiting for them to emerge. Farr-Jones's words came to them over the clatter.

'Guys, if I can have your attention for a moment, just a few quick words. Today is something like, as a team, we've never experienced before. Fellas, this is all different for us; it's all new and it's so important that in the next hour we remain really focused on what we're doing today . . . on how to do your job as well as you possibly can. This is a place we've never come to, a people we've never played, and the stands are filled with people we know nothing of but who badly want to see us go down. The only way forward for us is to keep together and keep doing what we have been doing without distraction. Good luck.'

No applause this time, it had been more of a warning than an encouragement, and the players filed silently off the bus.

'I mean it was all just so *eerie*,' Farr-Jones recalls now. 'I kept thinking of that movie *Deliverance*—these were a strange people who we had no experience of. It seemed that South Africa was in a bit of a time warp—it was like we were back in the '70s—and these people from the past were just out to get us.'

The inside of Olen Stadium, where the game was to be played, exacerbated that feeling. The field was hard, yellow and dusty, prompting one Wallaby, Tony Daly, to describe it as 'looking like that part of the paddock where the shearer lets his sheep go down the shute after he's shorn them'.

Simply, the Wallabies had never seen a field like it ever—nor for that matter had they ever heard such catcalls from the passing crowd as when they were warming up on a side paddock before the game. In thick Afrikaaner accents, yet: 'We're going to get you!' 'Wait till the Boks get a hold of you lot, you won't be so smart then!' 'Remember now, don't get on the bottom of any rucks, boys!'

Some of them were even wearing a T-shirt that was selling out all over South Africa at the time which showed a leaping Springbok engaged in coitus with a bedraggled Wallaby, above the words: 'You can't say you are world champions until you beat the Boks.'

It was all as motivational a diatribe as they could ever hope to hear and a thumping 46–13 win to the Wallabies was the result, even though they felt they had to overcome a certain hometown parochialism of the referee. His name, as they delighted in, was Mr Frik Burger. They were a strange bunch these South Africans all right . . .

It was odd for the Wallabies to be in a country where it seemed the entire population was focusing on a coming Test match in which they themselves were not involved. A little 'like being in Switzerland during a world war', as someone said at the time, and yet that was their curious position.

The Australians had been preceded by a week into South Africa by the same All Black side they'd just beaten back in Australia 2–1 in a three-Test series to reclaim the Bledisloe Cup. The Springboks were due to play the All Blacks a week before the Australians, and as the day got nearer the Wallabies got an ever clearer impression of just how seriously the South Africans took their rugby.

Nothing else that happened on the planet seemed to matter that week; for the South Africans there was only one conversation point—what was the likely result of the Test?

Some of the New Zealanders in South Africa were no better— most particularly the All Black supporters' group staying in the same hotel as the Wallabies, who seemed to spend a large amount of their time drinking in the bar, loudly wondering how the Australians could have been so *lucky* as to beat the All Blacks, and by just what sort of an amazing score their lads would beat the Springboks on Saturday.

Lucky? *Lucky?* When the Kiwis got out of hand in this way the Australians found at least one sure way to shut them up. Typical of the 'quaintness' of the Burgespark, the hotel had a paging system which featured an eighteen-year-old black South African, dressed in all the finery of a maitre d, regularly walking through the bar, ringing a bell and holding up a blackboard with a name on it. And what a splendid fellow he was.

In on the joke after a quick briefing from Farr-Jones and Tony Daly, the lad headed off into the middle of the All Black supporters, tinkling his bell and waving his blackboard, asking if they knew where 'Lord Bledisloe' was, or perhaps 'Mr William Webb Ellis'?

'They're over here!' the Wallabies then yelled. 'We've got them both!'

Fun? *Fun?* Boy, did they have fun.

Only three days before the All Black/Springbok test one extraordinary meeting took place.

In the presence of F.W. de Klerk, the South African president, the Black African leader, Chief Mangosuthu Buthelezi, and one of the heavyweight leaders of the African National Congress, Steve Tshwete, the Springboks, Wallabies and All Blacks met in the one room. The fact that that room was half a kilometre underground, at the bottom of a disused gold shaft, just added to the richness of the atmosphere, as did the barbecue in a place without proper ventilation . . . as did the numerous scantily clad young women serving drinks, who every now and then when the music started would throw their legs in the air for a quick can-can before resuming. All up there was *definitely* an odd feeling in the air.

To have de Klerk, Buthelezi and Tshwete in the same room at the same time for what was essentially a social occasion, was extraordinary enough in the context of South African politics, but if the room and the crowd was big enough that those three could essentially keep away from each other in the course of the evening, there was no escaping the Boks from the Blacks from the Wallabies.

For all rugby's renowned camaraderie after the game, in the time immediately before Test matches it is standard practice to stay away from your opposite number so as not to allow any troublesome humane feelings to grow. The All Blacks and Springboks, then, did not want to talk, as they were to be engaged in mortal battle in three days' time, which left only the Wallabies as kosher to talk to.

Through the smoke and the music and the regular intervals of the can-can girls with their legs in the air, Farr-Jones soon found himself in a smoky corner with President de Klerk.

'Well, we say welcome to you to South Africa', President de Klerk says to Farr-Jones, as the cameras rolled upon them to record the occasion. 'You bear the crown of being world champs . . . '

'. . . but you want to dethrone us very quickly,' Farr-Jones breaks in, laughing.

'Perhaps, but I have some inkling of what it is to bear a crown,' the President replies, just a fraction woodenly, 'and it's a heavy load to bear.'

If Farr-Jones was impressed to be engaged in such easy

conversation with the head of state of such a pivotal power in the world as South Africa it did not show.

When, at one point their tête-à-tête became a tête-à-cinq-têtes, as they were joined by three others, Farr-Jones happened to notice that de Klerk was pulling out a cigarette, and hesitated not a moment.

'Excuse me do you mind if I have a ciggy?'

'Not at all,' the president replied, gave him one and lit it for him.

The journalist from the *Johannesburg Sunday Times* Edward Griffiths, whom Farr-Jones had just been speaking to, looked at him in amazement.

'Do you realise what you just *did*?'

'No, what?'

'You asked the president of the Republic for a *ciggy*.'

Indeed he had.

'I just couldn't believe it,' Griffiths says now. 'As a non-South African, I wouldn't expect Farr-Jones to be quite so overtly respectful as we are, but it seemed extraordinary nevertheless how casual he was to the president and how much the president seemed to enjoy that casualness. I warrant that the number of times he has been asked for a cigarette like that since he's been president would be . . . well, that would be the only time.'

This familiarity was also evident in the official speeches. While on the microphone Farr-Jones happened to notice that de Klerk was already wearing the All Black tie he'd just been presented with, and promptly handed over an Australian replacement with the words 'We want that silver fern tie off right now and here's one of ours' to the amusement of all, including the South African president.

While Farr-Jones was getting to know de Klerk throughout the evening, the rest of the Wallabies were acquainting themselves with some of the other leaders. The man they were most impressed with was Chief Buthelezi, whom they'd only previously heard about through newspaper reports about South Africa's troubles. But now here he was, out in a back room with some of the boys, grooving to the music as those can-can girls put on a bit of a dancing show.

All up it was an amazing evening, and perhaps the most memorable of the tour. Coming out of the goldmine, the Wallabies couldn't help but notice President de Klerk's enormous 'car' parked near the entrance of the mine and guarded by a man with blond spiky hair, a grimace and a suspiciously bulky trenchcoat.

Later, back in the bus, Tony Daly and Ewen McKenzie, who had preceded the others out of the mine by some ten minutes, were able to fill the others in a little about both man and car. The man was one of the president's bodyguards, who also acted as his driver, and in the course of making idle conversation with him they chanced their arm in asking what he had under his coat.

Amazingly, no problem. He unbuttoned it for them to see. A compact little machine-gun on one side of the coat and a hand grenade in a pouch on the other. And that was just what was *visible*, there being still other unexplained lumps here and there.

Then he showed them the car. All eight metres of it. Daly swears to this day that the glass on the windows was 'six centimetres thick', capable of withstanding even a mortar attack. The rubber on the tyres was similiarly thickened to withstand bullets, there was another machine-gun on both doors and when the bodyguard opened the boot for them there was a bazooka right where the spare tyre should have been. Not only that, the whole thing was able to go at 280 kilometres an hour at top speed and in the opinion of Daly, 'It wasn't so much a car as a high-class tank.'

Though no one said out loud what a good thing they came from a country where the chief politician didn't have to be so protected from the population, the thought crossed a few minds, Farr-Jones's among them.

The morning after the game it is not unusual for a rugby player to feel as if he has spent the night sleeping on the camel track that Ali Baba and the Forty Thieves used to make their get-away on. Sore, very sore.

In this instance, though, the damage to Farr-Jones had been done by the Blue Bulls of the Northern Transvaal team. A very physical side, their forwards had been on average six kilograms heavier than the Wallaby forwards, and when they hit, they hit hard and heavy.

The Wallabies had eventually won 24–17, but in some respects they had been lucky to triumph. By awarding no less than twenty-five penalites against them, the referee had bought to mind another favourite Wallaby saying, vulgar as it is, that 'the five most useless things in the world are the Pope's balls and three cheers for the ref', and but for Northern Transvaal missing 8 penalty goals, the Wallabies might well have tumbled to a humiliating defeat. Not that Farr-Jones was thinking particularly about that now.

Instead, as he raced in a car from Pretoria to Johannesburg, he was thinking about meeting *the man* ... Nelson Mandela himself. The phone call had come through the previous night, saying that a small contingent of the Wallabies was invited to meet Mr Mandela at ANC headquarters in Johannesburg.

After a wake-up call at 6 a.m. Farr-Jones, together with Wallaby fullback Marty Roebuck and other Australian team officials, headed by ARU president Joe French and including Bob Dwyer, were on their way to meet him.

As usual in South Africa, the ANC building was not quite what they were expecting. Rather than the expected solid concrete building fitted throughout with your basic bunker decor, it was really just a nondescript, standard-brand office building on a standard-brand Johannesburg Street. The only difference being that ANC posters seemed to cover every available inch of wall space.

Ushered to the boardroom on the seventeenth level, they didn't have to wait long before a rustling at the door signalled Mandela's arrival. The ever-present press and film crews sprang into action.

Suddenly there he was—looking good for a man who had spent no fewer than twenty-seven years in assorted South African jails, but still a tad older and frailer than Farr-Jones had expected.

'Somehow you always imagine people like that to be almost invincible. They won't age; they won't die; they'll always keep going. But my first impression was "he's aged", even though of course I'd never met him before.'

Still, there was a twinkle in Mandela's eye as he stepped forward and gripped the hand of Joe French and said, 'Ah, Mr French ... I've heard many things about you. But I have concentrated only on the good things.'

There was a momentary pause as the whole room tried to determine whether the great man was making a small joke or delivering the mildest of all mild rebukes, until Mandela laughed ... and they all laughed, partly in relief that it was the former.

The man definitely had presence and, after shaking hands with Farr-Jones and the other members of the Australian contingent, Mandela sat down next to the Australian captain for the press conference proper.

One of the first questions from the floor was, 'What's it like to have the Wallabies in the country?' and in the ever-so-slightly embarrassed silence that followed, Farr-Jones for a moment had the impression that Mandela might not have been sure who the Wallabies were and jumped in, jokingly, with, 'That's us, Mr Mandela!'

'I mean, you could well imagine,' Farr-Jones says now, 'that with his background he might not have known much at all about rugby, and his days must have been filled with a lot more important things than our visit.'

Things went better, though, when Farr-Jones changed the subject to one that he had heard was a Mandela favourite—Sir Donald Bradman.

Sure enough, Mandela immediately warmed to the topic and recounted how in the 'old South Africa' such Australian cricketers as Sir Donald Bradman and Neil Harvey had been favourites of the black population because they could always be counted on to humiliate the hated South African white man on the sporting field, and the more they were humiliated the more Mandela and his friends had loved them.

However, now, in the 'new South Africa' everything had changed, and he was once again supporting the white South African team, and he was sure the Wallabies would find that all the country's Blacks would now be supporting the Springboks against them.

But perhaps most importantly, he also publicly endorsed the Wallabies' trip to South Africa, saying that 'sport is one of the most important weapons that we have . . . not because we want to use sport for political purposes, but because it can bring together people of various ethnic groups of various political persuasion. It is the one language which we can speak and which has the hearts of everyone throughout the country.'

As the press conference ended Farr-Jones, clearly by now enchanted in the presence of the ANC leader, at least had the presence of mind to halt proceedings momentarily to say, 'Mr Mandela, may I present you on behalf of our team a Wallaby cap and one of our big ties.'

As footage of the press conference shows, no sooner has Mandela received the cap and finished shaking the Australian captain's hand than he put the odd little Wallaby cap on his head and turns back to face the cameras. A comical sight to say the least.

And the room is already politely laughing as Mandela breaks into a broad grin beneath the cap, grips Nick's hand once more and says, 'Thank you . . . and I'm behind the best team.'

Farr-Jones pauses for a minute, while he realises who Mr Mandela means, then laughs uproariously.

'So are we, Mr Mandela, so are we!'

Only hours after this historic meeting with Nelson Mandela occurred an incident that went very close to derailing the entire Wallaby tour. From the moment the Wallabies arrived at Ellis Park in Johannesburg for the Test match between the Springboks and the All Blacks; it was obvious something was very odd indeed.

And it wasn't just that the only black faces in this much vaunted 'new South Africa' belonged to the waiters who were serving the whites drinks.

It was the continuing hostile roar, even before the game had begun, from the 80,000 spectators who packed Ellis Park, Johannesburg. Countless times before kick-off some of these spectators would jump the fence and run on to the pitch, aggressively waving South African flags. The South African police gave an early exhibition of crash-tackling to bring them to the ground, but for every one brought down there seemed another two to take their place as the crowd yelled even greater encouragement.

The famed South African-born author Bryce Courtenay, now an Australian citizen, recently wrote in the Australian magazine *Inside Sport* that 'To the Afrikaaner . . . [of which the Ellis Park audience was substantially made up] rugby is not a game. It is commitment, a chosen battlefield, a gesture of collective self-assertion against a hostile and unsympathetic world. It is a rally and call to arms. It is the initiation into manhood. It is a sacred covenant.'

Well, the Wallabies knew that day even before kick-off, it was certainly *something* that was not quite cricket. Up in the corporate BMW Box, where Nick was sitting with David Campese and Bob Dwyer, there was little speaking as they simply looked around them in amazement.

But to the coup de grâce.

The two teams ran out on to the ground for the first sanctioned Test match on South African soil for more than eight years and, if it were possible, the crowd roared even louder.

What happened next was very odd. The man on the loudspeaker had just announced that there would now be a one-minute silence to commemorate all the people killed at the Boipatong Massacre— a pre-condition for allowing the tour to go ahead, as agreed with the ANC in the place of anthems. But the static had not even faded from the announcement when the crowd began to sing the Afrikaaner anthem 'Die Stem' in full voice. They were barely a quarter-way through the spirited rendition when the loudspeaker again crackled to life. Not to rebuke the crowd for failing to observe even a few seconds of the minute's silence but, amazingly, to add official sanction to the singing of the anthem by piping through the musical accompaniment to 'Die Stem'.

Around the stadium thousands of voices took up the song with even greater vigour, and on the field many of the Springboks openly cried at the emotion of it all.

All anthems are emotional, of course, but 'Die Stem', in this context, was something else again. In the words of Bryce Courtney,. 'it is an anthem which celebrates the White Tribe and its love of a land it believes it won from the Black Tribes and for which it is willing to die.

'Make no mistake,' he says, '"Die Stem" is a war cry.'

Though the Afrikaan language skills of the Wallabies were not up to deciphering the words, they knew enough to know that you don't start singing the national anthem, *any* national anthem, in the middle of a one minute silence, and they were shocked.

Farr-Jones remembers thinking at the time, 'How hard can it be to keep your trap shut during a one minute silence? Whatever you think of the ANC, whether you agree with them or disagree with them, this was about having a minute's silence for people that had been massacred at Boipatong. To sing the national anthem, or to do anything other than be silent, was outrageous, and the SARU deserved whatever they had coming to them.'

What the SARU had coming to them, in fact, was a torrid time from an outraged ANC, though their official response would wait until they could officially meet. At least the Wallabies were glad, as their bus took them back to Pretoria, that the All Blacks had won the game 26–23, silencing the uppity Afrikaaners for a bit. But they were sure they could do better the following week.

It was with relief that the Wallabies escaped to Port Elizabeth on the South African coast the following morning. They were leaving, they thought, most of the fuss about the anthem behind them. And, besides, Port Elizabeth was a bit more like it. Far more English in character than the Afrikaaner stronghold they had come from, suddenly the feel in the air right from the airport was a lot more friendly, with less breast-beating and a lot more warmth.

And for the first time the black and coloured people of the population were out in force—Willie Ofahengaue, the only member of the Wallaby touring party with dark skin, claimed them all as his 'cousins' and professed to be very happy to see them . . . as were all the Wallabies.

At the airport they cheered, they waved welcoming placards, a twenty-member black choir sang in harmony, in their own tongue. Again, the Wallabies didn't understand the words of the song—'something, something, Walla-beees, something, something, Walla-beeeees'—but this time it made them feel good.

Not that the anthem episode was left behind. Far from it.

At two o'clock on the Monday morning, some thirty-six hours after the test, the phone rang in Nick's room. Ever since Jessica had been born Nick had particularly hated to get calls in the middle of the night when he was away. He'd always have a momentary fear that something was wrong at home.

'Mate, it's Breeny. I'm in Joe's room. Can you come to my room now for an urgent meeting? This is no joke. It looks as if the tour is going to be called off.'

Scrambling into a tracksuit, Farr-Jones got to Joe French's room soon afterwards and he, John Breen, Executive Director Bob Fordham and French chatted quietly for ten minutes as they awaited Bob Dwyer.

If there was a tinge of tension in the conversation between Farr-Jones and French, it was understandable. Though normally close, their relationship had been strained in the time leading up to the tour when the public pronouncements of the two in the press had been in direct contradiction. In the weeks before the Wallabies departure, French had said that the Wallabies would happily comply with the ANC's request that they visit Boipatong and wear black armbands during the Test. Farr-Jones had said the Wallabies would do no such thing. 'Sympathy obliged is no sympathy at all', he'd written in his *Herald* column, and he said he did not want the Wallabies to be used for any political purposes at all in South Africa, be they white or black'.

A few days later when that issue had been settled, in Farr-

Jones' favour, French had said the tour would definitely go ahead but Farr-Jones, concerned at a spate of deaths during South Africa's national strike, countered with, 'I want the tour to be re-assessed. I am going to have a very good look and ask a lot of questions in the next couple of days to see what's going on . . . '

Just who was running the show? Eventually it came to a stand-up verbal stoush between the Australian Rugby Union President and the Wallaby captain in front of the entire team just prior to departure at their airport hotel, with Joe French saying to Nick, 'I don't care who you are, or what you've done, if you open your mouth on this tour about political issues then the repercussions will be severe,' and Farr-Jones, bloodied but unbowed, replying, 'Thanks, Joe, I'll bear that in mind.'

With a bit of a bouffant hair-do at the best of times, Bob Dwyer's hair almost stands on end when he is roused from sleep in the middle of the night, but this was no time for levity . . .

The news was bad, Joe French explained. As president of the ARU, he had been informed a short time before that the African National Congress was going to meet later that morning at ten o'clock with a view to withdrawing approval for the tour because of what had happened at Ellis Park.

Citing the non-observance of the minute's silence, the playing of the anthems and the flying of the flags as a general breach of conditions agreed upon, the ANC maintained they were quite within their rights to withdraw the support.

If that happened then the tour was killed stone dead, of that there was no doubt, and the safety of the players could no longer be guaranteed. The Wallaby management was therefore duty bound to get them out. On the morrow if necessary.

The question was twofold—what stance should the Wallabies take to the whole anthem imbroglio, and how best to ensure the safety of the Wallabies, should things suddenly turn nasty?

'There was a real feeling in the air,' Farr-Jones recalls, 'like . . . this might be it. The possibility was that at a certain point we'd stop being the Wallaby football team in a stable country and suddenly turn into thirty-five Australians overseas in a nasty unstable situation, trying to get the hell out.'

The final decision was, then, that first thing in the morning the Wallabies would release a statement giving full support to the ANC position. After all, to the Australians it really did seem clear cut that the behaviour of the white South Africans had been beyond the pale—whatever one's political persuasion.

And on the safety front it was decided that at first light John Breen would look into the possibility of securing thirty-five seats on the afternoon flight from Johannesburg to London, as they had no desire to wait until the following Saturday when the next flight to Australia was due to leave.

When the meeting broke up at about 3 a.m. there was a sense of fait accompli—a 75–80 per cent certainty that the tour was all over. As they walked along the corridor back to their room, Bob Dwyer and John Breen discussed whether they should start contacting other scattered Australians, such as the television commentators and those with various supporters' groups, to inform them of the possibility that the Wallabies were going to pull out and it would be a good idea if they came too. It wasn't quite a question of a mass exodus, hanging from the helicopter skids as their feet left the embassy roof, but then again . . .

For Farr-Jones's part he went straight back to his room and phoned Angie back in Australia to say, 'I should be seeing you in about two days' time.'

Always the bloody phone. This time it was a regular 8.30 wake-up call. Training was on that morning, as every morning, and they had to keep preparing as if the Test match were still on, even though the four at the meeting the night before knew it was now only a slight chance.

Before training began Joe French informed the rest of the team what had gone on, and set out just what their position was. If the ANC withdrew their support that day, Joe explained, then they would be on the plane that very afternoon, no questions asked. In the meantime he knew they were all professional enough to keep preparing for the Test match as if it was still on and he thought it a good idea they should now get to it.

The news still hadn't come through to the Wallabies by the end of training, but at least Joe French, reported back when they got to the hotel that the first noises out of the ANC at Johannesburg were unexpectedly tolerant, and that it had been decided to keep to the original tour schedule until further notice.

From that point on the day got immediately better. In fact Farr-Jones would later claim it as one of the most enjoyable afternoons he has ever spent on a rugby tour.

It began with John Breen anouncing that after lunch he would like some volunteers to go out to a nearby black township to 'teach' some of the kids about rugby. Of course there was no question really of raising the standard of rugby in the township with one training exercise, but if there was one thing the Wallabies had gained from their time in South Africa thus far it was a greater affinity for the country's black people, as opposed to the whites, and there were many volunteers.

The captain was particularly keen to go. Not only did he feel the same growing affinity as the others, but before the tour had begun he had been particularly vocal in resisting all attempts by the ANC to have the Wallabies trucked from massacre site to massacre site, saying that, 'We're happy to go out and meet the people and hold a couple of clinics, but we're not going to be forced to.'

Now was the chance to be as good as his word.

The minibus set off from the genteel confines of their four-star hotel in Port Elizabeth at 2 p.m., with sixteen Wallabies and Bob Dwyer on board. Through the bus windows the scenery passed them by like a long panning shot in a movie. Concrete buildings, white faces, paved streets, expensive suits, parking meters, white, white, black, white, Mercedes, brick houses, gardens, black, white, black, fields, more fields, black, black, black, black, dirt tracks, tin shacks, hessian walls, wooden tables laden with meat, flies, flies, flies, *lots* of black faces now and, finally, a field.

Not that it was like any field the Wallabies had seen to date in South Africa. For starters there were some 400 black kids on it, with more streaming in from the township as word spread of their arrival—boys and girls, aged from five years old to, say, fifteen. The field itself was in a poor state of repair in a desolate patch of ground on the edge of the township, but it was at least basically flat, with a stark concrete stand on its western edge.

Back to business. Seventeen coaches into 500 kids just did not go, but they did the best they could. Bob Dwyer and Tim Gavin took some of them for lineouts, Willie O. and Phil Kearns were in charge of scrums, Tim Horan and Jason Little did the skills training and Campese and Farr-Jones went to the far end of the field to organise a shambolic game of touch.

The touch all went terrifically well, with seemingly all the kids having an instinctive feel for it, until the two senior Wallabies made a crucial tactical error by pulling out a couple of large packets of lollies that they'd bought back in Port Elizabeth. All thoughts of rugby were entirely lost for the time it took for the lollies to disappear, and both players realised that for many it was probably the first time they'd ever tasted them.

But to the touch again. They ran, they passed, they yelled out, they swerved back and forth, they giggled constantly, they showed off what they could do, they had a wonderful time, with the kids seeming to enjoy it too.

If for the Wallabies it was a wonderful break from the travails of tour life and the deadly serious business of preparing for a Test they weren't even sure was going to take place, for the kids it was simply a chance to run with their friends in the sunlight with a ball in their hands and the added oddity of being guided by friendly white people.

In Farr-Jones's estimation, 'Ninety per cent of them would have had no idea at all who we were or where we were from, and that too was part of the joy of the whole thing. They just loved running at each other with the ball and it maybe reminded all of us, too, why we loved the game so much in the first place. All of the other stuff of Wallabies and Springboks and anthems and hype was stripped away and it was just back to the basic joy of the game . . .'

As the sun started to sink and the time came to leave, all 500 children—together with parents, grandparents, aunts and uncles—gathered together with the Wallabies for a sit-down singalong of African songs, with speeches of thanks from all sides, Phil Kearns doing the honours for the Australians.

It was only two days earlier that Farr-Jones had been told by Nelson Mandela that he would find all the black South Africans would now be supporting the Springboks, but that was not his experience at all, particularly on this occasion. Many of the older people of the township who had now gravitated to the field to see what all the fuss was about made sure to tell the Wallabies in general and he and Campese in particular to be good and sure to beat the Springboks on the coming Saturday. Still, it was all said in such a *calm* way. Not with outright hate, so much as a long-suffering desire to see the white South Africans beaten. Part of it, too, must have been the simple goodwill they felt towards the Wallabies for having made the effort to spend the afternoon with them.

The atmosphere was very warm as the Wallabies piled back onto the bus, to the applause of the adults and the laughs of the children, and the Australians were on a 'high'. But ineffably, their spirits soon fell again as they drove back through the township, to see once more the way black people lived in a township with an unemployment rate of sixty-five per cent among the non-whites.

All in a day in the life of your average rugby player on tour in South Africa.

After all that wonderful feeling and bonhomie, the following day they found themselves in the middle of it again. The men of Eastern province coming hard at them, as if *they* would assume the mantle of World Champions if they won.

The Wallabies put them down, but as with all South African teams it was only as a result of huge physical effort. The brutes just didn't seem to know when to give up.

Still there had been no official word from the ANC as to whether or not they would withdraw their support for the Test, but unbeknownst to the Wallabies at the time, the ANC had in fact given private assurances to both Joe French and the Australian ambassador to South Africa, Colin McDonald, that they would not prevent the match taking place.

'But we were not allowed to announce this to anyone at all,' says McDonald, now posted in Egypt, 'because they wanted the white South Africans to stew on the possibility that it might be stopped for another few days.'

So on to Cape Town for the Test. And something of a shock.

Just out of Cape Town airport, sitting in his usual position on the bus, three back on the right, Farr-Jones was among the first to see them. There were only about thirty of them, but still it wasn't nice, not nice at all to see by the side of the road, blacks and coloureds holding up an assortment of placards: 'Disgusting Aussies', 'Go Home Aussies', 'Australians Have No Conscience', 'You Have a Vote, We Don't'. A fair point, the last, but *hell*—if it was all right with Nelson Mandela that they come, surely it was all right with them?

Obviously not. To this point one of the most comforting aspects of the whole crazy tour had been the warm support that they had enjoyed from the black members of the population, and even though this was only thirty people against them, that was thirty too many.

It was all getting a bit much—the threats of cancellation, the Afrikaaner hostility, the media intrusion, the constant chorus that 'you're not the real World Champions until you beat us', and now *black* protesters against them too.

Part of the strain showed up in press reports back in Australia the following day, quoting the Australian captain.

'I just want to play this Test and then go home,' Farr-Jones said. 'There are always going to be some groups who don't approve of what is going on as far as international rugby contact with South Africa is concerned. We can't do much about those groups.

'The demonstration was peaceful. The only surprise I had was that it was targeted at us a bit.'

Which was understating it a bit. In fact Farr-Jones was appalled that the Australians had been thus targeted, though he was at a loss as to know quite what to do about it. He'd half a mind to jump in a taxi and go straight back to the demonstration and talk to them, explain to them that they had come here in good faith and, furthermore, that after two weeks in South Africa they were more pro-black than ever.

But naturally there was the inevitable training to attend.

Not even in the few days leading up to the World Cup final the year before was the atmosphere within the Wallaby camp so intense. In that game they were, after all, up against a side, England, which they had already beaten that year by some twenty-five points. They had their measure.

But on this occasion they were up against a side that was after their title of rugby heavyweight champeen champions of the world, a side beaten by only three points by the All Blacks the week before, a side that was on their own turf, surrounded by their own people. A people that seemed to have risen as one in support of the Springboks—at least the white people had.

As the Wallabies prepared, sticking close to their hotel and venturing out only for the training sessions, they were always conscious that an entire country seemed to be following their every move. No sports page in the country was complete without at least two articles bearing news from the Wallaby camp, and no electronic media bulletin went to air without a similarly wide coverage. No sooner had the Wallabies disgorged from the bus to begin training than the media would be all over them. And the players they wanted to talk to most were Campese and Farr-

Jones. Campese because he was Campese, and as likely as not to say something controversial enough that would create a headline, and Farr-Jones because he was not only captain but also articulate.

On the Thursday before the Saturday test the ANC finally released a statement that the Test match could go ahead with their support, and it was gratifying to the Wallabies that it made a special point of stating that it was 'grateful to the Australian people, government, rugby players and officials for their understanding of the extent to which black South Africans were hurt'.

The conditions demanded by the ANC were essentially the same as for the previous week's Test, except that this time the SARU was on notice that any further breaching of the agreement and the ANC would shut down all further tours for good. The SARU agreed that a minute's silence for victims of violence would be observed, that there would be no official playing of 'Die Stem', that the official flag would not be hoisted, and that a statement expressing the SARU's support for peace and democracy would be inserted in the official program.

The people, though, had agreed to nothing, nothing at all, and in the time leading up to the Test there was a great deal of tension as to whether or not they could be counted on to 'behave themselves'.

The signs were not good. Never before had so many South African flags been sold in Cape Town over such a short period of time. Despite the warnings of the ANC as to the consequences, every flag supplier and manufacturer in Cape Town sold out a full twenty-four hours before the Test, with one enthusiastic flag seller claiming that he had sold 800 a day, every day, since the Wednesday of the previous week.

Even more worrying than all this was a certain complicity in the white media that *wink, wink, nudge, nudge*, it was all all right, that the authorities had once again got the bloody ANC off their backs, and now the rest of us can just get back to breast-beating, business as usual. For example, on the Friday the leading Afrikaans daily newspaper of Cape Town, *Die Burger*, printed a picture on their front page of a young lady showing off flags of various sizes, and the same paper also printed daily reports of 'The Great Flag Sale'.

In the face of it all the ANC was predictably angered, with

Steve Tshwete publicly warning that 'if spectators go to the Test not to watch rugby, but to challenge the new South Africa, the ANC will have no option but to oppose all future tours to and from South Africa, including the 1995 World Cup'.

It was in such an atmosphere that the Wallabies prepared for their most important match of the year.

The aim of the game, Farr-Jones kept repeating, was to keep totally focused, not to do anything different from the way they normally did things before a Test match. Forget the hype—each man do just as he had done before and get himself mentally and physically right for the Test. Business as usual, prepare normally. Yet, as the players themselves noticed, Nick himself was totally different from the way he usually was.

The Wallaby winger, Paul Carozza, for one, had long been impressed at how calm Nick usually was before a Test match and had drawn strength from it.

'But for this one,' Carozza says, 'Nick was like I'd never seen him. Jumpy, edgy, running around trying to make sure that everything that could be done had been done, trying to look after every last detail—it was like he wanted to win this game so badly he could think of nothing else.'

Marty Roebuck also noted that Nick was acting oddly when sitting next to him on the way to the test. But even more so.

'Nick was crying,' Marty recalls. 'Not sobbing outright or anything, just quietly brushing away the tears rolling down his cheeks. I had never known him to be so emotional and couldn't work out what was wrong.'

Their brief conversation went like this:

'Mate, is there something wrong, something at home, something you want to talk about?'

'No mate, it's all right. I just want to win this Test very, very badly.'

And he did. But there was more to his emotion than just that.

Over the last few days the feeling had grown stronger within him that if the Wallabies won the Test, the time might be right to 'pull the pin', to definitively retire from international rugby. By the Saturday that feeling was just short of being a conviction . . .

'There were a lot of things that made me feel like that,' he says. 'If we won we would have proved ourselves to be the very best and I'd always thought I wanted to get out right at the top.'

Hence the emotion.

'Just about everything I did that day leading up to the Test I was thinking, "this'll be the last time I'll do it . . ." Going to the team breakfast, packing my boots in my bag, going to the team meeting, all that sort of stuff . . . When I was on the bus with Marty I couldn't get out of my head that if we won then "I might never be doing this again . . ."'

'The other thing was that if we didn't win, everything we'd achieved over the previous two years would have been devalued, it would have taken the sheen off the lot, and the South Africans would never have let us forget it and would have claimed the "World Champion" tag for themselves. I remember feeling for this game that we *had to win*.'

Nick at least gained a lot of confidence when he saw how wet and muddy the ground was when they went out to inspect it before kick-off. To see that the match would be played under slippery and heavy conditions like that gave all the Wallabies heart. Oddly enough, it meant that the South Africans would be playing on a field far more suited to the Australian game than their own, for, with the exception of their centre, Danie Gerber, the Springboks were all from the far north of the country where they were used to playing rugby on the dry hard veldt.

But for the Wallabies this was the same beautiful mud that they'd learnt how to play on particularly in campaigns in New Zealand, and during other wet seasons at home. Perfect. Wet ground below, air with plenty of oxygen in it all around them. While the All Blacks had struggled the week before to fire on all cylinders while playing 2000 metres above sea level at Ellis Park, the Wallabies would be presented with no such problems at the sea level of Cape Town.

Farr-Jones could take at least some credit that the Wallabies would be playing in such advantageous conditions. In February of that year when the agreement had first been reached to hold a one-off Test against South Africa, he had written to the executive director of the ARU, Bob Fordham, with his own suggestions as to how the venture should be approached.

The third paragraph of his letter read . . .

The main purpose of my writing to you is to insist on the player's behalf that the test against South Africa be played at sea level. In March of 1990 I played a game in Pretoria, and having recently spoken to [Wallaby second-rower] Rod McCall about his experience with the World XV in 1989, I can assure you that acclimatising to altitude takes considerable time. It is my opinion that on such a short tour we would be jeopardising our prospects of success by playing anywhere other than at sea level.

After consultation with many sporting luminaries including marathon runner Robert De Castella, who had had a lot of experience competing at high altitude, Bob Fordham had become similarly convinced and succeeded in making the South Africans agree to a sea level venue.

After filing back to the dressing rooms and getting changed and warmed up, there remained little left to do. A small speech from Farr-Jones—but not much because 'everybody was totally "up" already, and it was just a question of getting them out the door in pretty much the same mood they'd come in—and then came the moment.

As captain, Farr-Jones started them off.

'Australians all let us rejoice,
'For we are young and free . . . '

Because of the agreement with the ANC that there would be no anthems before the game, it had been decided by the Wallabies that they would sing theirs in the dressing room. Which they did, with gusto. Renditions of the anthem when representing your country abroad are always emotive, but this one more than most. Do or die. Were they the true World Champions or not?

'In joyful strains then let us sing,
'Advance Australia Fair.'

Then out and into it.

(Meanwhile in the stadium outside, before the two teams had emerged, the one-minute silence had thankfully passed without a hitch.)

Sometimes in Test matches between fierce opponents that don't know each other well, there can be an unexpected calm in the opening minutes of the game. The teams are like two heavyweight fighters circling each other in a ring, each wanting to feel the other out before committing.

'It was very very strange,' Farr-Jones recalls now, 'I remember being very surprised that the encounter wasn't more physical in the opening twenty minutes.'

Still, that hardness would come . . . most particularly in the forward exchanges as the two packs continually clashed in the wet conditions, with the Wallabies gradually gaining the upper hand.

The first real breakthrough came just before half-time with the score at 3–3 when, from the base of a ruck on the Springbok line, Farr-Jones let the ball out to Phillp Kearns on the burst. As he was hit by the defence, Kearns still managed to get the ball back to Farr-Jones again, who passed to Michael Lynagh. Lynagh moved only a few metres forward and to his left and, just as he was hit, got the ball out to winger Paul Carozza. *In extremis* Carozza went in for try of prodigious team effort to make the score 8–3 to the Australians at the break.

Tiring now, both sides' legs getting very heavy after hurling themselves around in the mud for so long, the Australians were holding on to an 11–3 lead with twenty minutes to go and seemed to be getting on top, though as Farr-Jones recalls 'they just kept coming back hard, it was like they were starting to get their second wind and the South African crowd were just going crazy giving them more energy.'

It might well have been Willie Ofahengaue's hit that did the trick for the Australians. With fifteen minutes to go, the famed Springbok hooker, Uli Schmidt, gathered the ball from broken play about twenty metres from the Australian line and made the beginnings of a ferocious charge, when the Tongan-born back-rower began moving towards him . . .

A small parentheses here. The usual way of tackles is for the tackler to move only slowly forwards into his target so as to still have the capacity to move to the left or right depending on the target's side-step. Ofahengaue's trick is to go fast forwards regardless, meaning that when he makes a 'hit' the target/victim *stays* hit. This was just such an occasion, though as Willie drove Schmidt backwards he also rolled his shoulders over and threw him on the ground at his feet. Close parentheses.

The impact as Schmidt went down and the ball went free seemed to shake both teams, Farr-Jones recalls.

'That tackle was just what we needed. Seeing Willie throw him down like a rag doll like that lifted us up a couple of notches and seemed to knock the stuffing out of them. You could see in the Springboks' eyes how shocked they were, not to mention Uli . . . and we were just delighted.'

It was Tim Horan's try that sealed it. With six minutes to go in the game, Horan regathered a kick by South African fullback Theo van Rensburg some thirty-five metres from the Wallaby's own line and set off upfield, slicing and jinking all the way before sending a kick behind the South African defence.

Danie Gerber fielded the ball just inside his own quarter, but Horan just as quickly tackled him, got back to his knees, and somehow, amid all the churning feet and arms, picked the ball cleanly out of the muddy maelstrom without knocking on and got away a perfectly timed pass to the man with the cleanest jersey on the field, shining out there like a flashing orange beacon, David Campese on the burst, who crossed for the try.

Only minutes later it was Horan again, who set the play in motion for yet another Wallaby try. From a Marty Roebuck tackle on the Springbok winger, James Small, Horan darted in and secured the ball for Australia. From the base of the mini-ruck the ball came to Ewen McKenzie, who let it out to the flying Paul Carozza—the diminutive Queenslander who was enjoying far and away his best year of international rugby. Screaming down the left touch-line, Carozza chip-kicked the ball past the oncoming defence, regathered just before the line, and once again *just* managed to get over the line for the try that turned the game into a South African rout.

When the smoke had cleared, the Springboks had gone down to their biggest defeat in 100 years, by the score of 26–3. The 23 point margin of victory fitted nicely with the 23 years that had passed since the Wallabies had last played them. Rarely has a Wallaby side taken such outright joy in the beating of a side.

After they had again belted out an even more rousing rendition of the national anthem, linked arm in arm, the press were let into the changing room. In one corner of the crowded dressing room the generally mild-mannered Michael Lynagh came straight to the point, and his words indicate the streak of retributive joy that the Wallabies felt in the win.

'We didn't have to look for any extra motivation than the South African supporters . . . they were our biggest motivation,' he told a group of journalists.

'All the guys have been pretty pissed off with the arrogant

attitude of the South Africans, as we have really been battered from pillar to post here. It has been relentless, with them showing a total disrespect for privacy and manners.'

Harsh words. But perhaps not overstated. Farr-Jones for one felt much the same, even if a little more restrained after his previous experience with the South African press.

He was quoted as saying: 'A large majority of people over here think they're pretty good, and it was up to us to show them they're not as good as they think they are.'

Still, in a brief ceremony shortly afterwards high in the stadium complex, the South African Rugby Union were gracious enough to personally present Farr-Jones with a gold Krugerrand and a touch-judge's flag as a momento of the day.

'You have been a wonderful player and ambassador in world rugby, and long may you continue to be both,' they told him.

In the aftermath there remained just one thing to do. Back at the Sun Hotel, where they were staying, as the others made ready to go to the Happy Hour, Farr-Jones returned to his room, closed the door, sat at his desk and took out some of the hotel stationery. And began writing . . .

In the bus on the way to the post-Test dinner Farr-Jones sat quietly looking out the window as the coast-line of the Cape slipped past—Table Mountain to the left, the sea and cliffs to the right, the traffic coming thinly towards them. Feeling sore, feeling good. But very, very quiet.

When they got to the dinner, he was glad to see that his parents were already there, as they almost always were. With his mother having seen fifty-eight of the fifty-nine Tests he had played for the Wallabies and his father having seen fifty-six, they hadn't missed much of his career at all.

Momentarily dodging the many people who wished to offer their congratulations he walked over to them, gave his mother a kiss and then said:

'Mum, Dad, this is for you,' handing them the gold kruger-rand, the flag and the envelope.

Rosemary put down her drink, opened the envelope, and with her husband Max looking over her shoulder, they began to read . . .

To Mum and Dad

It's been a great day—a great nine years when we look back on that unexpected first Test at Twickers. Thanks for all the wonderful support.

Please put these two items in the cabinet back home to remind us of 22 August 1992—the day we can look back on and say we got to the top of the rugby tree and got out!

All my love,
Nick.

CHAPTER THIRTEEN

The Return

*'Once more unto the breach
dear friends, once more.'*
Henry V

O oops.
It didn't actually transpire quite the way Nick had planned.

Some nine months later, and now well away from playing representative rugby, Farr-Jones was watching Australia play Tonga in the first Test of the season from high in the Ballymore stands. It wasn't the greatest of all games, this particular one, but what the hey?

With his headphones on and a microphone before him, he was there in his new incarnation as television commentator—and was at least enjoying *describing* the shots instead of calling them out on the field—when something happened that stopped him cold.

Out on the field, Peter Slattery, the man who had replaced Farr-Jones as Test half-back, dived upon a loose ball and suddenly was badly crunched by a big Tongan knee driving hard down into his back and ribs.

'I could see that Slats was injured,' Nick recalls now, 'though at first I thought maybe it wasn't so bad, and he'd get up and resume playing. It was only when he didn't move and they signalled for help that I really thought he must be crook.'

As the ever-faithful physiotherapist, Greg Craig, soon

afterwards led Slattery from the field, Farr-Jones found himself inadvertently thinking about the fact that the biggest match of the year, a one-off Test against the All Blacks at Dunedin, was only two weeks away.

The actual call came less than twenty-four hours later, at about 10.30 a.m. on Monday 5 July when Farr-Jones was back in his Sydney law office. It was the Australian assistant coach, Bob Templeton, and he delivered the news without preamble: the injury to Peter Slattery's ribs was serious, and the doctors' advice was that he would be sidelined for a minimum of six weeks.

Farr-Jones knew what was coming next, even before Templeton began his run-up . . .

'Bob Dwyer's on a flight back to Sydney, and asked me to talk to you now. We had a long chat at the after-match dinner last night. We want you to play against the All Blacks.'

It was with mixed feelings that Farr-Jones received the news. Part of him, of course, had missed it. Part of him had continued to whisper that his natural place in the world on any cold winter's day when there was a Rugby Test on involving Australia, was right there in the middle, barking behind the Australian pack.

On the other hand, a luxurious feeling of relaxation always engulfed him now when waking up on the morning of a Test, and realising that this day he would not be called upon to hurl himself into the whirling maelstrom. Instead he could enjoy the marvellous spectacle like everyone else.

'We *need* you, Nick.'

'Tempo, give me a couple of days to think it over. I've just got to have a little time to make sure that whatever I do is the right thing . . .'

They said their goodbyes, and Nick put the phone down. It was going to be a very difficult decision, but at least he had two days to think it over which would be . . .

'OUT of the QUESTION, Nick!' Bob Dwyer told him in the same law office only an hour later, where the coach had come direct from Sydney airport.

'I need to know *today*, tonight at the absolute latest. All of us selectors want you, but we haven't got time to muck around waiting for you to make up your mind.

'And anyway, what's the problem? You never "retired" did you? You told me that you'd "bowed out unless something happened to Slats". Well, something's happened and I want you to make yourself available again, like you said you would.'

Dwyer continued in this vein for another twenty minutes or so and they finished by agreeing that Nick would phone the coach at nine that night to give him his answer.

Farr-Jones used that time to do two things. Firstly, to talk to his wife Angie about her views on the matter, and secondly to sound out a few Wallabies as to their feelings on the advisability of his return. The last thing he wanted to do was to go back into the Test team if the current team-members felt that instead of him, the team would be far better off with Brett Johnstone, the young Queenslander who had come on and played so outstandingly after Slattery had been injured.

Angie's advice was as he expected, that 'whatever you wish to do, you have my full backing'. It wasn't great guidance, no, but it was totally supportive which he needed. Then another call.

'Yes, hello . . . could I speak to Phil Kearns, please?'

'Phil . . . ? It's Nick. Listen, Bob wants me to come back into the side to play the All Blacks, and I was wondering what you thought . . .'

Kearn's basic reply was that it would be great to have Nick back in the side, no mistake about that, though he did have a few reservations about whether it was the absolute best thing for the future of the team.

Given than Nick was obviously not going to be around forever, and most unlikely to play in the 1995 World Cut to begin with, the team may as well start trying to cope with that now as any time else.

Oddly enough, Nick's mother, Rosemary, concurred with Kearns's reservations, though for different reasons. 'Why', she wanted to know, 'go back into full Test Rugby now . . . when you've played no more than club rugby all year for Sydney University? Why?'

Basically, Mum, because it just might be that they need me, and if the 'three wise men' who are the Australian selectors think I'm the player who will inject the most into the half-back role, it just may be that they're right.

Farr-Jones continued his ring around to senior Wallabies including Michael Lynagh, David Campese and Tim Horan— all of whom were unequivocal in their support for his return. To have him back, they said when he called, would definitely be the best thing for the side.

Thus heartened in a decision that in all probability he'd made deep down at the moment that Templeton had phoned him that morning, Farr-Jones called Dwyer and told him he had his man.

After going to bed that night, he remembers reflecting long and hard while staring at the cracks in the ceiling that 'while it really was exciting to be back, the thing was that win, lose or draw against the All Blacks, nobody could take away what we'd achieved as a team over the previous few years.'

He eventually dropped off to sleep well after midnight, with his sandshoes under the bed, the better to find them easily in the early morning light when he intended to go for a hard run.

What happened in the ensuing days was a burst of concentrated publicity unprecedented in the annals of Australian rugby. At the press conference held the following day to announce his return to the side, word had already leaked out, and from his chair behind the table at the Rugby Club, he looked out to see some forty or fifty assembled members of the media—most of whom he had never seen before.

Usually, for such an event, one might expect an intimate gathering of the four or five journalists in Sydney who cover rugby full-time, but this was something else again.

There was something about the 'come back from retirement of the Wallaby World Cup-winning captain to answer the desperate call of his team' which seemed to pique the interest of every media chief of staff on the Eastern seaboard. On Wednedsay 7 July, Farr-Jones photograph was on the front *and* back page of, in turn, the *Sydney Morning Herald*, the *Daily Telegraph-Mirror*, and the *Australian*. That night he led all the sports reports on the TV news, as well as going on such prime-time current affairs shows as 'A Current Affair' and 'The 7.30 Report'.

Viewers of the latter show were charmed when, in the middle of a live-cross from the Farr-Jones' living room, little Jessica Farr-Jones suddenly ran into the picture of Nick on his couch talking to the show's host, Geraldine Doogue. Jessica was yelling something entirely unintelligible in adult language, but which probably meant in toddler talk: 'Daddy, daddy, there's a lot of strange men with lights and cameras in the house!!!'

Farr-Jones, without missing a beat, plopped Jessica up on the couch beside him, saying quickly to his daughter 'Yes, yes, darling,

Daddy's *talking* right now, so let's be quiet', before continuing talking to Geraldine Doogue 'and sorry, Geraldine, you were saying . . . ?'

In reply, Ms Doogue beamed with merriment, and the rest of the interview went even more swimmingly than before.

Just beneath this wave of good, if hyperbolic, publicity though, ran a very strong undercurrent of an entirely different make-up. Farr-Jones had 'lost the plot' it said, and should never have come back to take the place of Brett Johnstone who, after all, had scored a try himself against the Tongans and generally looked very impressive.

Even Farr-Jones' own former Wallaby captain, Andrew Slack, went public in a newspaper column: with a private conversation the two had had on Monday afternoon, when Slack mentioned that Nick had asked him his opinion and he had told him not to do it.

'When Nick telephoned me to hear my thoughts on the matter, I suggested he refuse Dwyer's request. . . . I believed Brett Johnstone, the man squeezed out of the starting fifteen, was up to the standard required.'

Farr-Jones made no public reply at the time, but his private feelings were clear: 'I respected Andrew's opinion, which was why I asked him in the first place before the decision was made. But I was still disappointed that at such a time he chose to air publicly what we'd discussed in private.'

Whatever, Slack was joined in his negative opinion about the Farr-Jones come back—by the Queensland coach, John Connolly, who publicly wrung his hands and said that once again the Australian selectors were turning their back on youth, and that the selection of Farr-Jones was 'a blatant no-confidence vote in the youngster (Brett Johnstone).'

The *Sydney Morning Herald* was moved enough by the debate to enshrine in an editorial its official opinion that Farr-Jones should *not* have come back. 'Farr-Jones is not going to be around for the next World Cup in 1995. When better to start preparations for 1995 than now?'

'The fault' continued the *Herald*, 'lies with the selectors. They have shown a lack of faith in all aspiring young Test players, not just Brett Johnstone . . .'

And so on. Initially, such a negative undercurrent did not affect Farr-Jones greatly, beyond the occasional pang of disappointment.

'At the end of the day,' as he was fond of saying at the time, 'it will all come down to how I play on the field, and there will be no problems there.'

If Farr-Jones sounded totally sure of his own abilities to play well against the All Blacks, it's because he was. He never doubted for a minute that he was up to the task. In fact, so sure was he that, despite the circumstance that he would shortly be playing in the toughest match of rugby going on in the world that year, he still felt no compunction in missing out on his regular game of club rugby for Sydney University on the Saturday preceding the Test. He'd long ago secured University First Grade coach Brian Burnett's accord that he would take his family that weekend to a popular coastal resort north of Newcastle, to join his parents and brothers, and he saw no reason to change those plans now. He'd run hard that week, gaining as much quick condition as he could, and felt that was sufficient.

In response, his old mate FitzSimons, for one, was almost apoplectic that Farr-Jones wasn't going to avail himself of every opportunity to improve his match fitness and that included a bare minimum of playing for Uni on the Saturday and *what the hell did Farr-Jones think he was doing*? FitzSimons may as well have been throwing marbles at the Great Pyramid. Farr-Jones did not move an inch.

'I'll be all right,' he said. 'And I'm plenty fit enough to play the All Blacks. Playing this weekend won't make one jot of difference, and I'm not going to change my plans for this weekend because my family comes first now, and that's all there is to it.'

And that's all there *was* to it.

Uni played without him, and Farr-Jones went north with his family.

He was to receive a rather nasty shock on the Sunday morning at his resort though, when his father took him aside to tell him about an article he'd just read in one of the Sunday papers. It quoted the great Australian half-back from the 1960s, Ken Catchpole who, under a banner headline of CATCHY: FLICK NICK!, said if he had been a selector he would not have picked Farr-Jones as he had many concerns over his fitness.

Hoping to retain his equanimity, Farr-Jones refused to read it, knowing how much an article quoting such a great would upset him, but his policy of evasion simply did not work. Over golf that morning the thrust of the article emerged bit by bit, and he became progessively more disgruntled as he comprehended it.

It was close on being the last straw. So much of the criticism to this point had revolved around the fact that Farr-Jones had 'retired', and therefore had no business coming back into it and taking the place of a younger man. It was precisely this kind of criticism that got Farr-Jones most. In fact, he felt he never really *had* retired and had always, 'left the door slightly ajar, leaving my way open to get back into the side if the occasion warranted it.'

His letter to his parents notwithstanding, Farr-Jones had never actually made any grand announcement to the world that he was retired and in fact had studiously avoided making any definitive statement whatsoever.

At the happy hour after the Test in Cape Town for example, his colleague of many years, Tom Lawton, had spoken to the team and announced that he was retiring. The team had had a drink in his honour, and Tom was given the warm send-off befitting someone who had had his distinguished career.

Though it would have been the perfect time to make his own retirement announcement, Farr-Jones had kept his peace, not wishing, in his words, 'to make any song and dance, knowing that there was still a slight possibility that I might in fact play again.' Back in Australia he'd continued to play regular club rugby, and played well enough to be leading the *Sydney Morning Herald*'s 'Best and Fairest' competition.

Yet his critics were now coming at him as if he was some punch-drunk old fighter out of the ring for ten years who had announced he was coming back to go after the world heavy-weight champion-ship of the world.

All up, the whole thing was starting to hit Farr-Jones hard, most particularly this last bit of criticism about his lack of fitness from someone so respected as Catchpole. And as one used to a fairly consistent diet of adulation in the rugby arena, Farr-Jones was ill-equipped to cope with such public criticism calmly, and for a couple of hours on this Sunday morning considered phoning up Bob Dwyer and telling him he had changed his mind and had decided that he wasn't going to play after all. Did he need such public criticism amid all the hoopla? Nossir, he did not, so they could find themselves a new half-back.

In the end though, he was persuaded out of such a rash decision for the most part by his own conscience, which told him that such a move would be a cop-out at best, betrayal at worst. He was going to play the All Blacks and prepare as hard as he could to ensure he was equipped to play as well as he possibly could and the hell with the Catchpoles and all the other nay-sayers.

As he was to say in a fit of pique to one of his brothers at lunch that day 'If ever you see me publicly tearing into current Wallabies when I'm fifty, please slap me around a bit till I come to my senses.'

In the afternoon he went for a hard, gut-busting run along the beach, only stopping when his legs all but gave out from under him. Bring on the Blacks.

And this was just like it had been in the old days, starting some ten years before—going off to the Camperdown Travelodge to join the Wallabies. On Monday morning, after getting from the resort, Farr-Jones again trod the familiar path . . .

The first time he'd done that was way back in 1984 when he was on his first Wallaby tour, to Fiji, and had had to introduce himself to a lot of players.

This was *deja vu* all over again. Even though Farr-Jones had been out of the system for only the last nine months, there were still six new players added to the Wallaby squad that he had not met before. Such was the attrition rate of modern rugby . . .

On the subject of attrition, Farr-Jones had five days of hard training to get through before the Test, as opposed to the more usual three days, the maximum time allowed in the rules set by the International Rugby Board. For, nominally, the first two days of the camp would be 'squad training', where another dozen players who were not part of the Test team or reserves, were also put through their paces. The main event though, would always be the preparation of the Test side.

If Bob Dwyer was exploiting the rules a little in gathering the Wallabies so early before a Test, it seemed only fair to enable the Wallabies to close the gap a little in the preparation that had been put in before this Test between the two teams. While the Wallabies had only had one Test against the comparatively minor rugby nation of Tonga, the All Blacks had been able to toughen themselves up and fine-tune their play with a full series against the British Lions which the New Zealanders had won 2-1.

Ten minutes prior to the team-meeting on Tuesday morning,

manager John Breen had taken Nick aside for a brief chat and dropped what tabloid journalists are pleased to refer to as 'a bombshell'.

Breen's news was that Michael Lynagh, the man Nick had played inside of for over fifty of his 59 tests, establishing a world record, was at this moment lying 400 metres up the road in the Royal Prince Alfred Hospital and was about to 'go under the knife' to determine the extent of hernia problem which had blown up. Lynagh was *out*, not only for this game, but also the foreseeable future.

His replacement was to be young Pat Howard, the 19-year-old son of the Wallabies assistant forward coach, Jake Howard, who had recently been impressing all with his incisive play and, most particularly, coolness under pressure. (A highly desirable quality when one was to make one's debut against the All Blacks on New Zealand soil.)

Howard's ascension to the five-eighth position changed entirely the perspective of the 'undecided's' in the debate that continued to rage as to whether or not Farr-Jones should have come back. With a 19-year-old at five-eighth, playing his first Test against the All Blacks, thank Gawd the man inside him was Farr-Jones, supremely experienced in the art of not giving the ball to his five-eighth when the latter had five All Blacks in his face.

The alternative, of having had a Johnstone/Howard combination at half-back/five-eighth, playing the All Blacks in Dunedin with only half of one Test experience between them was all but unthinkable.

Farr-Jones was *back*.

Following the usual practice of the Wallabies before Test matches, players who would be linked together on the field were also roomed together and Nick, naturally enough, found himself rooming with the 19-year-old debutante, Pat Howard. To Farr-Jones, it seemed rather nicely symmetrical that some ten years later he should be in a position to return the favour of what Mark Ella had done for him before he'd played his first Test—be calm, cool, controlled and nurture confidence in the younger player.

Not that Farr-Jones had to try too hard for all that, for Howard seemed naturally a very relaxed character—All Black Test or no All Black Test. And the content of their conversation was equally beside the point of the coming battle.

'We talked about a lot of things,' recalls Nick, 'from university life to family. Pat had plenty of questions, but they weren't about the All Blacks. We hardly spoke about the rugby and the upcoming match.'

There was perhaps one echo of Mark Ella's advice to him ten years previously of 'whether it's good ball or bad ball, just fling it over your shoulder and I'll be there.'

When on one occasion going down in the lift to training Howard had asked him where he should position himself from the scrum to make it easiest for Nick to get the ball to him, Farr-Jones reply was succinct: 'Stand wherever *you* feel most comfortable, I'll put the ball right in your breadbox . . .'

And was as good as his word.

In the opening minute of the game, Farr-Jones gathered the ball from the base of the scrum and arrowed it perfectly out to Howard on the fly, just as he had done for Ella all those years ago.

Not that his problems were over, not by a long shot . . . The All Blacks swarmed, surged forward in the opening minutes and immediately pushed Australia back to a position where they had to defend their own line.

There is an intuitive moment at the beginning of all Rugby matches where each side instinctively sizes up the hardness and will to win of the other side. It is the way the opposition enter a ruck, make a tackle, take the ball up, it is *something* they collectively do where you're able to gauge just what you're up against.

For Nick that moment came very soon after the start. Relentlessly surging forward, onwards ever onwards, the All Blacks were in wonderful form this day, and hard, and to Nick it felt a lot like he was playing against a bunch of big rocks in jerseys. Rocks, incidentally, which wasted little time in beating the Australian door down. When the eighty minutes of fury had passed, the final score again was 25–10.

It hurt as they trudged off the field, but at the very least, Farr-Jones had vindicated the decision to bring him back to the side. In the final half particularly, he had been one of the few Australian players to actually make headway into the teeth of the All Blacks defence and get the ball *across* the advantage line. For whatever reason a lot of the other players seemed un-characteristically quiet on the day, the way it sometimes happens in Test Matches for reasons no one can discern.

The difficulty for Farr-Jones now was whether or not to make himself available for the coming Test against South Africa, who had already arrived back in Australia and were in the early stages of their three-Test tour.

Coming back on the plane from New Zealand the following night, his inclination was not to announce whether or not he was available, but instead again talk to Angie and then announce his decision on the morrow. He was dissuaded from this plan by a journalist friend who pointed out to him while standing in the customs queue at Sydney's Kingsford Smith airport that this would just prolong the media hoopla and what he had to do was make his decision *now*, one way or another, and bloody well live with it for better or worse.

'Ok, tell 'em I'm available for the whole series,' Farr-Jones said after a long pause, and that at least put that issue to rest for good. The *Sydney Morning Herald* deemed the news important enough to put on their front page the following day—and for better or worse he was in for the series.

Four days before the First Test against South Africa, Nick lay drunk, prone on the back seat of a limousine purring over the bridge to his home on Sydney's North Shore.

He had been the star turn at a long lunch that day at the Regent for 650 people which had launched his biography, and spent the evening at another exclusive Sydney hotel with the other Wallabies and team management at a gala event called— regrettably without tongue-in-cheek—'The Greatest Night in Rugby History'.

The basic theme of the evening was to fly in thirty of the biggest legends in rugby from all over the world and sell tickets at $1000 a head to the corporate world so as to raise money for the Wallabies themselves, in the form of a company they'd recently formed, called Wallabies Promotion and Marketing Limited.

What with drinking, singing, and hob-nobbing with all the rugby legends, a good time was guaranteed to all and Nick had done plenty of all of the above. So much so that one of the invitees, John O'Neill, the Managing Director of the State Bank, had decided it would be a good idea to get the Wallaby half-back safely home by putting him in the care of his own limo and driver.

The driver, Craig Smith, pulled up outside Farr-Jones house

only to find the former Australian captain sprawled all over the back seat and entirely dead to the world.

'Mr Farr-Jones, Mr Farr-Jones,' he said, shaking him by the shoulder to bring him back from the land of nod, 'we've arrived at your home, sir. It's time to get up.'

Slowly, slowly, Farr-Jones surfaced from wherever it was he was at and peered glazedly at this strange face peering over him.

'Wh . . . wh . . . what?' he said.

'We're at your home, sir. You've got to wake up.'

'Just give me ten more minutes,' said the half-back, before slumping his head back down on to the seat.

Four nights later, in the middle of the First Test against South Africa at the Sydney Football Stadium, the situation was rather more sober. Sober to the point of dire.

The South Africans seemed amazingly energised from the sound of the opening whistle and it was all the Wallabies could do to hold them out as they continually drove towards the Australian line. What the *hell* was going on here? This didn't seem like the stolid, solid, occasionally stodgy play the South Africans had shown on the tour to date. Why were they going berserk now?

Because it was a Test match, and while the Wallabies had gone into this game perhaps over-confident that they had the measure of the visitors, the South Africans themselves had more than risen to the occasion. It was a cold clear night, with that particular feel in the air that follows heavy rain, and the Springboks seemed curiously enervated by the whole thing, while for some reason the Wallabies seemed to move as if through deep water—slowly and with difficulty.

Even so, at least one player on the Australian side of things, Marty Roebuck, was up to the task at hand and through expert long-range use of his goal-kicking boots, had put Australia ahead by 9–0 after 16 minutes with three penalty goals. It was a lead entirely unjustified on the pattern of play, but if it was a quirk of modern rugby that a good goal-kicker could conquer all, then so be it—the Wallabies had been on the wrong side of that equation often enough that they were happy enough to be on the right side now.

It was not to last. Ten minutes before half-time, South African inside-centre Heinrich Fuls jabbed a neat kick end over end through the Australian back-line and followed through hard. The first player to get to the ball was Wallaby winger David Campese, who fumbled it, allowing the South African outside-centre Pieter Muller to regather and plunge over for a try. Converted, the score stood at 9–7 in the Wallabies' favour, but worse was shortly to follow.

Seconds before half-time, the South Africans launched a blind-side scrum movement which, after clever passing, saw the ball come to the South African winger James Small on the fly. Farr-Jones, knowing that he was in the first line of defence against the attacker, instinctively calculated as he had done so many times in the past, that precise point that Small would be at when he passed him.

Then the denouement.

He hurled himself towards that point, grasping outwards with his hands as he went and . . . came up with thin air. Small, too, had made his split-second calculations of where Farr-Jones would dive, and at the last possible instant had darted inside him.

By the time Farr-Jones had picked himself up off the ground, the South African had gone in for the try that put his team on top for the first time. Farr-Jones had missed other tackles in his long career—not many, but a few—but this was perhaps the most damaging. It proved to be the turning-point of the game and the South Africans came home strongly to win the Test 19–12.

Doom. Gloom. Devastation. In the dressing room afterwards, there was little discussion, for there was simply little to be said—they would have to regroup and try to come back to level the series in the second Test.

Late that same night, after leaving a rather downcast reception at the stadium, Farr-Jones was with team-mates Marty Roebuck and Phil Kearns looking for a taxi to take them back to the team hotel. No chance. Eventually though, they were picked up by a huge Mercedes—a government public bus—which took them in more or less the right direction and the three sat in a rough kind of silence, contemplating what might have been.

It was an appropriately humble return from such a game.

On the Monday, two of the senior partners of Nick's law firm, Michael Holden and Steve Martin, took Farr-Jones aside and made a novel suggestion: why not, for the duration of the South African series, give up drinking all together?

Why not indeed? Farr-Jones considered the novel suggestion for a moment, then readily agreed.

'I don't think drinking socially like that had had a great deal of physical effect on me,' Farr-Jones says, 'but I think *psychologically*, to cut out drinking was a great idea, because it was a reminder that what I was engaged in here was a very serious business and there wasn't much room in it for someone who wasn't continually focused on the task at hand.'

In the interim between the First and Second Test, all of the Wallabies felt the pressure. Another loss in the coming Test would see the South Africans win the series and that generation of Wallabies would have lost all possible claim to being the world's best.

Just as Slack had made public his disaffection with Nick's comeback before the New Zealand Test, now another old friend in Alec Evans—who had at that time returned from his Welsh base where he was coaching the Cardiff team—also went public with his considered opinion that no less than nine of the Wallabies from the First Test should be replaced, and he named Farr-Jones as one of them.

Nice one, Alec, and thanks for the memories.

Not that Farr-Jones' naming for the first time in his career, as one who should be dropped from the Test team, seemed to unduly upset him.

'I think perhaps I was too focused at that time on the upcoming Test to worry any more about what was being written in the press. In the end what was said there was pretty inconsequential and we were all just totally committed to getting ourselves physically and mentally right for the Test at Ballymore.'

And if perchance the Wallabies did lose the Second Test to the South Africans, there was no question of Farr-Jones being dropped, as he would immediately have fallen on his own sword and stood aside.

'There would simply have been no point,' he says. '*That* would have been a good time to blood a younger player, and I would have been more than happy to stand aside, albeit devastated at what have then be three losses on the trot to the Wallabies.'

If there was one other complication for Nick in the lead-up to the Second Test, it was that Peter Slattery had recovered from his injury sooner than expected and had resumed playing in Queensland. By the reckoning of some, with Slattery now available, the loophole by which Nick had returned from 'retirement' had now closed and Nick should have again stood aside.

The man himself felt otherwise.

'Absolutely not,' Farr-Jones says. 'For better or worse I'd declared myself available for the series and that was it. If Slats had come back and then injured himself again, what was I going to do, come back *again*? It would have been ridiculous. No, I was available if the selectors wanted to pick me and that's all there was to it.'

Peter Slattery, to his eternal credit, was entirely supportive of the Farr-Jones' approach, and was never heard to utter a peep in public to the effect that his former captain should step aside now that he was recovered. In private he was equally gracious, and in a conversation the two had had over the phone prior to the second Test, Slattery assured Farr-Jones that there were no hard feelings at all.

In the bus on the way to the Second Test, the atmosphere was, Farr-Jones remembers, 'as good as I can ever remember it being prior to a Test match.

'It's always difficult to compare of course, but I just remember the feeling in the air was absolute *steel*. Like, whatever happens, *whatever* happens, we simply were not going to allow ourselves to lose. We'd all put up with too much in the preceding two weeks to allow it to happen, and while the South Africans already had a big win in their bellies to sate their hunger a bit, we were just STARVING to win.'

So good was the feeling between the players in fact, that there was little said in the dressing room before the game. The previous evening Dwyer had made an unusually emotional address to the team on the importance of winning this day but, together with the captain Phil Kearns, recognised that nothing they could say could possibly improve the already totally committed approach of the players and so held their fire.

Out on the field, the South Africans scored an early intercept try after an awry pass by Wallaby centre Jason Little to go to an initial lead, but in Farr-Jones memory, 'it didn't matter a damn.'

'Neither our resolve nor our confidence wavered a jot and we just set about going straight back at them,' he says. 'What I particularly remember is how fantastic the atmosphere at Ballymore was throughout the game. The people of Brisbane had seemed to ignore all the preceding criticism of us, were giving us 100% support, and I think we could *feel* how badly they wanted us to win.'

No problems. Coming on strong like thunder, the Wallabies finished the game with a handsome 28–20 win, and all was right with the world once more.

With victory, the series had been levelled at 1–1, Dwyer's faith in his men had been vindicated, and Farr-Jones felt he had ample justification for having a small celebratory drink that night when he had dinner in Brisbane with his wife and parents.

But he still didn't.

'Of course I could have had a few wines and it wouldn't have made a damn of physical difference in my performance in the Third Test the following week, but psychologically, I still wanted to hold tight to me that feeling of being *totally* committed to winning the next Test, even while celebrating our victory in the last.'

Not that they didn't celebrate hard that night anyway . . . (WAITER! Bring me *four* mineral waters on the rocks and make it snappy!)

In the aftermath, the accolades for Farr-Jones performance in the Second Test were satisfyingly many, and from all quarters. Even the highly-esteemed Sydney journalist, Evan Whitton, who had been yet another to have been critical of Farr-Jones return, just as he had often been critical over the half-back's career, was generous in his praise in the *Sun–Herald* the following day:

'The selectors' gamble on Farr-Jones paid off,' he wrote. 'They had obviously hoped that constant play at this level would finally bring him into fitness and form. His play, particularly in the first half was a significant factor in the result.'

Whatever. Just bring on the decider and let's be done with it.

The Third Test: Australia vs South Africa at the Sydney Football Stadium. The result: Australia 19, South Africa 12.

Again, there was a nice bit of symmetry to the scoreline— as it was an exact reversal of the score in the First Test, when South Africa had triumphed. It was the first time Australia had come back to win *any* series after losing the first Test and the Australians, with Farr-Jones in the thick of it, had played a storming game throughout.

The previous evening Farr-Jones had broken his own rule of

never addressing the team, in the manner of his previous role as captain, and had indeed had a few words to say. At the team meeting after dinner at the Wallabies hotel, he had stood up and implored his teammates to be URGENT in everything they did. Not to hold anything in reserve, not to hesitate an instant in anything they did, but HIT! HIT! HIT! and THROUGH! and OVER!

'Basically I thought it was important that whatever else happened we had to retain the momentum we had from the Second Test where we did everything at pace and swarmed all over every Springbok that poked his head up over the parapet. If we went back to the way we'd played in the First Test and *assumed* things would happen instead of *making* them happen, I thought we'd be in trouble.'

No trouble at all. The Wallabies had indeed been frenetic throughout and had rattled the South Africans from first to last with their intensity and purpose.

But it was over.

Phil Kearns, as captain, had the microphone on the podium set up on the field, and was thanking the South Africans for the spirit in which they'd played the series as well as congratulating the efforts of his own team. When he came to Farr-Jones' name as part of his speech, to thank him particularly for his efforts, he was interrupted by an immediate roar of appreciation from the crowd, and resumed with a public aside to his former captain: 'I think they like you, Nick.'

They did indeed.

There followed a wonderfully spontaneous moment when the entire stadium seemed to stand as one to salute the career of one who had played well, done fine.

Amid the tumult, the Wallabies ran to each end of the Sydney Football Stadium to thank the crowd for their support, as had become the Wallaby custom. Farr-Jones, as always, was in the middle of the team, but when they ran towards the eastern side of the stadium something instinctively made the rest of the Wallabies hold back without Nick's knowledge, meaning that he ran the last ten metres on his own. It meant he was suddenly on his own, between a solid wall of standing Australian rugby supporters and the current generation of the team he'd graced for the last ten years.

Farr-Jones looked round, realising what had happened, only

to see the Wallabies themselves applauding him, then looked back to the crowd to see they were doing the same with ever more gusto.

If this was the end, it was a wonderful way to leave the stage.

INDEX